'TIL 1850 STUDY OF ARISTOTLE'S RHETORIC LIB ED'N 35
MEDIA AS CONTEXT FOR EXTRA-PARL'Y RHETORIC 35
PUBLIC (POOR LAW) ASSISTANCE = DISENFRANCHISEMENT 36
DRIVE TOWARDS ORATORY 37
EXPANSION OF (PROVINCIAL) PRESS 37, 41
1870S DECLINE IN PARL'Y COVERAGE 38
GROWTH IN EXTRA-PARL'Y SPEECHMAKING 39, 40
SUCCESS OF PART. STYLE OF ORATORY → UNIFIED 39
INTEGRATED POL COMM'Y
CONTEXT OF LIVE SPEECH & PRINTED VERSION DIFF 39-40
'STAR' SPEAKERS 41, 57 fn13
MEDIA OF VICT POL'N: SPEECH | PRINTED WORD [CARTOON] 40
↳ PHOTOGRAPH | PORTRAIT ?

[...] 2 AUDIENCES ← (A HAPPENING)
↓
[...] ASSEMBLAGE ELOQUENT UTTERANCE OF POPULAR FEELING' [42]
↓
[...]KE GROWTH OF [O]RGANISED TEAM [S]PECTATOR SPORTS [43]
↓
[']VULGARISING' POLS

# POLITICS AND SOCIAL CHANGE IN MODERN BRITAIN

PRESS AGENCIES & TELEGRAPH 43
↳ SPEECHES PROFIT-MAKING 45
↳ 'FIXTURES'
SPEECHES GIVEN ON BASIS OF BRIEF NOTES 44

PRESS AGENCY LOSSES AFTER WEG'S RETIREMENT 46
POL POS'N → COMMONS PERFORMANCE AS MEDIATED BY PRESS INTEREST 46
PRESS UNIONIST BY 1886-90 47 (FULL/VICT 'VERBATIM' REP'G ESP IMP TO LIBERALS!)
LONDON DOM. 1870S-80S 47
FORMAT 'UNCHANGED' 1860-1900 ?? 48
TORIES & IMPORTANCE OF SYMBOLS IN POLS 50
VERBATIM REP'G — STIMULUS TO RAT'L PRES'N 50
RHETORIC ESP. IMP'T FOR LIBERALS (DISCUSSION) 51, 52
LATE 20TH C BRITAIN — V. DIFF POL CULTURE 52
WEBER & GLAD 53 (NOT 'CAESARISTIC PLEBISCITICAL ELEMENT')
CHANGING STRUCTURE OF POLS & MEDIA 53
↳ DAILY MAIL & NEW STYLE POL REPORTING (SIZE; NAT'L DISTRIB'N; SIMPLICITY OF PRES'N) [PACKAGED POLS WAY UNLIKE VERBATIM REP'G]
1918 → BOTH (ALL) PARTIES APPEAL TO DELIB. EXPLOITATION OF NON-RAT'L INFERENCE 54
↳ EXTRA-PARL'Y DEBATE NEVER RECOVERED AFTER WWI
↳ JNLSTS VIEW COMES BETWEEN READER & POL'N 54-5
RADIO — SHORT ACCESS — NOT CONDUCIVE TO EXPOSITION OF LIBERAL RAT'M 56
TICKETING 42-3.

MANCHESTER GUARDIANS — LANCS DIALECT STORIES 20
LABOUR, 'THE PEOPLE' & UNAFFECTED SPEECH 24
IRISH & SCOTTISH 'GENTLEMEN' 25
[CONDITION OF THE PEOPLE] SOCIAL REFORM 59, 81 fn2
'HEALTH' [1864] 61, 67, 72, 75
EDUCATION (+ INT'L COMP'N) 65
'VOX POPULI... ASSISTED AND AIDED US' 75
EXTRAORDINARILY INDISTINCT EMERGENCE OF CLASS-BASED ELEMENT IN POLITICS 81
LIB'M & SHIFT TO CLASS POLITICS 118
1892-5 GLAD-ROS. ADMINS & RUFF OF PROGRESSIVE POLS 121
IMPERIALISM & BREAKING OF PROG. MVT 122

A. F. THOMPSON *Photograph: P. S. Derow*

# POLITICS AND SOCIAL CHANGE IN MODERN BRITAIN

## ESSAYS PRESENTED TO A.F. THOMPSON

EDITOR

P. J. WALLER

Fellow of Merton College, Oxford

THE HARVESTER PRESS · SUSSEX

ST. MARTIN'S PRESS · NEW YORK

First published in Great Britain in 1987 by
THE HARVESTER PRESS LIMITED
*Publisher: John Spiers*
16 Ship Street, Brighton, Sussex
and in the USA by
ST. MARTIN'S PRESS INC.
175 Fifth Avenue, New York, NY 10010



*British Library Cataloguing in Publication Data*
Politics and social change in modern
Britain: essays presented to A.F. Thompson
1. Great Britain—Politics and government
— 19th century 2. Great Britain—
Politics and government—20th century
I. Thompson, A.F. II. Waller, P.J.
320.941 JN216

ISBN 0–7108–1133–0

*Library of Congress Cataloging-in-Publication Data*

Politics and social change in modern Britain.
Festschrift for A.F. Thompson.
Bibliography: P.
Includes index.
1. Great Britain—Politics and government
—1837–1901. 2. Great Britain—
Politics and government—20th century.
3. Great Britain—Social conditions—
19th century. 4. Great Britain—Social
conditions—20th century. 5. Thompson, A.F.
I. Waller, P.J. (Philip J.) II. Thompson, A.F.
DA550.P58 1987 941.081 87–14014
ISBN 0–312–01251–9

Typeset in 11/12pt Garamond by Input Typesetting Ltd, London
Printed in Great Britain by Mackays of Chatham Ltd, Kent

# Contents

Notes on Contributors vii

Preface: Appreciating A. F. T. xi
*C. S. L. Davies and L. G. Mitchell*

1. Democracy and Dialect, Speech and Class 1
*P. J. Waller.*

2. Rhetoric and Politics in Britain, 1860–1950 34
*H. C. G. Matthew.*

3. Style and Substance in Disraelian Social Reform, *c.* 1860–80 59
*P. R. Ghosh.*

4. The Movement for the Higher Education of Women: its social and intellectual context in England, *c.* 1840–80 91
*Gillian Sutherland.*

5. Conflicts and Change in Liberal Theory and Practice, 1890–1918: the case of Bertrand Russell 117
*Richard A. Rempel.*

6. The Labour Party, Capitalism and the National Debt, 1918–24
*R. C. Whiting* 140

7. The 'Social Psychology' of Unemployment in Interwar Britain 161
*R. I. McKibbin.*

8. Trade Unions and Corporatist Politics: the response of the TUC to industrial rationalisation, 1927–33 192
*Gordon Phillips.*

9. Sweethearts and Scabs: irregular trade unions in Britain in the twentieth century 213
*Robert J. Waller.*

Index 229

# Notes on Contributors

C. S. L. DAVIES read History at Wadham College, Oxford under A.F.T. and Lawrence Stone, 1956–59. Since 1963 he has been Fellow and Tutor at Wadham, working on the fifteenth and sixteenth centuries. Published *Peace, Print and Protestantism, 1450–1558* (Paladin, London, 1976).

P. R. GHOSH. Educated Merton College, Oxford, 1973–6; Student and Junior Research Fellow, Nuffield College; Fellow and Tutor at St Anne's College since 1981. Published articles on Gibbon and on Disraeli. Research on Victorian financial politics supervised by A.F.T.

R. I. MCKIBBIN. Educated University of Sydney, then Oxford. Thesis supervised by A.F.T. Fellow and Tutor at St John's College, Oxford since 1972; published *The Evolution of the Labour Party 1910–1924* (Oxford University Press, 1974).

H. C. G. MATTHEW. Fellow and Tutor of St Hugh's College, Oxford and Lecturer in Gladstone Studies at Christ Church, Oxford. Author of *The Liberal Imperialists* (Oxford Historical Monographs, 1973), originally a thesis supervised by A.F.T.; *Gladstone* 1809–1874* (Oxford University Press, 1986), and editor since 1972 of *The Gladstone Diaries with Cabinet Minutes and Prime-Ministerial Correspondence* (Oxford University Press), whose publication is supervised by a Committee of which A.F.T. is a member.

L. G. MITCHELL. Educated Wadham College, Oxford, 1962–8; Salveson Junior Research Fellow, University College, Oxford, 1968–71; Fellow and Praelector in Modern History, University College, since 1971. Author of *Charles James Fox and the Disintegration of the Whig Party, 1782–1794* (Oxford Historical Monographs, 1971), and *Holland House* (1980); editor of *The Purefoy Letters, 1735–1753* (1973), and joint-editor of *The History of Oxford University*, vol. 5 (Oxford University Press, 1986).

GORDON PHILLIPS. Educated Wadham College, Oxford, then Nuffield College, encountering A.F.T. first as an undergraduate tutor, then as a doctoral examiner. Taught at Lancaster University since 1966, where he is currently Senior Lecturer. Publications include *The General Strike* (Weidenfeld and Nicolson, 1976) in A.F.T.'s series 'Radical Men, Movements and Ideas'; and, with Noel Whiteside, *Casual Labour: The Unemployment Question in the Port Transport Industry 1880–1970* (Clarendon Press, Oxford, 1985).

RICHARD A. REMPEL. Educated University of Saskatchewan, then Oxford. DPhil. thesis supervised by A.F.T. Currently Professor at McMaster University, involved in the Bertrand Russell Editorial Project. Published *Unionists Divided: Arthur Balfour, Joseph Chamberlain and the Unionist Free Traders* (David and Charles, Newton Abbot, 1972).

GILLIAN SUTHERLAND. Educated St Hugh's College, Oxford, 1960–63; then Nuffield College, working on her DPhil. thesis under A.F.T.'s supervision. Since 1966 she has been Fellow and Lecturer in History at Newnham College, Cambridge. Publications include *Policy-Making in Elementary Education* (Oxford Historical Monographs, 1973), *Ability, Merit and Measurement: Mental Testing and English Education 1880–1940* (Oxford, 1984) and (as editor and contributor) *Studies in the Growth of Nineteenth Century Government* (London, 1972) and *Government and Society in Nineteenth Century Britain: Commentaries on British Parliamentary Papers: Education* (Dublin, 1977).

P. J. WALLER. Educated Wadham College, Oxford, 1964–7; Prize Fellow, Magdalen College, 1968–71; Fellow and

Tutor in Modern History, Merton College, since 1971. Author of *Democracy and Sectarianism: A Political and Social History of Liverpool 1868–1939* (Liverpool University Press, 1981), and *Town, City and Nation: England 1850–1914* (Oxford University Press, 1983). Tutored and supervised by A.F.T.

ROBERT J. WALLER. Educated Balliol College, Oxford, 1974–78; Senior Scholar, Merton College, 1978–80; Prize Fellow, Magdalen College, 1980–84; Lecturer, Trinity and Wadham Colleges, 1984–86; Director of Social and Political Research at the Harris Research Centre since 1986. DPhil. supervised by A.F.T. Published *The Dukeries Transformed* (Oxford University Press, 1983), *The Almanac of British Politics* (Croom Helm, London, 1983), *The Atlas of British Politics* (Croom Helm, London, 1985).

R. C. WHITING. Educated Wadham College, Oxford, 1970–73, Nuffield College, 1973–76; Lecturer at Heriot-Watt University; Lecturer in Modern History, University of Leeds, since 1979. Published *The View from Cowley: the Impact of Industrialisation upon Oxford 1918–1939* (Oxford Historical Monographs, 1983); 'The Suez Canal and the British Economy 1918–1960', in K. M. Wilson (ed.), *Imperialism and Nationalism in the Middle East* (Mansell, 1983). Tutored and supervised by A.F.T.

# Preface: Appreciating A.F.T.[1]

*C. S. L. Davies*

Born in Preston in 1920, Pat (Alfred Frederick) Thompson was brought up in Belfast, the son of a Londonderry-born Ulsterman working as a Treasury official in Northern Ireland. He moved from Campbell College to Dulwich in 1935, when his father was transferred to Whitehall. He went on to get an exhibition at Magdalen, arriving there just after the outbreak of war, faced therefore with doing History Schools in two years. He duly got his first in 1941. At Magdalen he was lucky to be taught by two of the outstanding historians of their generation, K. B. McFarlane and A. J. P. Taylor, and to be taken up by both of them as a friend. Living on the same staircase as McFarlane, Pat found himself invited for after-dinner chats or music, occasionally taken to the theatre and supper. Taylor had him to stay at his house at Holywell Ford over the fateful summer of 1940.

McFarlane had hopes of Pat as a medievalist, and he diligently ploughed through Stubbs' *Charters* in his first year. He clearly imbibed the contempt for the eye-catching, the meretricious or the merely shoddy which was so marked, indeed so inhibiting, a feature of McFarlane and his school. The master's sceptical, commonsense, view of history, his distaste for over-arching explanations, his insistence that historical characters deserved to be recognisable as human beings, not patronised by either adulation or denigration, would certainly have been congenial. Some remarks of McFarlane to an undergraduate society in 1938 are worth quoting as prefiguring many of Pat's own working assumptions. He instanced

> two misconceptions that are bound to produce havoc if allowed to luxuriate in our minds. . . . The first is the belief that it is possible and desirable to write the history of institutions apart from the men who worked them. They are born, develop, change and decay by human agencies. Their life is the life of the men who make them. Constitutional history is concerned with men. . . . The other misconception is perhaps more widespread. It is the habit of assuming a simplicity of behaviour and of motive in medieval politicians that is wholly unwarranted by our knowledge. . . . It is doubtful, to say the least, whether human nature has changed at all between the fourteenth century and the twentieth. Success in politics demanded then much the same qualities as it does now, powers of persuasion, a sense of an audience, good nerves, a willingness to compromise, and the habit of application to business. . . . It is a great mistake to picture the medieval baronage as if the House of Lords was something like the prefects' room of a public school . . . [2]

It is a recognisable recipe; though Pat's version would include a *soupçon* more vinegar.

To McFarlane's irritation, Taylor seduced Pat into the modern world; indeed, provided a sense of psychological relief after the intellectual austerities of McFarlane, encouragement to chance his arm rather than always asking, 'What is the evidence?' None the less, although Taylor's influence is obvious (not only in Pat's pride in lecturing without notes) he clearly remained in spirit more akin to McFarlane; he never shared Taylor's contempt for the tutorial system or the examination game.[3] More profoundly, McFarlane's withering perfectionism contributed, as it did in his medievalist pupils, to Pat's most un-Taylorian reluctance to publish. What Taylor did provide was an introduction to the wider world. Holywell Ford functioned as something of a refuge from London during the summer of the fall of France. There Pat met Stephen Spender and Dylan Thomas as well as such Oxford figures as Isaiah Berlin and A. L. Rowse; also a host of Central European refugees, including that improbably leftish *grand seigneur* Count Michael Karolyi, briefly first President of independent Hungary in 1919, with whom Pat played chess.[4]

Other influences were R. B. McCallum of Pembroke, who took Pat for the 'Peel' special subject, Harry Weldon, the hard-nosed Magdalen philosopher, who had led the campaign to transform Magdalen from old-fashioned leisurely gentility to the active pursuit of intellectual distinction and success in the Schools, and C. S. Lewis, improbably but fruitfully engaged in teaching political thought to Magdalen historians. Pat played rugby for the College, squash for the University, and frequented the Labour Club of Roy Jenkins, Tony Crosland and Denis Healey. His generation was determined to extract the maximum advantage from Oxford before the inevitable call to the colours, and, despite wartime conditions (less draconian than might be imagined retrospectively), succeeded in their aim. In Pat's case that included meeting Mary Barritt, then reading Botany at Somerville. Their marriage in 1942 became the bedrock of his life.

War service involved a commission in the Worcestershire Yeomanry, a territorial unit of the Royal Artillery. The regiment was attached to 6th Airborne Division and Pat underwent parachute and glider training. He served in Normandy in 1944, where he was wounded. His remaining war service was spent in intelligence at GCHQ at Bletchley. Demobilised in November 1945, he returned to Magdalen to begin research under McCallum's direction on the general elections of 1865 and 1868. This involvement in what McCallum had just christened psephology attracted the sometimes overbearing interest of Lewis Namier. First fruits of the research were the article published in 1948 on 'Gladstone's Whips at the General Election of 1868'.[5] Time for research was short; Magdalen recruited him as a lecturer in 1946 to help coax the mass of returned warriors (many his senior in age and rank) through Schools. Other careers beckoned; he passed high into the Civil Service and nearly entered the Treasury, and he dabbled with an offer from the *Manchester Guardian*. But in 1947 he was elected Fellow and Tutor in Modern History and Politics at Wadham.

Wadham was a small college in terms of its fellowship (ten all told, only seven of them 'tutorial fellows' responsible for teaching undergraduates), large in terms of undergraduate numbers, swollen by the post-war bulge, then by the influx of grammar school beneficiaries of the Butler Act. Pat worked first with William Deakin, recently returned from making history in Yugoslavia, an intimate of Churchill's and heavily involved in preparing Churchill's *Second World War*. Deakin soon left to become the first Warden of St Antony's. He was succeeded by Lawrence Stone, championed by Pat in a hard-fought fight which pitted him against the Warden, Maurice Bowra. Pat was nominally teaching a twenty-hour stint, in practice much greater; while the social life of the College in Bowra's day was invigorating but strenuous. Bowra demanded total commitment to the College from fellows, and indeed their wives. Within a year, Pat found himself with the heavy additional responsibilities of Domestic Bursar, a job he held with considerable panache for six years (1948–54); shortly after he gave it up it became a full-time, non-academic appointment.

Pat this year (1987) has achieved forty years as a mainstay of a remarkably successful History School, cheerfully shouldering the chores of administration, to the relief of Lawrence Stone and, since 1963, his successor Cliff Davies. For twenty years, until the appointment in 1967 of Robert Currie as Tutor in Politics, he was also involved in P.P.E. He continued to play more than his share in college administration, Senior Tutor twice (1955–57; 1962–64), Tutor for Graduates (1964–67), Sub-Warden during a tricky period in 1968–69, and again between 1975 and 1978, the latter including a spell as acting-Warden. Interspersed have been three visiting professorships at Stanford, and one at McMaster.

Lawrence Stone sums up Pat as college tutor:

> His devotion to his students, in both an official and an unofficial capacity, was legendary, and he was fortunately endowed with the memory of an elephant. He never forgot a name or a face, and could usually be relied upon to provide an anecdote, not infrequently unrepeatable in polite company, to go with them. He followed the subsequent careers of his pupils with paternal interest, and was always ready to pull a string or bend an ear to help them to jobs or promotions. He was, in fact, the very model of a modern college tutor, working long hours, the only reward for which has been the gratitude and affection of his pupils.

But if Pat's first priority has been to his undergraduates, his second has been to the remarkable number of graduate students he has supervised, formally and informally. He has been extremely active in academic publishing; especially as an editor (and in fact the workhorse of the editorial board) of the rejuvenated *Oxford Historical Monographs*, and as a member of the Gladstone Diaries Committee. Pat produced, fortuitously, his own self-portrait when he described Kitson Clark:

> The man who inspired, cajoled or bullied [his students] into producing work of distinction can still draw upon a combination of pervasive enthusiasm, wide learning, robust common sense and plain unselfishness rare among supervisors of research in any period. The one drawback of the unfashionable dedication to the subject through his pupils has been that the rest of us seldom hear from Kitson Clark himself.[6]

The priority he has accorded to his pupils, to the college and to the History Faculty at Oxford, has inevitably affected his own work; so, too, has that perfectionism which makes him so constructive a critic of the work of others, and too destructive a critic of his own writing. His contribution to the writing of modern British history has, however, been a major one. This book can provide only a pale reflection of that achievement.

## *L. G. Mitchell*

In the early 1960s, a prominent Oxford historian, surfacing from the experience of examining in the Schools, wrote a piece for a Sunday newspaper, in which he purported to demonstrate that each college had a distinctive, historical style. Wadham men, he thought, were marked by 'corrosive ingenuities'. The pupils of Pat Thompson and Lawrence Stone seemed to apply acid to the past, droplet by droplet. The writer of this newspaper article found such an approach not to his taste. The Wadham tutors would not have been dismayed. For them, and for Pat in particular, better acid than syrup and waffle.

Pat's rooms in Wadham were not designed for sentimental discussions. Bare walls suggested a sense of despatch without the fussiness that too often accompanies the owners of water colours and prints. A portrait of Frederic Harrison, not everyone's idea of a congenial companion, was the only point of relief. Sensible Windsor chairs, a sofa, two armchairs and a plain table made up the furnishings. Piles of papers, in boxes or loose, covered the window seat, most of the table, some of the chairs and a certain part of the floor. On the mantelshelf, there were two brass candlesticks and, occasionally, a model steam-engine. Three doors led out of the room, and pupils wondered 'what on earth he kept there'. One presumed that it would be more boxes, more papers. Finally there were ashtrays to catch the fall-out from the pipe ritual, which Pat may have learnt from Reggie Lennard: 'In 1949, Pat had not then yet mastered his "pipe technique" – Reggie took *much* longer and filled *his* pipe from a one-pound tin of *John Cotton No 4;* Pat would be brought to blush slightly when one referred to this, as he fiddled with his 2 oz tin of *Navy Cut.*' It was a room in which to give working tutorials.

Pat was what might be called a 1945 don, a distinctive and rather special breed. He was not a prewar don, for whom teaching was something that gentlemen might or might not indulge in. Nor was he a modern don for whom teaching is too often an irritating diversion from research. Pat was a teaching don. History, at one level, was a day's work to be done. One ex-pupil remembered 'feeling a bit bleak and asking if he ever had black days. "Every day," he answered with a chuckle.' Therefore 'it was just not the done thing to go unprepared for a tutorial with Pat.' At another level there was a game to be played, and 'the message was that all games could be won if correctly played.' The Cup Final was the Schools, and Pat was the Captain of the examinees' team every year. Tutorials, in which Pat spoke a good deal, were functional and Schools-oriented. Pupils came away from tutorials in the confidence that they now knew something that the examiners might find acceptable. Each tutorial was 'an intricately phrased summing-up of the whole subject'.

Beyond the functional demands of examinations was an intellectual style. History was the study of the virtues and vices of people who had really lived. Abstractions and generalisations were vicious in their subordination of individual complexities and small triumphs. Of course, the historian had to be something of a cynic because human nature was quite often less than heroic. Sentimental approaches to the past were preposterous. On the other hand, what made one man different from his fellows gave that man a historical dignity worthy of study. In other words, 'the immediate lesson was a deep hostility to any of the ideas which made history more simple – applications of class consciousness or of "the Labour movement" uncritically handled, for example – with a real emphasis on the human qualities of the people involved.' Or again, 'in my time at least, he wouldn't have been very interested in theorising about the art of history *as* an art or discipline; and I suppose he was untypical of the historical profession in the last thirty years in not erecting any barriers between contemplation of the present and of the past.' What some thought 'corrosive' was in fact a knowledge of how the world wags and a belief that it wagged very much the same in the past.

This approach to history could produce devastating comments on essays and Collections. A suggestion that Cavour might have had some genuine interest in the ideal of Italian unification led Pat to offer the comment, 'or a predatory Piedmontese exploiting the diplomatic opportunities available?' Prolixity brought an invitation to 'cultivate terseness and not to ignore the need for the telling phrase.' A purple passage was described as 'a marginal tendency to patronise and pontificate.' A very purple passage was dismissed as 'too much Wardour St.' A sloppy Collection could only be remedied by 'sweat and tears, if not blood.' What pupils came to realise was that Pat wanted well-researched, no-nonsense discussions of the topic set. There was no reward for humbug, affectation or cant. People in the past, like people in the present, deserved better. They had a claim to our sympathies and understanding and should not become the sport of our neuroses. This was not necessarily a comforting message for eighteen year olds who tend to think in categories and look for heroes and villains. It was hard to sustain an enthusiasm in Pat's presence. He simply pointed out that that enthusiasm would be more securely based and more productive if the limitations of the people on whom it was bound to operate were clearly appreciated. For Pat's generation and for the generation of his Magdalen tutors, many gods had failed. Wadham men must be removed from the temptation of setting up new ones.

Such were bracing views for eighteen year olds to confront. They were made tolerable and attractive by not always being purveyed in tutorials. Outside the formal teaching was the wider tutorial responsibility. From the sherry party for those about to die in Prelims to the party for those who had survived Schools, the Thompsons were a real part of undergraduate life. One refers to the Thompsons, because Mary was a crucial element in the experience of reading history at Wadham. Her 'alert, crisp interest in Pat's pupils reinforced one's sense of belonging to a team.' Dinner in Wychwood Lane was an entertaining and formidable matter. If the Webbs had had a sense of humour or the Duff Coopers more solidity, they might have come near the Thompsons. Although Pat 'would never have wasted tutorial time with gossip', neither he nor Mary had any objection to it over a meal. And it was instructive gossip. A kind of conversational tennis would develop. Pat would throw out an outrageous remark about someone known to the company. Mary would register surprise and murmur a disclaimer. This demur simply allowed Pat to expand his original remarks. All was immensely amusing until the diners became aware that it was their own personalities and foibles that were being debated. The Thompsons preferred to talk about someone in front of their faces rather than behind their backs. This was both flattering and character-forming. As one contributor recalled, 'I suspect I won't be the only one of your correspondents who believes that as a tutor Pat knew – somewhat unnervingly – one's strengths and weaknesses better than one knew them oneself.'

It might be thought that, in order to read History at Wadham in Pat's years, a thickish skin might have been in order. Certainly most undergraduates were conscious of a thickening process as time went by. But this was a crucial aspect of the tutorial method that Pat so successfully employed. Having established, through a lot of time and effort, what the preoccupations and interests of his pupils were, he then taught history through the prism of those preoccupations and interests. It was a flattering notion to feel that events in the past could be related to one's personal idiosyncracies. Needless to say, undergraduates responded to that style of teaching with spaniel-like enthusiasm. Pat and Mary invited confidence and confidences. Historians worked for them because, having taken the trouble to sort their pupils out, it appeared that they found all of them moderately agreeable. As an undergraduate from the 1950s notes, their 'extraordinary loyalty to those whom Pat had taught seemed to me exceptional thirty years ago and seems to me even more exceptional now.' That loyalty, that stripping away of pretension by irony and anecdote, was an essential adjunct to the formal tutorial. The theory seemed to be that better history would be written, if the writers of it had few illusions about themselves.

More tangibly, this knowledge of pupils' characters and aspirations allowed Pat to give practical expression to his definition of a wider tutorial responsibility. When a former pupil resigned an Oxford Fellowship in difficult circumstances, Pat let him borrow his Wadham rooms, so that he could continue to teach. He could be very helpful if, by any chance, he knew the result of a DPhil. viva in advance. Nothing specific would be said, but he would manage to convey the reassuring knowledge that the world was not about to fall in. To one man he could suggest that changing to P.P.E. was unlikely to do much to cure the ills of the world; to another that to take a job in the Levant had probably too much Lawrence Durrell in it. By the same token, a DPhil. was something to be got and got out of the way. It was not wise therefore to set off for three years of paddling in the murky waters of Chateaubriand's Romanticism. Better by far was it to hold to the dry land of politics as something more sustaining for the feet of a young researcher. None of these points would have been made in the form of an absolute prohibition. Rather the wisdom or unwisdom of a particular course of action would have been suggested with a certain amount of verbal winking and nudging. Pat's style was 'avuncular, a steadying influence in times of stress, the calming pipe, the sound advice', playing Baldwin to Lawrence Stone's Churchill. When C. P. Snow's *The Masters* first appeared, Wadham historians awarded Pat the role of Brown 'the most sympathetic of all the characters in Snow's academic *galère*.'

It can hardly be an accident that so many of Pat's pupils have gone on to careers in teaching. Many who now follow his craft openly acknowledge that they also follow his methods. 'He not only shaped one's attitude to history, but also to students. The idea of a shared commitment, the genuine interest and concern that was never suffocating and confining.' Or again: 'my own views about what an exemplary history tutor should be were inescapably formed by the experience of tutorials with Pat.' The 'corrosive ingenuities' of Wadham have spread far and wide. This is hardly surprising. Pat's pupils tended to do well, better, as many of them will readily admit, than they probably would otherwise have done. What they recognised in him was someone who was first and foremost a teacher, whose enjoyment in life was in part measured by the success of those he taught. It was a compelling example, one which has been followed widely.

After 1987, there will be no Thompson 'school', no set of orthodoxies or even fully-fledged heresies associated with his name. That is not the memorial he would wish. Even the thought of it would probably lead to the raising of an eyebrow in reproach. What there might be is a Thompson 'style'. If history is written in clear recognition of the well-meaning imperfection of most of the people who lived it, that would, in all likelihood, be enough. If, in addition, that history could lead the writer to an amused awareness of his own imperfections, Pat would be well pleased indeed.

## *Notes*

1. The authors would like to thank all those Wadham historians who have written to them with memories to relate.
2. K. B. McFarlane, *The Nobility of Later Medieval England* (Oxford, 1973), pp. 280–1.
3. A. J. P. Taylor, *A Personal History* (London, 1983), pp. 138–9.
4. Ibid., pp. 165–9; Michael Karolyi, *Memoirs: Faith without Illusion* (London, 1956).
5. *English Historical Review*, LXIII (1948), pp. 189–200.
6. *History*, lvii (1972), p. 291.

# 1 Democracy and Dialect, Speech and Class[1]

*P. J. Waller*

'It is impossible for an Englishman to open his mouth without making some other Englishman hate or despise him.'

So George Bernard Shaw prefaced *Pygmalion* (1912). He was writing during a period when one regional and class dialect – Standard English in Received Pronunciation – confirmed its supremacy over all others. This essay considers three questions: why the study of language matters for historians; how Standard English extended its authority; and what consequences resulted.

No historian of nation-building ignores language. Speech cleavages carry implications for hegemony. Historians have not neglected the clash of English with Celtic cultures in Ireland, Scotland and Wales, or with Québecois and Afrikaans in Canada and South Africa. But the collision of English dialects has never struck historians with equal force. This is surprising because, though there was no official imposition of a standard,[2] it is clear that one developed and that it gained unrivalled prestige. Indeed, the convention resulted, preposterous in any scholastic sense, that Standard English speakers spoke 'without accent'. There were no pitched battles in England's language civil war – unlike Greece where riots occurred between classical purists and vernacularists – but there were casualties. The wrong speech, Shaw noted, barred people from high employment. And deservedly so, the egregious Gissing implied in *Demos* (1886), when he remarked of 'Arry – one of that 'distinct class, comprising the sons of mechanics who are ruined morally by being taught to consider themselves above manual labour' – 'He pronounced the work "clerk" as it is spelt; it made him seem yet more ignoble.'[3]

How speech affected social relations and, by extension, political and economic power, requires close assessment. An accent is as striking as outlandish dress or physical deformity. Language is an instrument of both communication and excommunication. It makes possible intimacy, also exclusiveness. All languages experience continuous shifts and revision, but the prevailing current in modern times has seen dialect retreat as cultural localism was breached and as social sensibilities were exposed. Through speech the manners of an age are recorded; so also is social mobility measured as speech communities meet and mingle. In the nineteenth century, both lexicographical authority and orthographical uniformity were strengthened and, in an increasingly literate society, these acted together to contain and reduce the diversity tolerated in written and, to an extent, spoken English. Whether England's regional dialects were linguistically distinct or constituted one family of cognate languages became chiefly a question for scholarly argument. Socially, what mattered was the stratification between refined and vulgar speech, such that the grammatical and lexical peculiarity and, even more, the pronunciation of the regional speaker were generally associated with low birth and defective breeding. As the larger differences between speech provinces were broken down and gradients of Standard English were established, surviving regional dialect speakers were liable to find themselves deemed 'substandard' or 'illiterate' speakers, vilified for retaining an uneducated argot as much as valued for representing a provincial heritage. Correctness in speech was determined by social convention not science. None the less, many students of the language, even Henry Wyld who abominated speech snobbery and insisted that there were no absolute standards of 'right' and 'wrong' speech, were persuaded that the very artificiality of Standard English constituted a genuine claim to be recognised 'good' English and more meritorious than vulgar English. Not because this was the speech of social superiors but because Standard English required intellectual discrimination – 'a more or less deliberate choice is exercised by the speakers in eliminating or adopting for use this or that particular pronunciation, word, phrase, or construction.'[4]

The subject attracted considerable attention in Victorian times, though its spirit was not disinterested. Schools of comparative philology flourished because of ethnological studies. They also inherited the rationalists' concern for spelling and alphabet reform.[5] This had practical applications, to accelerate universal literacy and to assist the deaf, the blind and learners of foreign languages. The lexicographical method was well established, but all past exercises were deemed inadequate by the Philological Society (1842). Their dissatisfaction inspired the *Oxford English Dictionary*, edited by J. A. H. Murray from 1878. The *OED* sought to establish current meaning, spelling and pronunciation, and to trace the descent historically; but dictionaries are not neutral, whatever their compilers' intentions. To label words slang, vulgar, colloquial, corrupt, literary, archaic or current is to be open to the charge of prescribing usage. The *OED* has been an authority for the social acceptability of words and for the standardisation of written English in modern times.[6]

It was not the sole lexicographical endeavour of the period. Another was Joseph Wright's *English Dialect Dictionary*, produced in six volumes between 1898 and 1905. This also derived from a philological society, the English Dialect Society (1873). Its eighty publications, abetted by 600 correspondents, furnished the archive of Wright's dictionary which was, the preface proclaimed, 'a complete vocabulary of all English dialect words which are still in use, or known to have been in use at any time, during the last two hundred years in England, Ireland, Scotland and Wales.' Wright documented 100,000 words which ran concurrent with, but below, the standard speech. The collection was undertaken just in time. In 1895, Wright wrote, 'Pure dialect is disappearing, even in the country districts, owing to the spread of education and to the modern facilities of intercommunication.' Later, in 1926, Wright complained: 'It is very difficult to find people who can speak a dialect without being seriously mixed up with the so-called Standard language.'[7]

Scholars were not content only to embalm language in dictionaries. Phonetics was established as an academic discipline. One pioneer was Henry Sweet who achieved posthumous celebrity as a model for Henry Higgins in *Pygmalion*. In 1877 he publicised his ambition for an English school different from the German in which he and Wright were trained: 'Our tendency is not so much toward the antiquarian philology and text-criticism in which German scholars have done so much, as towards the observation of the phenomena of living languages.' 'The vastness of our Empire', he declared, 'forces us incessantly to grapple with the difficulties of spoken, often also unwritten, languages.'[8]

Phoneticians were recognising a cardinal linguistic principle, that because people in one age were no longer thinking and acting as people in another they no longer wrote or spoke as they did. Language change was ceaseless and inevitable but, Sweet noted, people 'can resist change, and retard it.'[9] Differences derived over time and territory and from social class and political and economic ambition. These differences were as striking within Britain as without in the Empire. This was the theme of a five-volume study by Alexander Ellis, *On Early English Pronunciation* (1867–89), of which the largest section examined current dialects. That sense of irretrievable pending loss which motivated Joseph Wright, drove Ellis too. It also inspired the Folk-Lore Society (1878) and Folk-Song Society (1898) to preserve memorials of disappearing cultures. Their interest, again, was not mere scholarship. The ambition burned that through such records the distinctive character of England might be read and a national musical style developed.[10]

The question was, how to gather and classify words and sounds? An orthography was required to indicate pronunciation. Ellis developed his own alphabet systems, Glossic and Palaeotype, to symbolise variants of sound. Modern students of linguistics consider Ellis's technique so flawed as to render his findings useless for the exact measurement of phonetic features.[11] This hardly matters for historians studying ambiance. It is not essential to reproduce the speech *viva voce*. The information which Ellis accumulated remains precious. Altogether, 811 persons reported about 1145 places where English was the ordinary medium. Different tests were used. The first was a specimen of typical words and constructions. This Ellis tried to get 'translated' into the idiom and pronunciation of each place. It was sent out in 1873; a revised version followed in 1875. From 1877 Ellis issued word lists and, after 1879, a dialect test. Always, Ellis had difficulties comparing the returns, because correspondents altered or misinterpreted instructions. None the less, he proceeded to divide the English-speaking area into six broad dialectal regions incorporating 42 districts. Twenty-one districts contained 89 varieties, within which he even marked 19 sub-varieties. Ellis's informants were mostly the professional and landed classes. All spoke a variant of 'received speech'; many also spoke, or had spoken, dialect. They took pains to seek out people who would now be targets for tape-recording by oral historians. When the Midlands correspondent, Thomas Hallam, visited Bewdley he listened to 'a nonagenarian, about 94, full of vivacity, reading and sewing without spectacles, when young a maker and seller of ling brooms.'[12] The occupations embraced by Ellis's survey included farmers, servants, labourers, cottagers, masons, carpenters, waggoners, miners, fishermen, slaters, textile workers, shoemakers, potters, lock-keepers, coach-builders, porters, grocers.

Ellis's work had an heroic quality, comparable to Jules Gilliéron's and Edmond Edmont's atlas of Gallo-Romance *patois*.[13] But scholars were only endeavouring to record scientifically speech habits which novelists, playwrights and poets depicted impressionistically. Their representation varied in accuracy. Ellis noted about George Eliot that 'quotations from her are far from being conclusive in Le.[icestershire] grammar.'[14] A concern with class shone through many writers' rendering of popular speech. Mrs Gaskell sharply deployed dialect in this way; later, the cockney school used slang and dialect to signify the separateness of working-class life from middle-class experience, even comprehension.[15] Did such separation exist? Dialect literature was not confined to working-class audiences. Its North country practitioners like Edwin Waugh, Ben Brierley and John Hartley earned fame by purveying working-class dreams and disappointments to middle-class readers; and in the South many a gentleman treasured dialect and folklore from county patriotism.[16] That it was more sentimental than erudite may be true. William Barnes' Dorset poems, once ranked with Horace, were esteemed less by the time of his death in 1886; nevertheless, the 1879 edition of his verse was reprinted seven times before 1905, and his bardic quality was recognised.[17] Tennyson embodied the highest union: poet of Lincolnshire and Poet Laureate.

The colloquial joined and largely superseded the dialectal as an influence upon literature. The banjo bards, Kipling especially, exploited music-hall vernacular to extend the popularity of verse.[18] Language concerned literary men as an educational instrument too, in the drive for national efficiency. In 1900 Robert Bridges told Henry Bradley, then president of the Philological Society and an editor of the *OED*, that he was experimenting with 'an aesthetic phonetic script so like our present literary spelling and writing that anyone with common education could read it.' Bridges published this in 1910;[19] and in 1912–13, with Bradley and Sir Walter Raleigh, he founded the Society for Pure English. Despite the name, this should be distinguished from the school of 'piddling and nibbling philology'[20] exemplified by Henry Alford, Dean of Canterbury and first editor of the *Contemporary Review*. Alford had written *The Queen's English* (1864) which arbitrarily laid down rules and decried as pollutions many modern usages. The profusion of such 'authorities' reflected both rapid language change and concern about 'correct' expression.[21]

The Society for Pure English was dedicated to Efficiency, which it aimed to achieve 'by inquiry and discussion rather than by authority.' Their proposals were 'conservative and democratic': conservative in wanting to preserve the classic core as English spread throughout the world, with the danger that 'our Elizabethan literature would come to be as much an obsolete language as Middle English is to us now, or as Homer or Aeschylus to a modern Greek'; democratic in repudiating 'foolish interference with living developments.' They contended that dialects enriched speech, that 'language is or should be democratic both in character and origin', and that 'its best word-makers are the uneducated classes.'

The Society for Pure English was tiny but influential. Its influence was transmitted through newspapers, publishing houses, schools and, perhaps most powerfully, broadcasting. This promised to be the greatest force for influencing language since the Book of Common Prayer and the Authorised Version of the Bible or, indeed, since the invention of printing itself. The BBC in 1926 established an Advisory Committee on Spoken English. Bridges was chairman and his colleagues included another founder member of the Society for Pure English, Logan Pearsall Smith, two professors of phonetics, Lloyd James and Daniel Jones, Sir Johnston Forbes-Robertson, renowned as the finest speaker of Shakespeare; and George Bernard Shaw.

Shaw's interest in phonetics was not confined to *Pygmalion*. Earlier, he can be found lecturing dockers, as he put it, 'to refine the oratory of the New Unionism.' A declaration in 1901 summarised his ambitions.[22] He advocated a phonetic alphabet to relieve the newly educated democracy of 'that worst of handicaps in life', Board School 'cockney' pronunciation. Shaw proposed 'the nationalisation of the existing class monopoly of orthodox English speech', which he termed 'the received Oxford-West-end pronunciation.' The Board School citizenry dismayed Shaw by its poor prospects – 'the young man who . . . in a political conference calls himself a delegite, or perhaps a dyollagite, will find these solecisms obstructing his way through life more than three or four sentences of imprisonment would obstruct a peer's.' Collective action might propel the working classes into social significance, but the future for language was hideous. Either working people would induce the smart set to speak like them – witness the fatuous Clara in *Pygmalion* – or they would endeavour to improve their elocution by the 'fatal process of imitation' and succeed 'mostly only in adding affectation to mispronunciation'.[23] Shaw, therefore, proposed formal instruction in a phonetic alphabet and a standard pronunciation. This seemed the most efficient solution, both to speed the process of learning to read, and to reduce the widening breach of colonial and American speech from English. The link with the Society for Pure English was plain. It too advocated phonetics in elementary education as 'a crying need'; its concern also was with global developments based on a common standard. Language was empire. Latin and Greek were the administrative instruments of the ancient world; likewise, Macaulay's Indian education minute of 1835 marked the onset of the British imperial system. Shaw and Bridges were not so dictatorial. Their goal was a speech commonwealth, elevated to a common level by consent and education rather than by imperial fiat.

A phonetic alphabet was conceived foremost as a means to improve the teaching and learning of the traditional orthography; but its promotion also excited more grandiose plans of the Simplified Spelling Society (1908) about introducing spelling reform into schools. Henry Bradley, for one, objected to this as 'a calamity';[24] but ideas of spelling reform had been boosted by the invention of phonographic shorthand systems. Outstanding here was Isaac Pitman whose one-time collaborator was Alexander Ellis. Henry Sweet invented a rival, Current Shorthand, and scorned the 'Pitfall' system. But Pitman triumphed through business organisation:

> there was a weekly paper to persuade you to learn Pitman: there were cheap textbooks and exercise books and transcripts of speeches for you to copy, and schools where experienced teachers coached you up to the necessary proficiency.[25]

In fact, the transition from shorthand training in business to spelling reform in the schools never made progress in England despite the occasional support given to it by the Philological Society, under Ellis's and W. W. Skeat's inspiration. Even in America where the American Philological Society, National Education Association (1898), and Simplified Spelling Board (1906) tried to build on Benjamin Franklin's linguistic nationalism, only a few innovations occurred.[26]

By contrast, changes in pronunciation made great strides. The BBC's committee observed,

> Out of the broad band that comprises all district and class variants, there is emerging a considerably narrower band of variants that have a very great measure of similarity. This narrow band of types has more features in common with Southern English than with Northern English. Those who speak any one variety of the narrow band are recognised as educated speakers throughout the country. They may broadcast without fear of adverse intelligent criticism.[27]

The BBC would broadcast 'dahnce' music, not 'dănce' music.

The BBC's committee was not a conspiracy of Home Counties or Oxbridge linguistic Tories, designing to overthrow the People's English and to establish a class dialect. Its members did not assert that there was only one right way of speaking. This was improbable since only Bridges had English parentage. Their primary aim was to identify the winning side and join it. Lloyd James reflected, 'The kilt is as conspicuous in Piccadilly as the silk hat upon the moors; there are, however, occasions when a black tie is considered suitable by all classes. What is true of dress is in some degree true of speech.' The committee's proclamation was defensive, 'to secure some measure of uniformity in the pronunciation of broadcast English, and to provide announcers with some degree of protection against the criticism to which they are, from the nature of their work, peculiarly liable.'[28] The BBC's Director-General, John Reith, seemed to follow their prescription literally, since radio announcers were fortified with both impeccable pronunciation and evening clothes.

According to the BBC's committee, the civil war of pronunciation was won before broadcasting arrived. How had dialect-speaking lost strength? Many dialect words were local names for plants, birds and animals, or technical terms associated with traditional husbandry and trades. These were most vulnerable to standardisation by formal education and by movements which eliminated uneconomic processes. The same was true of many sayings, superstitions and customs. These diminished with the spread of science and medicine and the supersession of folk pastimes by commercial entertainment. As for vulgarities, the glossarists perhaps never fully registered these riches,[29] though if Hazlitt is believed, England was 'rather a foul-mouthed nation'.[30] Evangelical prudery covered the traces. Thus, John Bright avoided Shakespeare, whose coarseness repelled him.[31]

The Wellington magistrate and churchwarden, F. T. Elworthy, denied that he had bowdlerised his Somerset glossary: 'the people are simple, and although there is a superabundance of rough, coarse language, yet foul-mouthed obscenity is a growth of cities, and I declare I have never heard it, so it cannot be recorded by me.'[32] Nevertheless, many glossarists projected a conservative bias, abominating 'the ghastly compounds of illiterate advertisers . . . the sweepings of the music-hall, the leavings of the prize-ring and the worst specimens of Americanisms' which were displacing 'good old English words.'[33] Glossarists seemed most interested in quaint expressions. Ellis judged them severely: 'Collecting country words is looked upon as an amusement, not as laying a brick in the temple of science; and, curiously enough, an accurate appreciation of their sounds is one of the last things thought of, and one which few glossarists give themselves any trouble about.'[34] But, treated cautiously, they remain for the historian indispensable guides; and their explanation of language change merits examination.

Urbanisation and the metropolitan influence were the first targets. London speech, from the concentration of the court, government and the law, was the ancestor of both literary English and the modern Received Standard. During the fifteenth and sixteenth centuries upper-class and popular London speech diverged. Thereafter, metropolitan demotic spread throughout the Home Counties. By 1876 Leveson Gower noted that Surrey dialect was 'almost confined to the old people and from the nearness to London and increased facilities of travel will ere long become obsolete'. In 1893, he reported, dialect-speaking was 'daily more circumscribed'.[35] From Essex, Hertfordshire, Sussex and Kent the account was the same. In Kent, dialect flourished only in the Weald, where strangers were rare. Otherwise, the 'dialectal sewage of the Metropolis finds its way down the river and is deposited on the southern bank of the Thames, as far as the limits of Gravesend-Reach, whence it seems to overflow and saturate the neighbouring district.'[36]

Counties further afield were not immune. Many Hampshire natives had been in service in London. A pupil of Henry Sweet reported from Andover in 1887 that even the oldest farm labourers were accustomed to London pronunciation.[37] Berkshire was said to be suffering cockneyisms in the 1860s. From Wiltshire came another account of 'the cockney misuse of H [which] is essentially foreign to our dialect. Formerly it was the rarest thing in the world to hear a true Wiltshire rustic make such a slip, though the townsfolk were by no means blameless in this respect . . .' Glossarists dated this process: virtually unknown before the 1830s, unusual in villages even in the 1860s and 1870s, common by the 1890s.[38] London was paramount, but every sizeable town controlled a linguistic field. Sheffield is one city for which evidence exists, though authorities disputed its dialect boundaries.[39] Small towns exercised influences too. Even northerners found Penrith speech obscure, a subdivision of Cumbrian dialect encompassing the area within which farmers attended Penrith market.[40]

The extension of urban dialect fields was a normal process of language change, but urbanisation now seemed so pervasive that rural England faced devitalisation. George Sturt thought villagers lay between civilisations, neither versed in traditional dialects, customs and trades nor coping with the new language of textbooks, official notices and procedures.[41] George Moore weighed the consequences for literature in 1913: 'The source from which language is refreshed – rural English – is being destroyed by Council Schools; and God help the writer who puts pen to paper in fifty years.'[42] Town speech was marching over larger tracts of countryside; it was also, many feared, converging. A standard genteel tone was spreading; so, to a degree, was a popular tone. Of course, the rough were always separable from the respectable, even in tiny places. At Berwick-upon-Tweed, 'the roughest part for the dialect and for social position is in the place called Greeses . . . , where the fishermen live outside the walls.'[43] Such dialect seclusions were becoming rarer in urban centres. Evidence from York and Leeds suggested that in towns the attempt was being made, by tradespeople especially, to speak a Standard English, although refinement was 'continually frustrated by dialectal tendencies and youthful habits'.[44] To the glossarists, therefore, town-speech was exceptionally corrupt. In the East Midlands this process seemed complete. Napier Reeve, a resident for thirty-five years, noted about Ellis's word-list that he could see no word whose Leicester pronunciation differed from the standard.[45]

The concomitants of urbanisation were improved communications, migration and industrialisation. All were blamed for the spread of alien usages and the disappearance of local expressions. In several areas the united process of industrial and speech colonisation was traced exactly. In north Cleveland, dialect was transmogrified by the introduction of iron works; in the Calder valley by the integration of the textile industry. Between 1840 and 1880 Colne and

Burnley came to share a common speech. Ellis's informant stated that as a boy he had

> opportunities of hearing the hand-loom weavers who lived in the small farm cottages on the hill-side in what was known in old times as Pendle and Trawden Forests. During the 20 years he had been away the dialect had completely changed and become a bastard Yo.[rkshire], from the mechanics who were engaged fitting the mill machinery and from the 'hands' who cross and recross the Pennine chain.[46]

Such movement occurred gradually in most places; but its impact on the remotest counties could be catastrophic. The dialect of eastern Cornwall was initially submerged by migrants to the mines; but after 1859 came the railways, whereupon 'cockneyisms' were rife.[47] Railways appeared ubiquitous and unifying. Ellis was told about Marklye in east Sussex:

> A railway has been opened for the last few months within four miles of us [at Heathfield], and already the change is very great. We have two old men who have worked on the farm in our family for many years, one for forty years. He is of an old superior family, but cannot read. He said yesterday [15 October 1885] that he was much put out at hearing people talk now, and he could not make out 'high words'. His wife, who is upwards of seventy and able to write, has much disgusted him by buying a dictionary to keep pace with the times. There are not a dozen people left in the parish who speak the real old dialect.[48]

By 1890 remoteness was measured as 13 miles from the nearest railhead.[49] Motor cars and telecommunications would quicken the commingling of speech and multiply the social contacts which railways advanced. Perhaps these were accelerated also by the dislocations of military service:

> When the soldiers return to their villages they will undoubtedly bring a greatly enlarged vocabulary, consisting partly of new technical terms, partly of the current slang of the Army, partly also of words picked up from their mates in the Regiment, who represent often a great variety of linguistic types . . . It is thus not improbable that the [1914–18] War will have destroyed, in many areas, the last frail claims of Vocabulary to be considered a specific characteristic of the dialect.[50]

In some respects, the glossarists were unduly alarmist. Was urban industrialisation inevitably inimical to dialect? The destruction of traditional occupations, mixture of populations, and introduction of new habits of thought and behaviour cumulatively made a difference; but many towns long retained rural features, and customary songs and festivals did not die overnight. Indeed, by extending literacy and purchasing power, industrial society provided means of preserving and diffusing this culture. The pre-industrial Lancashire dialect writer 'Tim Bobbin' (John Collier, 1708–86) found a larger audience in the industrial nineteenth century when his works were reprinted umpteen times.[51] It may be that by fixing upon the urban, industrial and transport revolutions' cardinal responsibility for the decline of dialect, glossarists missed the target. They supposed that prior to urban industrialisation dialect was 'pure', whereas the mobility of people and mixing of speech were continual. Towns might multiply dialects by generating new combinations and permit migrants to protect their heritage or even mount a cultural recovery, as did the Liverpool and London Welsh and Glasgow Gaelic.

Another agency of change was education. Its influence was prophesied early enough, by the Rev. Joseph Hunter who in 1819 and 1829 investigated the Sheffield region: 'The Madras and Lancasterian schools will make mighty havock among the relics of our primitive tongue.'[52] After the 1870 Education Act the threat was magnified: Jago, the authority on Cornish, wrote of 'that arch-enemy of all dialects, the modern school-board'.[53] The school-board teacher was excoriated as the determined eraser of dialect, rather as the French counterpart who allegedly promoted republican anticlericalism together with the French language. But villagers also encountered commercial travellers with their town speech. The clerical author of a Cotswolds glossary noted this. Moreover, he did not absolve the clergy, who countered local dialect by 'a latinised slip-slop.'[54]

The quality of public elementary education was not high. H. G. Wells recalled that the 1870 Act was 'an Act to educate the lower classes for employment on lower-class lines, and with specially trained, inferior teachers who had no university quality.'[55] It seems likely, before the profession raised its standards and became more mobile, that many teachers taught at schools located within regions where they were born, and only marginally modified their diction. Securing a regular attendance and lengthening the child's school life was also a long, slow process; and we may guess at the persistence of sub-literacy, the inability to read and write fluently and to articulate without awkwardness.[56] We should neither exaggerate the impact of the Education Acts nor pretend with Lady Bracknell that 'in England, at any rate, education appears to produce no effect whatsoever.'

Where compulsory education prevailed before 1870 – in the Scilly Isles, for example, since the 1840s – dialect speaking apparently perished. The islands' proprietor, Dorrien Smith, maintained: 'I know of no place in the British Isles where the Queen's English is less massacred by the lower classes than it is in these islands. There is no dialect or any peculiarities of speech worth mentioning . . .'[57] More sensitive observers were less absolute about education's transforming effects. In 1875 came this judicious account of west Somerset:

> Now although a process of levelling may be going on, as respects quaint words and local idioms, which board schools in every parish will surely accelerate, yet . . . this process is slow, and at present very far from complete. As regards pronunciation, intonation, and those finer shades of peculiarity which mark divergencies from the Queen's English almost more than the words used, I maintain that the changes are far slower than those which are constantly going on in what we call received English itself.[58]

By 1886 philologists agreed that

> our hereditary pronunciation will survive, together with our grammatical peculiarities, long after board schools and newspapers have brought English as a written language to one dead level. . . . The Education Act has forced the knowledge of the three R's upon the population, and thereby an acquaintance in all parts of the country with the same literary form of English, which it has been the aim and object of all elementary teachers to make their pupils consider to be the only correct one. . . . There is one written language understood by all, while the inhabitants of distant parts may be quite unintelligible to each other *viva voce*.[59]

Differences were marked between the old and young. Their accent was similar, their range of expression dissimilar. A schools inspector, Thomas Darlington, reported from Cheshire in 1887 that 'the very broadest and most thoroughly dialectal pronunciation is to be heard in the playgrounds of our common schools. On the other hand, the vocabulary of the folk-speech has suffered terribly of late years.' Darlington reckoned that over half the words in his glossary 'are never in the mouths of persons under twenty-five, and will consequently be obsolete in another generation. It is no uncommon thing for a boy to be unable to understand words and phrases which his grandfather has used all his life.'[60]

The education system was establishing a uniformity in writing;[61] but speech habits persisted, so that many appeared bilingual. It was reported of Worcestershire in 1882:

> Under the teaching of certificated masters in government schools the dialect is being rapidly modified; perhaps on the whole it is strange it does not disappear faster. Young people educated in these schools will often talk among themselves in broad Worcestershire, while they address their pastors, masters, and betters in the nearest approach to Queen's English to which they have been able to attain.[62]

Hardy noticed the same in Wessex. Of Tess, he observed: 'the dialect was on her tongue to some extent, despite the village school.' He contrasted Tess and her mother: 'Mrs Durbeyfield habitually spoke the dialect; her daughter, who had passed the Sixth Standard in the National School under a London-trained mistress, spoke two languages: the dialect at home, more or less; ordinary English abroad and to persons of quality.'[63]

Class relations, therefore, have a part in explaining speech patterns. Dialect was dying, not simply because old people were dying. Ordinary folk were becoming as conscious about speech as dress: agricultural labourers discarded the peasant smock as a menial badge. This mood glossarists were well qualified to register. The Rev. Sir William Cope observed

> among the old people a growing disinclination, when speaking to educated persons, to use . . . their vernacular dialect. So that when asked to repeat a word, they frequently – from a sort of false shame – substitute its English equivalent. And it is only perhaps my habit of being much with my workmen and cottagers, and frequently using their own words and names of things, that has enabled me often to overcome this shyness.[64]

The class aspect had several sides. Within the working classes different types of talk were reserved for the workplace and among mates, for the home and among women, and for public or social gatherings, though only the syntax and vocabulary, not the accent, might change.[65] Further differences were audible in communication between classes. Ordinary people might talk 'fine' when addressed by those whom they thought superior, while the quality guarded against dialect lapses and plebeian slips. About this latter proclivity, regional and town–country differences may be recognised. Country gentlemen once easily mixed rustic and courtly English, and the regional dialect of Northern manufacturers was famous. By the late nineteenth century a change was notable. Tenant farmers in Cheshire spoke dialect to servants and labourers, more or less standard English to their families, social equals and superiors. Status was at issue. For those of established rank there was less anxiety. Herbert Knatchbull-Hugessen, as proficient in north Kentish as Sir William Cope in Hampshire dialect, was not thought less of a gentleman for conversing with tenants and labourers in the local manner.[66]

In towns this freedom was circumscribed. Consider the Greys, mill-owners of Burnley. James Grey, active in the firm until 1923, spoke emphatic Lancashire; his son, Sir John Grey, spoke what his obituarist delicately called 'cultured Lancashire'; his grandson, another James who entered the business in 1935, spoke with a mild public school accent outside the mill but the broadest Lancashire he could muster inside, because 'it is better to get the points across'.[67] The mutuality of these mill communities represented a special case, although it deferred rather than defeated the general trend towards a class division of speech. The world of finance, commerce and big business, with less personal contact between masters and men, registered the change earlier. There was no tolerance for City bankers who spoke like cockney costermongers. And middle-class women everywhere lived in dread of being thought vulgar. So Ellis believed – he attributed several mutations in educated speech to the strength of this concern among women.[68]

Class feeling was one inspiration of Received Standard English. Henry Wyld actually defined it as a class dialect, or public school English.[69] It was also characteristic of a geographical area, more south than north, although various Modified Standards, influenced by provincial capitals like

Birmingham, Manchester and Newcastle, were admitted. Technically, these Standards remained dialects, actually mongrel though the claim was pedigree English. In the 1870s, though he used the term 'received pronunciation', Ellis was sceptical when listening to public figures in the pulpit, in Parliament, at the bar, at university, and in learned societies, whether there really was such a thing.[70] Certainly, regional, group and generational peculiarities existed then as they persist now. There was no uniformity but there was a new variety because, Wyld contended,

> the old Regional Dialects of England were disappearing, . . . their place . . . being taken by a totally different form of English, not developed normally from the several Regional Dialects, but one of different origin, acquired through external channels. The old dialects were not growing like each other, but were vanishing. In their places various forms of Modified Standard have arisen.[71]

The degree to which larger differences were long ago broken down in educated speech was underlined by Sebastian Evans in 1881 when revising his father's 1848 Leicestershire glossary. Evans noted how Leicestershire dialect had slid into those of neighbouring counties, while the distinction between educated and uneducated Leicestershire speech had hardened. Mid-Midland educated speech, he concluded,

> was decided by the fact that it was the form most 'agreeably intelligible' to the greatest number, but the moment the national unity by demanding a national standard language had made this fact distinctly apparent, it was no longer possible for the educated classes in any town or city to remain permanently on the side of the minority.

The public schools and universities reinforced this, each a 'powerful engine for rendering the educated dialect homogeneous from one end of England to the other'.[72] Tom Brown never returned to the Vale of the White Horse speaking as he had done, after his Rugby schooldays.

Many distinctive features of Received Standard English seemed determined by class conditioning. Ellis speculated that it might only be 'the classification of "dropping *aitches*" among social sins which keeps the aspirate alive in the received dialect.'[73] The Received Standard which Wyld celebrated as a widespread educated dialect was a middle-class triumph. Their influence he detected in two directions from the eighteenth century, eliminating both popular vulgarities and aristocratic profanities.[74] These culminated in that fastidious speech which G. K. Chesterton recognised in his upbringing; indeed he argued that by attaching such 'enormous importance' to speaking correctly the bourgeoisie cut themselves off from the classes above as well as below them.[75]

It is appropriate to ask again the questions, how was the authority of Received Standard English established and how did dialects decline? There are parallels to be drawn from the fate of Gaelic speaking. In Scotland, the dissemination of English forms was speeded by institutional influences, the Reformers' Bible and monarchical and parliamentary fusions of 1603 and 1707; but economic and demographic dislocation and social aspiration supplied additional force. The *Gaidhealtachd*, for long roughly coterminous with the Highland line, was progressively confined within a diminishing zone of the maritime north-west and adjacent islands. Outside this region a Scots English hybrid developed, most luxuriant in Robert Burns' poetry which blended the literary and colloquial, Lallans and what J. A. H. Murray styled fancy or spurious Scotch, that is English spelled as Scotch.[76] A Scotch literary tradition continued; but self-consciousness snuffed out more than sentimentality spared. Here the representative Scots were the Enlightenment philosopher, David Hume, who died seeking forgiveness not of his sins but his Scottisms;[77] Samuel Smiles, who preached the central sermon of Victorian endeavour, *Self Help* (1859); and J. M. Barrie, who observed few more impressive sights than a Scotsman on the make. Under this twin movement, the English invasion of Scotland and the Scotch invasion of England, accents lingered, but the language was reduced and confused.[78]

In Ireland, the Great Famine, which fell most severely on the *Gaeltacht*, tended to obscure the social processes at work. Irish nationalists complained that English governments sought to exterminate the Irish language via the National Schools. Clearly, the anglicised bias of education counted; but decline was already advanced before this system was established. F. S. L. Lyons explained the effective cause thus: 'economic betterment and social advancement of all kinds depended upon mastering the tongue of the foreigner.'[79] Welsh had greater tenacity. Some 8500 books were published in Welsh in the nineteenth century; a vernacular press and *eisteddfodau* flourished; and chapel and work communities gave the language protection and vitality.[80] The number of Welsh speakers was in relative decline from the late nineteenth century and in absolute decline from 1911; none the less, Welsh continued to be taught in schools owing to the exertions of the separate Welsh Department of the Board of Education from 1907 and subsequently the Welsh Office. Here the central state was not the enemy. By capturing state resources, Welsh language partisans arrested the speed of its decline.[81] Indeed, in parts of the economy, the public domain especially, Welsh-speaking proved a talisman for getting jobs.

As for Cornish, use of the complete language, as distinct from odd words and idioms, was restricted to Land's End villages by 1700 and dead altogether by 1800, although Cornish folk still talk of going to England when they cross the Tamar.[82] Manx survived longer because it had institutional protection in the courts, Tynwald and pulpit – the Bible was translated into Manx – but the Manx Society acknowledged in 1870 that to uphold Manx as a spoken language was 'hopeless' and 'doomed'.[83]

Cultural nationalism preserved these languages from extinction and even led to revivals as emblems of nationhood, in Ireland and Wales especially, to a minor degree elsewhere. England's dialects had no such compelling reason for survival or recovery. They were outflanked from two directions, crushed from above and cast off from below. That some used the public authority as well as private schools to reform speech is indisputable. 'At the present time', wrote Henry Wyld in 1906, 'it will not be denied that to inculcate the speaking of correct English is the chief solicitude of a very large number of persons engaged in Primary and Secondary Education in this country.'[84] When Edward Lyttelton, headmaster of Haileybury, advocated phonetic training at the Northern Education Conference in 1904, the *Manchester Guardian* agreed that current dialects were wretched,

> urban hybrids, the products of a conflation which tends to corruption, produced moreover amid surroundings which do not foster either charm

> of sound or charm of imagination. The dialect spoken by the masses of the people in Manchester is not the fine speech of Edwin Waugh. Cockney, the most odious of the bastard forms, is swallowing the dialects of South-east England like an Aaron's rod; even in the villages of remoter Wessex you will regularly hear Cockney songs sung in the public-houses. For persons who mournfully recognise these facts the question is coming to be, not 'Shall we replace the old dialects?' but 'Shall we concern ourselves as to what language replaces them?'

All that remained was whether to level up or down:

> Doubtless it is odious and un-English to level at all, but we have to face facts. And on the issue of what is now a rapid development depends not only the tie between future England and the best of her own past, but the tie between her and the younger nations whose language is at present still identical with hers.[85]

The *Manchester Guardian* in practice was ambivalent. As a newspaper which served a proud region it continued to publish stories in Lancashire dialect;[86] as the country's leading organ of liberal opinion it believed that Standard English might extend communication between classes and unite nations. That the educational system might be used to purge dialect-speaking was evident; indeed explicit recommendation issued from a committee of the Board of Education in 1921, under the chairmanship of the one-time Coefficient, the poet Sir Henry Newbolt, 'regard being had to (1) the requirements of a liberal education; (2) the needs of business, the professions, and public services; and (3) the relation of English to other studies.' Newbolt's committee censured dialect and vulgar speech partly on aesthetic and moral grounds, referring to it as 'disfigured', a 'perverted power', 'lip laziness', in sum, 'evil habits of speech contracted in home and street.'[87] The committee appeared unsympathetic to the communal loyalties which sustained dialect-speaking; but it was not unsympathetic to working-class aspirations. Had it been so, its natural course would have been to recommend *preserving* dialect and the demotic, thus to ensure that the working classes were permanently confined within local quarters as an undermass deprived of access to national resources. The committee's assumption about the superior authority of Standard English may have been linguistically baseless but functionally its case seemed strong. Dialect-speaking, to this kind of liberal mind infused with Edwardian Efficiency, was a barrier to national integration, a linguistic tariff which impeded easy communication, perpetuated obscurantism, and denied its adherents full intellectual satisfaction, social mobility and economic and political power. Pressed further, the logic of this linguistic free trade position led beyond a Standard English, ultimately to an internationalism based upon Esperanto or Novial.[88] The Newbolt Committee's primary purpose, however, was meritocratic, to make available to working-class children the nation's literary heritage and to frame an educational ladder for individuals to glimpse wider horizons.

Speech training through education would be ineffectual without social experience. Those who reformed their speech required opportunities to practise it. If not the removal of class exclusiveness, then at least more frequent mixing of classes and upward social mobility were necessary preconditions. The education system thus only confirmed a decline of dialect already incipient through a diffused spirit of improvement and self-help. According to Gladstone, 'that was the most desirable condition for the working classes that would enable its worthiest members to most easily rise out of it.'[89] Language was a liberator for the individual. To better your speech was to better your station, given the terms on which society's judgements were arranged. The affectations and solecisms of clerical workers, petty shopkeepers and domestic servants invited snobbish humour; but the individual intent was serious. Eliza Doolittle called on Henry Higgins because the dustman's daughter wanted a place in a genteel florist's shop. Likewise the Liverpool urchin, Benny Bates, 'was anxious to speak correctly, and not be a disgrace to the gentleman who employed him and the butt of the clerks.'[90] So, too, the son of a Cheshire farm-worker, born in 1874, Ernest Barker, and the son of a Cornish clay-miner, born in 1903, A. L. Rowse, determined to improve their spoken English. Both had the scholarship boy's psychology. Ever since Rowse received the shattering revelation that 'the word "chimley" was wrong, and that it should be "chimney" ', the struggle to abandon dialect utterance was pursued without regret, 'for was it not the key which unlocked the door to all that lay beyond – Oxford, the world of letters, the community of all who speak the King's English, from which I should otherwise have been infallibly barred?'[91]

The consequence for class development should be weighed. Some might suppose that, shorn of dialect vocabularies and left only with modified regional accents, the working classes were becoming more homogeneous. The late nineteenth century evinced plentiful variety still. The style of address to fellow workers in different areas – mates, lads, chaps, boys, and numerous less general forms – was only one index tabulated by Ellis from his dialect test.[92] It remained possible to localise a speaker from indicative intonation and stress, as well as from surviving dialect words and constructions. To attend the annual mops like the Doncaster Martlemas Fair, where workers gathered from south Yorkshire, north Nottinghamshire, north Lincolnshire, and parts of Derbyshire, was to hear 'the biggest babel of dialects since the time of Noah'.[93] Lancastrians and Cockneys were still plainly separated on any language scale, although not so distantly as during Samuel Bamford's prison encounter in 1817, when two Londoners confounded him with their v's and w's and rhyming slang, and they 'stood wide agape when I opened upon them in broad Lancashire; the old man put on his spectacles, and peered at me as if I were uttering barbarous Russ, or a Lappish incantation.'[94]

The variety of voices was less striking by 1940, George Orwell remarked with his usual abruptness –

> After 1918 there began to appear something that had never existed in England before: people of indeterminate social class. In 1910 every human being in these islands could be 'placed' in an instant by his clothes, manners and accent. That is no longer the case. Above all, it is not the case in the new townships that have developed as a result of cheap motor cars and the southward shift of industry.[95]

The linguistic ascendancy of southern English was accelerated by inter-war economic trends, as the northern industrial staples shrank in the Depression; but this only confirmed a centuries-old metropolitan predominance since London had continued to generate greater wealth and to attract most wealth-holders even during the heyday of the industrial revolution.[96] The extent to which regional dialects survived into the 1950s and after was measured by Harold Orton and his colleagues, whose surveys concentrated on older (over 60 years) inhabitants in small rural settlements.[97] In 1978, they noted how Standard English pronunciation was 'itself being redefined within a larger range of acceptability than formerly';[98] but this was a consequence of its near universality, and evidence everywhere pointed to a rapid ousting of vernacular vestiges.

Regional accents and idioms, none the less, remain and reproduce, as among Asians who acquire Bradford or Birmingham accents. London's West Indians have blended a metropolitan demotic and Caribbean patois, to produce a Black British speech. Thus new distinctions have replaced old, reminiscent of times when near neighbours were incomprehensible, like the inhabitants of Leeds and Heckmondwike or the mid-Derbyshire man who migrated to Sheffield in the 1830s and suffered several months' solitude before he could converse with workmen whose dialect differed so much from his own.[99] What also remains is tension between speech provinces, a pecking order of melodious and execrable accents. Gissing recoiled from cockney as from the vile. Another might judge Yorkshire crass and Brummagem cretinous with as little authority; but for long periods cockney was regarded with especial disdain, perhaps because it was that popular accent heard most by the quality and therefore deemed most deadly.

Another general observation might be advanced. Vertical social divisions survived longer perhaps in places where masters and men spoke a common dialect; horizontal divisions grew where the employing and managerial classes spoke in the national 'educated' patronising manner and the dialects of their workforce merged into a common colloquial style, generating perceptions of 'us and them'. Here was the rock of class. The withering away of dialect words was relatively speedy, but dialect accents and unceremoniousness masquerading as dialect were located in impermeable class layers. The London Head Teachers' Association noted in 1938 that least progress had been made since the 1880s in improving the pupils' spoken English, though 'more and more engaging the attention of teachers'.[100] Deep down there was resistance, ridicule or resentment of those who talked 'la-di-da'.[101] Or perhaps it was just physiologically impossible. No training could counteract heredity and environment in the Lancashire girl who, after an elocution examination, exulted before her mother, 'Ee ma, Ah've past.'[102]

The role of the trade unions and Labour Party requires final comment. Unaffected speech vindicated Labour's claim to represent ordinary people against the exclusive governing classes, as J. H. Thomas's studious underemployment of aspirates exemplified. The Establishment made some accommodation by abandoning classical tags in speeches, but increasingly Labour claimed a monopoly of the popular style.[103] Nevertheless, that part of Labour's striving which grew from Liberal self-improvement should not be forgotten. In pursuit of Northumberland dialects in 1876, Ellis interviewed two Bebside pitmen. Both spoke well and Ellis asked if they spoke so in the colliery. They replied, 'Oh no! in the pit you must speak as they speak or you will be laughed at. We are allowed to speak properly at the weekly meetings of the Trades Union'.[104] Thirty years later, we can find in the Poplar branch Labour Party an elocution class run by R. C. K. Ensor, the Wykehamist and Balliol-educated Fabian.[105] He aimed to educate working men in socialist literature; but another purpose was to improve their diction, to gain assurance in public. Slovenly or dialect pronunciation would deny speakers a national audience, devalue the force of the argument, or simply lessen their Party's prestige.

Qualifications about this assumption are curious. The Labour Party was led first by two Scots, Keir Hardie and Ramsay MacDonald. Likewise, Irish and Welsh rhetoricians flourished on the parliamentary stage. Their regional accents ceased to have derogatory connotations as the English became particular about their own refinement. They were classless, even charming.[106] The low-born Celt was thus emancipated before the low-born English provincial. David Marquand describes how easily MacDonald entered Society. He had come a long way from Lossiemouth but

> It would have been much longer if he had been born in a working-class district in Leeds or London. Like many Scots – and, for that matter, like many Irishmen and Welshmen as well – he almost certainly derived a certain sneaking satisfaction from the thought that he could move at will up and down the English social scale, and storm the heights of London society.[107]

This was a Pyrrhic victory for Celts who regretted the colonisation of their lands by English settlement and speech; but it is widely evident as the twentieth century progresses that a Standard English speaker who retains a provincial quality enjoys compensation where once his dialect-speaking forebear suffered censure. The maxim which James Boswell enunciated for the Scotch and Irish professional and gentry classes who aspired to succeed in England in the eighteenth century, eventually became applicable for all. Correct your pronunciation only so far as it may be thought not offensive, was Boswell's recommendation. Then he elaborated:

> let me give my countrymen of North-Britain an advice not to aim at absolute perfection in this respect; not to speak *High English*, as we are apt to call what is far removed from the *Scotch*, but which is by no means *good English*, and makes, 'the fools who use it', truly ridiculous. Good English is plain, easy, and smooth in the mouth of an unaffected English Gentleman. A studied and factitious pronunciation, which requires perpetual attention and imposes perpetual constraint, is exceedingly disgusting. A small intermixture of provincial peculiarities may, perhaps, have an agreeable effect, as the notes of different birds concur in the harmony of the grove, and please more than if they were all exactly alike. I could name some gentlemen of Ireland, to whom a slight proportion of the accent and recitative of that country is an advantage. The same observation will apply to the gentlemen of Scotland.[108]

To the Welsh too and so, eventually, to the English.

## *Notes*

1. I am grateful to many friends and colleagues who debated interpretations: Professor J. Carey, Mr T. Griffiths, Dr B. H. Harrison, Mr Alan Hindle, Dr R. I. McKibbin, Professor S. Romaine, Dr G. Sutherland and Professor K. V. Thomas.
2. The most celebrated advocacy of an official standard, to be decided by an English Academy modelled upon the French (founded under Louis XIV's patronage), was by Jonathan Swift, 'A Proposal For Correcting, Improving and Ascertaining The English Tongue . . .' (1712), in *The Prose Works of Jonathan Swift, D.D.*, edited by Temple Scott, vol. XI (George Bell, London, 1907). Dryden and Defoe also made entreaties.
3. George Gissing, *Demos: A Story of English Socialism* (1886) (Harvester Press, 1972), pp. 405, 407. Gissing's heavy-handed social

comedy, *The Town Traveller* (1898), offended 'the great order of minor clerks', one of whom protested to the *Daily Chronicle* about the character of Christopher Parish. Foremost of the complaints was that 'We are not in the habit of dropping our aitches, we do not pronounce "rain" as "rine" . . .' The correspondence is quoted in Pierre Coustillas' notes to the 1981 Harvester edition, pp. 315–18.

4. H. C. Wyld, *The Historical Study of the Mother Tongue* (John Murray, London, 1906), p. 358.
5. J. R. Firth, 'The English School of Phonetics', *Transactions of the Philological Society*, 1946. Reprinted in Firth, *Papers in Linguistics 1934–1951* (1957), ch. 8. See also J. W. Burrow, 'The Uses of Philology in Victorian England', in Robert Robson (ed.), *Ideas and Institutions of Victorian Britain* (G. Bell, London, 1967), pp. 180–204.
6. The first part of the letter A issued in 1884; Z was reached in 1928, after 240,165 main words had been defined. The official title was *New English Dictionary*, though *Oxford English Dictionary* found common adoption after its appearance on the cover of the section 'Deceit to Deject' in 1895. Even more people felt the influence of the allied *Concise Oxford Dictionary of Current English*, first edited by H. W. and F. G. Fowler in 1911.
7. Quoted in Elizabeth Mary Wright, *The Life of Joseph Wright* (1932), vol. 2, p. 424. Wright's dictionary was vitiated by this failure to sort out regional dialect from 'corruptions' and 'mistakes' – see H. C. Wyld, *A History of Modern Colloquial English* (Basil Blackwell, Oxford, 1920; 3rd edition 1936), p. 14.
8. Quoted in Firth p. 120. About 120 millions spoke English round the world; and the Empire gave many new words to the language. See *The Cambridge History of English Literature*, vol. xiv, Part III (1916), ch. xv; William Crooke (ed.), Henry Yule and A. C. Burnell, *Hobson-Jobson* (1903); and Mary S. Serjeantson, *A History of Foreign Words in English* (Routledge & Kegan Paul, London, 1935).
9. Henry Sweet, *A New English Grammar: Part I, Introduction, Phonology and Accidence* (Clarendon, Oxford, 1892), p. 186.
10. Richard M. Dorson, *The British Folklorists* (Chicago, 1968); Maud Karpeles, *Cecil Sharp* (Routledge, 1967); John Bird, *Percy Grainger* (Faber, 1976).
11. On this problem, see A. J. Ellis, *On early English Pronunciation*, IV, p. 1185; V, pp. 38, 54, 638, 640, 748; Wright, vol. I p. 137; Wyld (1920), pp. 190–2.
12. Ellis V, Preliminary Matter, p. 59.
13. W. B. Yeats nominated Ellis 'perhaps the last man in England to run the circle of the sciences without superficiality', *Autobiographies* (Macmillan, 1980), p. 159. On the striving for linguistic unity in France, see Eugen Weber, *Peasants into Frenchmen* (Chatto & Windus, 1977), chs. 6, 18. Gilliéron's and Edmont's *L'Atlas linguistique de la France* was published in seven volumes (Paris, 1902–10).
14. Ellis, V, p. 463.

15. P. J. Keating, *The Working Classes in Victorian Fiction* (Routledge, 1971).
16. Martha Vicinus, *The Industrial Muse* (Croom Helm, 1974), ch. 5; Brian Hollingworth, 'Lancashire Writing and the Antiquarians', *The Journal of Regional and Local Studies*, vol. 6, no. 2 (Autumn 1985), pp. 27–36; R. C. K. Ensor's diary (Bodleian Library), 20 January 1917, for his wife reading aloud to him Edwin Waugh's poems; and L. S. Amery, *My Political Life*, vol. I (Hutchinson, 1953), pp. 22–3, for his cousins' proficiency in Devon dialect.
17. John St Loe Strachey, *The Adventure of Living* (Hodder & Stoughton, 1922), pp. 19–20; Chris Wrigley (ed.), *William Barnes, The Dorset Poet* (Dovecote Press, Wimborne, 1984), p. 5.
18. Lord Birkenhead, *Rudyard Kipling* (Weidenfeld & Nicolson, 1978), pp. 95, 123–4, judges Kipling's cockney spurious and his Irish of the stage kind, but his Yorkshire more authentic because scrutinised by his father.
19. Memoir by Robert Bridges, in *The Collected Papers of Henry Bradley* (Clarendon, Oxford, 1928), p. 24. Also, Shaw to Bridges, 4 February and 24 March 1910, in Dan H. Laurence (ed.), *Bernard Shaw, Collected Letters 1898–1910* (Dodd, Mead & Co., New York, 1972), pp. 895–8, 916–17.
20. FitzEdward Hall, 'English Rational and Irrational', *The Nineteenth Century*, vol. 43 (1880), reprinted in W. F. Bolton and D. Crystal (eds.), *The English Language*, vol. 2 (Cambridge, 1969), pp. 30–53.
21. See K. C. Phillips, *Language and Class in Victorian England* (Basil Blackwell, Oxford, 1984).
22. G. B. Shaw, 'A Plea for Speech Nationalisation', *Morning Leader*, 10 August 1901; reprinted in Bolton and Crystal, pp. 80–5; also Shaw to Archibald Henderson, 3 January 1905, in Laurence, pp. 484, 504–5.
23. For the pressures placed on working men to graft a 'cultivated' accent onto a local one, see Wright, vol. 2, p. 610; and *Bolton Journal and Guardian*, 26 September 1924.
24. *Collected Papers of Henry Bradley*, pp. 27–8, 164–93.
25. Shaw, *Pygmalion*, Preface. For a police sergeant's son taught to speak from formal grammars and Pitman's rules, see C. H. Rolph, *London Particulars* (Oxford, 1980), pp. 95–7.
26. On the English Simplified Spelling Society, see *The New Age*, vol. 13 (1913), p. 234 and vol. 23 (1918), p. 334, reprinted in Wallace Martin (ed.), *Orage as Critic* (Routledge, 1974), pp. 159–60. William Archer, the Scots rationalist and enthusiast of Ibsen, was the Society's secretary.
27. A. Lloyd James, 'Broadcast English', BBC pamphlet (1926); reprinted in Bolton and Crystal pp. 100–13. See also A. Briggs, *The History of Broadcasting in the United Kingdom*, vol. II, 'The Golden Age of Wireless' (Oxford, 1965), pp. 467–9.
28. Lloyd James, op. cit.; Robert McCrum, 'The English Language', *The Listener*, 2 October 1986, pp. 10–12.
29. J. S. Farmer and W. E. Henley attempted a record in their

*Dictionary of Slang and its Analogues* (1894–1904) but this remained incomplete, partly owing to the refusal of publishers to risk printing obscenities. See John Connell, *W. E. Henley* (Kennikat Press, New York, 1949), pp. 191, 212, 264, 288.

30. W. Hazlitt, *Table Talk*, XXII, 'On Criticism'.
31. R. Barry O'Brien, *John Bright* (Nelson, 1910), p. 437. So did Samuel Butler's father, see *Selections from the Note-Books* (Cape, 1930), p. 68.
32. F. T. Elworthy, *The West Somerset Word-Book* (1886), p. xii. See *D.N.B.* (1901–11) for Elworthy (1830–1907); and Karpeles, pp. 51–3, for a similar defence.
33. Rev. W. D. Parish, *A Dictionary of the Sussex Dialect* (Lewes, 1875), preface.
34. Ellis, IV, p. 1087, n. 2.
35. G. Leveson Gower, *Surrey Provincialisms* (1876), p. 79, *A Glossary of Surrey Words* (1893), p. viii.
36. W. D. Parish and W. F. Shaw, *A Dictionary of the Kentish Dialect and Provincialisms in use in the County of Kent* (1887), p. viii.
37. Ellis, V, p. 99.
38. On Berkshire, Ellis, V, p. 129, and R. W. Huntley, *A Glossary of the Cotswold Dialect* (1868), p. 4; on Wiltshire, G. E. Dartnell and E. H. Goddard, *A Glossary of Words used in the County of Wiltshire* (1893), pp. xvii, 72. Dartnell was a bank clerk in Salisbury; Goddard a clergyman.
39. Ellis, V, pp. 404–5; S. O. Addy, *A Glossary of Words used in the neighbourhood of Sheffield* (1888).
40. P. H. Reaney, *A Grammar of the Dialect of Penrith* (Manchester University Press, 1927), pp. 1–2; cf. W. W. Skeat and J. H. Nodal (eds.), *A Bibliographical List* (English Dialectt Society, 1877), p. 104; and W. Dickinson, E. W. Prevost and S. Dickson Brown, *Dialect of Cumberland* (London and Carlisle, 1899).
41. George Sturt ('George Bourne'), *Change in the Village* (1912). For Sturt's anxiety to purge dialect solecisms from his own literary English, see his correspondence with Arnold Bennett in 1898, in James Hepburn, *Letters of Arnold Bennett*, vol. II 1889–1915 (Oxford, 1968), p. 110.
42. A. R. Orage debated Moore's contention in *The New Age*, vol. 14 (1914), p. 498, Wallace Martin, pp. 160–1.
43. Ellis, V, p. 645.
44. Ibid., pp. 63, 394, 396.
45. Ibid., p. 46. In part, this was because the metropolitan standard itself comprised a Midlands element.
46. Ibid., pp. 62, 340. See also Harold Orton, *The Phonology of a South Durham Dialect* (Kegan Paul, Trench, Trubner & Co., 1933), pp. xiii-xviii for the influence upon the speech of Byers Green of miners from Ireland, Scotland, Wales, Yorkshire, Lancashire and the Midlands.
47. M. A. Courtney, *West Cornwall Words* (1880); F. W. P. Jago, *The*

*Ancient Language and the Dialect of Cornwall* (Netherton & Worth, Truro, 1882), p. 49.

48. Ellis, V, pp. 182–3.
49. R. PPearse Chope, *The Dialect of Hartland, Devonshire* (1891).
50. Wyld (1920), p. 15; Edward Fraser and John Gibbons, *Soldier and Sailor Words and Phrases* (Routledge, London, 1925).
51. See W. E. A. Axon in Skeat and Nodal, p. 54; Vicinus, ch. 5; and *D.N.B.* entry for J. H. Nodal (1831–1909), secretary of the English Dialect Society, 1874–96. Brinley Thomas, *Migration and Urban Development* (Methuen, 1972), pp. 179–81 makes a similar point for Wales.
52. Quoted in Addy, p. x.
53. Jago, p. 49. The Rev. H. C. Beeching, whose *Pages from A Private Diary* (Smith, Elder & Co., 1898), was serialised in *The Cornhill Magazine*, ranked Board schoolmasters along with railway porters as chiefly responsible for new-fangled pronunciations, p. 129. See also Wyld (1906), pp. 377–9 for the railway pronunciation of place-names.
54. Huntley, pp. 1–2. The eponymous heroine of George Meredith's *Rhoda Fleming* (1890), daughter of a poor Kentish farmer, learns 'correct' speech by copying the rector and his wife ('highly grammatical people'), and by mimicking the phrases and manner of characters in 'the courtly French fairy-books', p. 4.
55. H. G. Wells, *Experiment in Autobiography* (Cape, 1934), vol. I, p. 93.
56. But see M. Loane, *From Their Point of View* (Arnold, 1908), pp. 80–7 warning against underestimating the fluency and vocabulary of the poor; Wyld (1906), p. 349, and Stephen Reynolds and Bob and Tom Woolley, *Seems So!* (Macmillan, 1911, 1913 edition), Introduction.
57. Quoted in Ellis, V, p. 174. The mixture of population on the islands was deemed a contributing cause.
58. Elworthy (1875), p. 4. For examples of sturdy survivals, despite education, see Cecil Torr, *Small Talk at Wreyland*, first series, 1918 (Oxford, 1979 edition), p. 55 for Devonshire, and Philip Snowden, *An Autobiography*, vol. 1 (Ivor Nicholson & Watson, 1934), pp. 11–12 for Yorkshire.
59. Elworthy (1886), pp. v-vi, xliii. In sum, Elworthy concluded in a paper to the Philological Society in 1888, 'the Board Schools had not tended to destroy the dialect but to develop it', *Athenaeum*, 10 March 1888. Addy, p. xi, who quoted this, concurred with respect to Sheffield; as did A. L. Lowell in general, attributing it to the unwillingness of the middle classes to send their children to public elementary schools – *The Government of England* (Macmillan, 1908), vol. 2, p. 339.
60. T. Darlington, *The Folk-Speech of South Cheshire* (1887), p. 14.
61. Belief in the power of the education system accounts for Henry Bradley's assumption that, while the vocabulary would continue to undergo great changes, English grammar was 'probably a finished

process [and] . . . will remain for centuries very nearly what it is now'. H. Bradley, *The Making of English*, (Macmillan, London, 1904), p. 78.

62. Mrs E. L. Chamberlain, *A Glossary of West Worcestershire Words* (1882), preface.
63. T. Hardy, *Tess of the D'Urbervilles* (Macmillan, 1891; 1965), pp. 14, 22.
64. The Rev. Sir W. H. Cope, *A Glossary of Hampshire Words and Phrases* (1883), p. v.
65. Harold Orton, *Survey of English Dialects: Introduction* (Leeds, 1962), pp. 18–19.
66. Darlington, p. 13; Ellis, V, p. 137. The upper classes always enjoyed greater freedom than the middle classes in their speech although, for instance, Curzon's retention of the Derbyshire short 'a' was regarded as a chink in his superior armour. See Michael Kennedy, *Portrait of Elgar* (Oxford, 1982 edition), pp. 141–2 for the upper classes' use of dialect/baby talk in intimate exchanges; and Phillips, pp. 114–15 for their delight in using servants' phrases. Wyld (1920), pp. 15–16 defines the limits of the upper classes' excursions into dialect.
67. Quoted in G. Turner, *The North Country* (Eyre & Spottiswood, 1967), p. 117. Some Yorkshire worsted manufacturers made the status transition (and speech refinement) earlier, see Eric Sigsworth, *Black Dyke Mills* (Liverpool University Press, 1958), pp. 72–3, quoting a scornful *Bradford Observer*, 9 June 1879. In fiction, the Dunfield (Wakefield) millowner, Dagworth, anxious to purchase refinement through marriage, in Gissing's *A Life's Morning* (1888), is a good example of the between stage: 'His utterance was that of an educated man, but it had something of the Yorkshire accent, a broadness which would have distressed the ear in the drawing-room' (Harvester Press, 1984 edition, p. 78). The novel repays study as an updated *North and South* in which the characters' speech establishes their station, prospects and ambition in life, and embodies Gissing's estimate of their moral worth.
68. Ellis, IV, pp. 1148, 1160. The latest survey notes the same for dialect speakers: 'men speak vernacular more frequently, more consistently, and more genuinely than women', Orton (1962), p. 15. Significantly, too, Jonathan Swift exempted women from his diatribe against purveyors of corrupted speech: ' . . . I would rather have trusted the refinement of our language, as far as it relates to sound, to the judgment of the women, than of illiterate court fops, half-witted poets, and university boys' (Swift, p. 14).
69. Wyld (1920), pp. 2–3; Wyld (1906), pp. 23, 99–102.
70. Ellis, IV, pp. 1208–17.
71. Wyld (1920), p. 7; Wyld (1906), pp. 104, 342–3, 346, 354–5.
72. S. Evans (ed.), *Leicestershire Words, Phrases and Proverbs* (1881), p. xxv.
73. Ellis, IV, p. 1332; Wyld (1920), p. 296.
74. Wyld, (1920), pp. 17–24; cf. Dean Hole, *Then and Now* (Hutch-

inson, 1901), p. 41, recalling when 'the conventional gentleman was as profuse in his anathemas as an Oecumenical Council or a Commination Service, but his maledictions were not pronounced against evil and unbelief, but against political opponents, inclement weather, forgetful servants, refractory horses, disagreeable duties, and tradesmen who wished to be paid. Those were days in which a Primate said to a Premier, "It may save time, my lord, if we assume before we commence our discussion that everybody and everything is damned".'

75. G. K. Chesterton, *Autobiography* (Sheed & Ward, New York, 1936), pp. 6–8.
76. Ellis, V, p. 731. A similar confusion characterised English North country writing which interlaced lexical dialect with Standard English misspelt in phonetic dialect.
77. T. C. Smout, *A History of the Scottish People 1560–1830* (Fontana edition, 1972), p. 461. See also James Boswell, *Life of Johnson*, 1791 (Oxford, 1980 edition), pp. 273–4, 404, 468–70.
78. J. Y. Mather and H. H. Speitel (eds.), *The Linguistic Atlas of Scotland*, 3 vols. (Croom Helm, 1975, 1977, 1986); M. Robinson (ed.), *The Concise Scots Dictionary* (Aberdeen, 1985).
79. F. S. L. Lyons, *Ireland Since the Famine* (Fontana edition, 1973), p. 88. The most sophisticated statistical study is Garret FitzGerald, 'Estimates for Baronies of Minimum Level of Irish-Speaking amongst Successive Decennial Cohorts: 1771–1781 to 1861–1871', *Proceedings of the Royal Irish Academy*, vol. 84, C, no. 3 (Dublin, 1984), pp. 117–55.
80. K. O. Morgan, *Rebirth of a Nation: Wales 1880–1980* (Oxford, 1981), chs. 4, 9, 12; R. Merfyn Jones, *The North Wales Quarrymen, 1874–1922* (Cardiff, 1981); John Langton and R. J. Morris (eds.), *Atlas of Industrializing Britain 1780–1914* (Methuen, London, 1986), pp. 202–5.
81. Timothy Williams, 'Whitehall and the Welsh Language – A Case Study', *Agenda, Welsh Journal of Business and Administration*, no. 5 (Summer 1984), pp. 10–17.
82. Jago, p. 45.
83. The Rev. W. Gill, *Kelly's Manx Grammar* (Douglas, 1859, 1870), pp. iv-v. Gill argued, however, that 'among the peasantry it still retains a strong hold. It is the language of their affections and their choice – the language to which they habitually resort in their communications with each other . . . In English, even where they have a fair knowledge of the tongue, they speak with hesitation and under restraint. In Manx they are fluent, and at ease.' See also *D.N.B.* entry for A. W. Moore (1853–1909), Manx antiquary.
84. Wyld (1906), p. 356.
85. *Manchester Guardian*, 9 January 1904. Lyttelton returned to the subject of speech training for all and for the clergy especially, in *Memories and Hopes* (John Murray, 1925), pp. 291–7.
86. A. J. P. Taylor, *English History 1914–1945* (Oxford, 1965; Pelican, 1970), p. 221.

87. Newbolt Report, quoted in Stephen Humphries, *Hooligans or Rebels?* (Basil Blackwell, Oxford, 1981), p. 54.
88. Wyld (1906), pp. 107–8, however, predicted that if Esperanto were established it would inevitably generate national and local dialects, thus impeding the international communication its advocates sought.
89. Quoted in H. M. Lynd, *England in the Eighteen-Eighties* (1945; 1968 edition), p. 249. Gladstone retained 'certain peculiarities of pronunciation; he always spoke of "constitootional" and of "noos".' Lord Frederic Hamilton, *The Days Before Yesterday* (Hodder & Stoughton, 1920), p. 204.
90. S. K. Hocking, *Her Benny* (1879; Gallery Press, Liverpool, 1968), p. 112.
91. A. L. Rowse, *A Cornish Childhood* (1942; Cardinal edition, 1975), pp. 102–7. Cf. Sir Ernest Barker, *Father of the Man: Memories of Cheshire, Lancashire, and Oxford, 1874–1898* (National Council of Social Service, London, 1948), p. 24, whose northern accent none the less persisted.
92. Ellis, V, p. 835.
93. Fred Kitchen quoted in P. Horn, *Labouring Life in the Victorian Countryside* (Dublin, 1976), p. 160.
94. S. Bamford, *Passages in the Life of a Radical* (1844; Harvester Press, 1967 edition), pp. 110–11.
95. G. Orwell, 'The Lion and the Unicorn' (1941), in *The Collected Essays, Journalism and Letters*, vol. 2 (Penguin, 1970), p. 98.
96. W. D. Rubinstein, *Men of Property* (Croom Helm, 1981), chs. 3, 8, 9.
97. Harold Orton (ed.), *Survey of English Dialects*, 12 vols. (University of Leeds, 1962–71); Harold Orton and Nathalia Wright, *A Word Geography of England* (1974).
98. Harold Orton, Stewart Sanderson and John Widdowson, *The Linguistic Atlas of England* (Croom Helm, 1978), Introduction.
99. Ellis, V. p. 403 for Leeds and Heckmondwike; Addy, p. xviii for the cutler's story.
100. *The London Head Teachers' Association 1888–1938* (University of London, 1938), p. 93.
101. The onomatopoeic 'la-di-da' was coined in the early 1880s in the music halls which gave a wider stage to the dialect comedian.
102. Quoted in Turner, p. 424.
103. It was never complete, of course. Dialect speech was valued by Lancashire Tory Democrats like 't'owd gam' cock' Hornby in Blackburn. See Snowden, p. 101 for Labour's efforts to present his candidature in similar terms in the 1900 General Election. Snowden esteemed dialect and always spoke it back home in Ickornshaw. On the other hand, he was married to an obsessive social climber, readily embraced establishment mores, and fastidiously criticised the mispronunciations of colleagues like Will Thorne. See R. I. McKibbin, 'Why was there no Marxism in Great Britain?', *English Historical Review*, vol. xcix, no. 391 (April 1984), pp. 325–6.
104. Ellis, V, p. 650; cf. the Edwardian engineering workshop: 'It was

an educative experience for every young apprentice introduced at a trade union branch meeting to witness the courtesy and decorum of his elders. Stiff and sober in their best rig-out, they hardly seemed the same men he knew at work. Here, in union discourse, even an escaping "damn" would be apologised for, and this, sometimes by journeymen who in the workshop used every obscenity they could lay a tongue to.' R. Roberts, *The Classic Slum* (Manchester University Press, 1971), pp. 38–9.

105. See Ensor's pocket diaries, R. C. K. Ensor Papers, Bodleian Library, Oxford. The elocution class was started in 1905.

106. The same applied to those Americans who so easily married into the English aristocracy, commended also, no doubt, by money and beauty.

107. D. Marquand, *Ramsay MacDonald* (1977), p. 404; cf. Barker, p. 74: ' . . . though I may exaggerate the barrier which it interposed, I have always noticed that the accent of Northern England (and especially of Lancashire) appears to be as much of a handicap (at any rate in Southern England) as a Scottish accent is an advantage.'

108. Boswell, p. 469.

# 2 Rhetoric and Politics in Great Britain, 1860–1950

*H. C. G. Matthew*

Rhetoric is the counterpart of logic . . . a kind of off-shoot of logic, and of that department of moral philosophy which it is fair to call the science of social life . . . Rhetoric is useful, because truth and justice are in their nature stronger than their opposites.

(Aristotle, *Rhetoric*)

Rhetoric is that Faculty, by which we understand what will serve our turn, concerning any Subject to win belief in the hearer . . . The end of Rhetoric is Victory, which consists in having gotten belief.

(Hobbes' *Digest of Aristotle's Rhetoric*)

The Journalists are now the true Kings and Clergy: henceforth Historians, unless they are fools, must write not of Bourbon Dynasties, and Tudors and Hapsburgs; but of stamped Broad-Sheet Dynasties . . . according as this or the other Able Editor . . . gains the world's Ear.

(Carlyle, *Sartor Resartus*)

It was pouring with rain, the wind was howling through the most ghastly hall and everyone knew that the Welsh vote had already been lost. Mr. Foot sat huddled in his overcoat until it was his turn to speak. He then delivered the most sparkling piece of rhetoric I have ever heard, though the content was negligible and he had never probably believed in devolution in the first place. The party loved him for it.

(M. Rutherford, 'Man of the Week', *Financial Times*, 15 November 1980).

Rhetoric – the presentation of argument – is an essential concomitant of representative politics, and its free exercise is the distinguishing feature of a liberal political community. The first of these epigraphs illustrates the liberal objective in argument, the second the conservative, 'realist' view of what that liberal objective actually amounts to, the third the factor in nineteenth-century rhetoric which distinguishes it from earlier eras and which made possible its general dissemination in a large and complex industrial society, the fourth its twentieth-century decline. The use of the word 'rhetoric' in the *Financial Times* well illustrates its common British twentieth-century use – contentless, windy, overblown, insincere and ineffective – a usage also commonly employed by historians. But this definition is misleading as to the historical meaning of the word, the means by which argument was publicly presented, summed up by Richard Whately as 'Persuasion . . . Style, Arrangement, and Delivery'.[1] Until the mid-nineteenth century, the study of Aristotle's *Rhetoric* was a necessary and central part of a liberal education; Chairs of Rhetoric were common, and, as Sir Robert Peel observed when discussing Cicero in 1837, classical rhetoric was of 'immense importance to all who aspire to conspicuous stations in any department of public or learned professional life'. Peel added perspicaciously that steam was 'fertilizing the intellectual as well as the material waste [ . . . and] supplying you, in the mere faculty of locomotion, with a new motive for classical study'.[2]

The subject of rhetoric has been little studied by historians. A few bearings can be taken from English literature scholars, who tend to use 'rhetoric' very generally to mean any form of communication, from studies of Nazi rhetoric,[3] and from American works, largely on Burke and the eighteenth century and largely non-historical. The aim of this essay is first to describe the phenomenon of late Victorian extra-parliamentary rhetoric, second to argue that its existence depended on a set of technical developments in the media, third to argue that the liberal political culture within which this phenomenon flourished was closely related to and largely conditioned by those developments, Fourth, I shall argue that when further developments occurred in the franchise and in the media, both the rhetorical phenomenon and the political culture to which it was related declined together.

Some discussion of the nature and extent of the electorate – the politician's raw material – is a necessary preliminary. The political community as it existed between 1867 and 1918 differed markedly in scale and tone both from its predecessor and its successor. The 1867 and 1884 Reform Acts, enfranchising about 55 per cent of adult males in the boroughs and rather more in the counties, had as their aims the enfranchisement of what Gladstone called the 'capable citizen', that is, an employed adult male, with a regular domicile, of some substance, the head of a household with the initiative to get himself registered.[4] Those who applied for public assistance (though not, after 1885, mere medical relief) under the Poor Law were automatically disfranchised: there was, therefore, a deliberate, explicit relationship between economic and civic competence, reinforced by the excluding power of the astonishing complexities of the registration system.

This electorate was a half-way house between the very limited electorate of the 1832 Reform Act and the achievement of what was effectively (though not completely) universal suffrage for men in 1918. The changes of 1867 introduced new problems for politicians: a change in numbers, and a change in system in the form of the accompanying secret ballot of 1872. Taken together, these changes posed problems of party organisation in the constituencies: there were more electors to manage and to bribe, and less was known about them. The ending of poll-books disadvantaged election agents and historians alike. The larger electorate was much less easy to know as individual electors, and thus not only more expensive but more difficult to bribe. The 1883 Corrupt Practices Act offered a way out acceptable to both Parties.

How did politicans cope with the post–1867 electorate? One solution was a more complex party organisation (already developing in some constituencies before 1867) to replace the solicitor with his 'face-to-face' knowledge of a propertied electorate, many of whom were his clients. Both Liberals and Tories developed their national and local organisations in the 1870s. At a local level, there was a marked development of political clubs, small versions of the House of Commons, flourishing in many towns and villages. Whereas before 1867 their function had been to demand entry into Parliament, now they imitated it, thus representing the successful incorporation into political life (defined in Westminster terms) of elements of the population which during the early part of the century had seemed in danger of being alienated. In these local parliaments, a high level of organisation and effort was involved. Members were allocated a parliamentary constituency, and some formed the government, issuing printed Queen's speeches, moving motions, and answering opposition criticisms. The movement was considerable and widespread. Blanchard Jerrold estimated in 1883 that there were over a hundred Houses of Commons (including four each in Glasgow and Manchester) with about 35,000 members overall; they constituted, he thought, 'an educational machine of national proportions, for constructing politically thoughtful members of the community'. Jerrold found a fairly even political balance: of 59 Houses in 1882, 26 (with 11,051 members) were Conservative and 33 (with 10,854 members) Liberal. Some of the parliaments were large – Glasgow, Lambeth and Hackney each having 1000 members.[5] The National Association of Local Parliaments, with offices at 14 Langham Place, London, coordinated from 1892 this remarkable experiment, which seems to have lasted from the 1860s (the first known local parliament was in Liverpool from 1860) until the First World War. A feature of these local parliaments was that men (those so far discovered had an entirely male membership) of both parties took part, suggesting a considerable homogeneity of the political community.[6] As the printed rules for the Croydon House of Commons said: 'It is earnestly hoped that members will bear in mind that the Croydon House of Commons is in the first place a debating society; and will assist the Council in every way in making it a success as such, and not endeavour to secure triumphs for their party at the expense of the Society.'[7]

The local parliaments show that the drive towards oratory was self-generated, and not merely an imposition from above. They were an important training ground and means of political and oratorical upward mobility, their most successful *alumnus* being Bonar Law (Member for N. Staffs. for a decade in one of the Glasgow parliaments). Their success partly depended on the expanding provincial press which reported their proceedings – for example, in 1867 in Yorkshire 66 out of 86 local papers (i.e. 77 per cent) had been founded since 1853, and in Lancashire 46 out of 74 (62 per cent).[8] The form these local parliaments took was the product of a mixture of the rules and conventions of the Oxford University Union and of the House of Commons, whose debates were widely reported. Guides to public speaking, such as the many editions of G. J. Holyoake's *Public Speaking and Debate*, directed the electorate into appropriate canons of behaviour. *The Times* observed on the jubilee of the Oxford Union (23 October 1873):

> In the course of these fifty years we have become a nation of public speakers. Everyone speaks now, and tolerably well too. Any country gentleman, or respectable tradesman taking a part in local affairs, might well compound for a speech a day, and be glad of that relief for the speeches of his neighbours. Even the clergy are throwing away their cork jackets, and interpolating with free speech, even if they must still ride at anchor. . . . Eloquence is but a facility, or instrument, or weapon, or accomplishment, or, in academic terms, an art. . . . We are now more than ever a debating, that is, a Parliamentary people.

But from the viewpoint of national political leaders, these societies, and the general enthusiasm for political action in the localities, had their difficulties: they had to be given a lead. Moreover, the enthusiasm for the newspaper reporting of Parliament was wearing off: the clogged timetable of the Commons was becoming more and more specialised – the old days of the 1840s and 1850s when leisured debates on the 'condition of the people' took up to ten days gave way to Parliaments dominated by the details of committee work. Government majorities, except at certain times such as 1885–86, became after 1867 more predictable: the role of rhetoric in the Commons in immediately influencing the survival of the ministry as in the 1850s and 1860 became less important, and consequently less exciting for newspaper readers. The press developed a resistance to anticipating *Hansard* (in turn diminishing the extent and accuracy of the latter, which was partly compiled from press reports). Alex Ritchie of the *Leeds Mercury* told the Press Association in 1870: 'It would, as a rule, be a great inconvenience to me to give more than two columns of a [parliamentary] debate. Gentlemen like to peruse their newspaper at breakfast time, and they will not always care to wade through 4 or 5 columns of Parliamentary matter.'[9] Summing up a debate on 20 April 1877 on the appointment of a committee on making *Hansard* official and verbatim, Hartington remarked, 'it is universally admitted that the reports in the newspapers . . . are not as full and as correct as they were a few years ago, and that what passes in Parliament is not known as fully by the public as it was formerly considered desirable it should be known.' When Lady Monkswell noted in her diary in January 1878 that 'The great men's speeches in this exciting time are the most interesting reading in the world,' she referred not to parliamentary speeches, but to the torrent of public-speaking generated by the Eastern Question.[10]

What is sometimes regarded as a golden age of parliamentary oratory – the gladiatorial clash of Gladstone and Disraeli, Randolph Churchill and Parnell, Chamberlain, Asquith, Balfour and Lloyd George – was in fact the era which saw the ascendancy of a new medium of communication long in genesis: this was the growth of regular extra-parliamentary speechmaking by leading politicians and by ordinary MPs. From 1872, the famous speeches – famous in their day and in the history books – are, on balance, extra-parliamentary speeches. Parliamentary speeches of general political significance are few compared with those of the Manchester Free Trade Hall, the Crystal Palace, 'peace with honour', the Midlothian Campaigns, the tariff reform campaign.

Fundamental to the successful use of political oratory of the type practised by the late Victorians – long, serious, detailed, well-informed – rarely demagogic, with few concessions to the audience in simplification of matter, style or language – was the notion of an integrated political community, using roughly the same vocabulary, interested in similar issues, willing to sustain a press which exploited the newly available telegraph to bring the words of the politicians to every educated household the morning after they were spoken. This integrated electorate the extended but still limited franchise supplied. The extension of the franchise made extra-parliamentary speechmaking necessary; the continuing limits on the electorate made it effective.

In 1863, when the platform system was in early development, Salisbury (then Cecil) presciently identified both the phenomenon of the two audiences and the difficulty it posed:

> The speechmaking usually takes place after dinner. The farmers or townspeople to whom the speeches are addressed are mainly drunk; and the speakers themselves are not wholly exempt, perhaps, from the

> moment's genial influence. The public . . . who read these speeches in the *Times* two or three days afterwards, usually get through their newspapers in the morning, when they are not only sober, but cross and critical. Is it possible for human ingenuity to construct a speech that shall suit both audiences – that shall be warm and slipshod enough to elicit the cheers of farmers who have dined, & yet calm and polished enough to extort the admiration of readers who have not breakfasted?

Later, the difficulty was equally often the other way round: could a complex speech given to an earnest meeting be understood by the electors reading the more popular newspapers? But the extent of extra-parliamentary speechmaking in the second half of the century, and the thoroughness of its reporting, suggests that 'human ingenuity' did indeed succeed in suiting 'both audiences', aided perhaps by a swing in the balance of the audience from drunk farmers to earnest nonconformists.[11]

Only two media were open to the Victorian politician – speech and the printed word (or cartoon). Regular speechmaking by all politicians in their constituencies each autumn came to reach a high proportion of the electorate. The thoroughness and regularity of the stump 'season' was new. In the mid-century, politicians, as a rule, visited their constituencies, and rarely any other than their own constituencies, at election times or for some special occasion. Thus Cobden found it necessary in 1849 to excuse his presence in his constituency; he told his constituents: 'There is peculiar advantage in Members of the House of Commons coming, from time to time, in contact with the people, and especially with their own constituencies.'[12] As in many aspects of Victorian politics, Palmerston, following his mentor, Canning, was an unsung pioneer, with a series of public speeches in the 1850s, but he was not at first followed up. Gladstone's speeches between 1864 and 1868 in Lancashire were the most prominent examples of a growing tendency of Cabinet Ministers to talk on a wide range of political subjects directly to the people. Salisbury indicated in 1864 the extent to which the process had developed; his metaphor, though used with characteristic distaste, caught the theatrical, spectacular quality of the speechmaking season: 'the stage manager . . . who arranges the appearance of Ministerial actors in the autumn performances evidently goes upon the principle of putting his best leg foremost. He begins the season with the stars, and leaves the sticks to the fag end.'[13] Care must be taken not to give Gladstone too prominent or original a role in the development of this process. The *Biograph*'s comment of 1879 gives a fair assessment:

> Provincial journalism entered upon a new phase with the repeal of the paper duties and the extension of the telegraph system. Daily newspapers soon became a necessity for all large centres . . . and with their establishment a change has followed, which Mr. Gladstone was, perhaps, the first public man to recognise, if by no means the first to discern.[14]

Disraeli made the first extra-parliamentary speeches by a former Prime Minister which had a really major impact – his speech in Manchester in 1872, which lasted three and a half hours (during which he drank two bottles of white brandy, believed by the audience to be water) and at the Crystal Palace in London, also in 1872: both of these speeches were, significantly, to assemblies of Tory Party workers rather than to open audiences. Speech series directly to the electors on a big scale began with Gladstone's orations on Bulgaria in 1876–77, and his Midlothian campaigns of 1879–80. By the 1890s, regular tours of autumn speeches – mini-Midlothians – had become the rule for most MPs, and for any MP who expected any sort of national prominence, a requirement which dismayed politicians who did not take naturally to the activity. There was, then, a codification and regularising of the stump oratory which had been developing haphazardly through the century.

At some of these meetings, politicians addressed vast audiences without any form of mechanical aid. These great occasions – for example, Gladstone's address to his constituents at Blackheath in September 1876 on Bulgaria – had in fact two audiences: first the audience actually present and, second, the audience to be reached through the press. The latter was clearly the more important.

For the audience present, a speech by a Party Leader was often as much an occasion – a 'happening' – as a detailed examination of the issues. At the Blackheath open air meeting, between ten and fifteen thousand people were present, but little could be heard of the speech for the rain on the umbrellas. At the Bingley Hall meeting in May 1877 when Gladstone spoke to the National Liberal Federation, he noted in his diary: 'A most intelligent and duly appreciative audience – but they were 25,000 and the building I think of no acoustic merit'; in fact the speech was inaudible to about half of the audience. When Rosebery made a famous speech at Chesterfield in 1901, a special train brought MPs and the press from London, and miners and railway workers assembled from all over Derbyshire to see his Lordship. The fact that the speech, given in a vast echoing railway repair shed, was completely inaudible to all but the big-wigs sitting on the platform (it was even inaudible to the stenographer) in no way diminished the success of the occasion, although the speech lasted nearly two hours. The *Daily Telegraph* (8 September 1876) commented generally about the phenomenon:

> In the open air, it is questionable whether more than 1000 to 1500 persons, in a gathering which may possibly exceed 30,000, will catch all that is said; but the mere assemblage is in itself an eloquent utterance of popular feeling; and, as all present will be assured, the next morning's papers are certain to contain full reports.

It would be misleading to suggest that huge meetings were characteristic of late-Victorian speechmaking. The routine speeches were given to rather specifically controlled audiences with three areas. First, tickets for the male party faithful were distributed and sometimes sold. Second, there was a women's enclosure, usually in the gallery, following what was still quite a common division in churches; the presence of politicians' wives on the platform, a custom made prominent by Catherine Gladstone in 1879, reflected the growing importance of women in politics as public encouragers and organisers and even, on the rare occasion, speakers, as well as reflecting, not always justifiably, the assumed orderliness of such meetings. Third, there was usually an open area at the back of the hall for all-comers; it was from this area that the 'heckling', a venerated and sometimes rather formalised part of the proceedings much welcomed by adroit speakers such as Gladstone and Lloyd George, was directed. Not surprisingly, electors had first call on the accommodation; when Gladstone spoke in 1880 in a church near Edinburgh, *The Scotsman* (20 March 1880) reported that 'admission was, in the first instance, limited to electors . . . of Cramond, of whom there are about 120, and to each of them was allowed the privilege of bringing a lady to the meeting', the doors being opened to non-electors half an hour before the meeting. A big speech was sometimes a two-tier affair: a solemn full-scale address to a restricted audience, followed by a short homily to a general audience (often predominantly working-class) afterwards in a separate hall or in the open air.

These political occasions, and especially the opportunity to see a national figure in the flesh, often generated considerable local excitement; they can be related to the general growth of organised team spectator sports characteristic of the period. The association of Cabinet Ministers with this sort of occasion caused alarm in high circles: what was in fact a remarkable exercise in political integration was seen as vulgarising politics and politicians, as in the Queen's objection to the Midlothian Campaign as 'democratic'.

But important though the occasion was in generating local interest and encouraging the party activists, the speech was not simply or even mainly declaimed to those present. Politicians' early appreciation of the nature of the vital audience is seen in this account by James Picton of a meeting in St George's Hall, Liverpool, in 1868: Gladstone was shouted down by the Tories in the hall: 'He proceeded, however, speaking to the reporters who were just below him.'[15]

Systematic extra-parliamentary oratory on the scale of late Victorian Britain, in which a great national debate was carried on over periods of weeks, was made possible by, indeed was the consequence of, technical developments in the press. The reporting of the speeches was largely done by the Press Association, the Central News Agency, and the Exchange Telegraph. The PA was set up in London in 1868 to act as a central news agency for the expanding, largely Liberal, provincial press.[16] Under the Telegraph Act of 1868 agencies such as the PA and Exchange Telegraph, which mainly acted for the London papers from its establishment in 1872, received very favourable rates of transmission, the Tories thereby making amends for their bitter opposition to the repeal of the duty on paper, which the Lords delayed in 1860. These agencies reduced the reporting to a fine art: in the 1860s over 70 reporters had been needed for Bright's reform speeches, now only a few teams were needed, one team for each agency. These teams were highly skilled – by Lloyd George's time a speech begun at 2.45 was included in four-and-a-half columns in the *Daily Leader* on the streets by 4.30, just after he had finished delivering it. The PA had a special team for covering Gladstone's speeches headed by the twenty-stone Walter Hepburn – it was through Hepburn that Gladstone in 1880 started a custom, new to Britain, though already common in the USA, of dictating a speech *after* the train had left the station – there having been no time to address it to the assembled crowds: the immediate audience could become superfluous.

Hepburn could not, in the manner of today, simply have been given the 'hand-out', for speeches usually followed the parliamentary convention of being delivered only from brief notes. Gladstone believed that such delivery, made after careful preparation, most accurately revealed the speaker's quality of character to the audience. Disraeli as a young man was said to have rehearsed his invective with friends; according to T. H. S. Escott's information from Montagu Corry, Disraeli's secretary, Disraeli changed this habit in later life: 'Lord Beaconsfield, to the best of my knowledge, deeply reflected on his forthcoming speeches long beforehand, and only put them mentally into verbal shape during a seclusion of two or three hours which he obtained before delivering an address of much importance.' Joseph Chamberlain was characteristically well-prepared; he told John Morley in November 1877 (before the platform arrangements had reached their most sophisticated form): 'For the first time in my life I have at the urgent request of the reporters (who say they fear a breakdown in telegraphic arrangements as Lord Hartington is speaking the same night) prepared an abstract of what I am going to say for the country and possibly for the London papers.'[17]

For some, such speeechmaking came easily. Cobden told Delane: 'it is known that I am not in the habit of writing a word beforehand of what I speak in public. Like other speakers, practice had given me as perfect self-possession in the presence of an audience, as if I were writing in my closet.' But for others, however experienced, meetings remained a strain. Randolph Churchill, like his son (who wrote out his speeches in advance), found speechmaking a great burden:

> I find . . . that addressing these large meetings is such anxious and exciting work that for a day or two afterwards I am quite useless and demoralised. . . . I have made up my mind to give up almost entirely attendance at these public meetings. It is simply killing and the constant necessity of trying to say something new makes one a drivelling idiot.[18]

As there was free trade in newspapers, so was there free trade in speeches. The agencies were profit-making and so, after a fashion, were the papers: they were certainly competitive. As Alfred Kinnear wrote: 'the market in great men's oratory is worked on sound commercial lines. It is a wholesale market. There is no retail business. Speeches are offered in bulk.' The financing of speech reporting worked in this way: the Post Office was paid £1 per column (reckoned at 2000 words) for the first report that the agency sold, and 3s 4d (16½p) per column for each subsequent report sold. The agency sold to all newspapers at 10 shillings (50p) per column; there was therefore a balance of 6s 8d (33⅓p) per column on each report sold beyond the first for the agency to cover reporting costs and make a profit. If there were insufficient orders, the profit margin would diminish or disappear, and it would not be worthwhile for the agency to send reporters to the meeting. As Kinnear observed, 'Newspapers regulated the trade by fixing the demand. They fix the demand on their part by testing the sale of the papers . . .'[19]

The demand for speeches was therefore of central importance to the culture of extra-parliamentary speechmaking. A sophisticated system developed for assessing it. On Saturdays each week each paper got a list of 'fixtures' – the whips arranged between themselves that there should not be clashes such as Gladstone and Salisbury speaking the same evening – and on Monday the papers sent in orders for the coming week. There were three kinds of report, (a) a verbatim (sometimes as much as five columns, (b) 'full' (first-person report but judiciously trimmed and shortened to about 1½ columns from the verbatim), and (c) third-person summary, usually half a column. On the basis of the papers' orders, the agency decided which of these sorts of report to arrange: if the number of orders did not justify a 'verbatim' report, the agency would switch to 'full' or summary. The elite of verbatim speakers was always very small; in 1885 the *Pall Mall Gazette* noted that only Gladstone, Salisbury, Chamberlain and Randolph Churchill were reported verbatim, and in 1897 only Salisbury, Rosebery, Balfour and Chamberlain created enough demand for the agencies to supply verbatim reports. Harcourt, much to his chagrin, was not on the verbatim list until he resigned the Liberal Party leadership, when renewed interest in his career, or lack of career, got him briefly promoted from 'full' to verbatim.

The reporting of speeches was thus conditioned by the law of supply and demand. Newspapers had to sell and the notion that they printed speeches out of a sense of duty, knowing that they would not be read, is quite false; news agencies exist to make profits. When Gladstone retired from public speaking, the PA reported a loss: its chairman explained:

> Last year [1895] was the dullest we have had for many years . . . The most serious loss we had was, no doubt, the withdrawal of Mr. Gladstone. . . . Probably two thirds of the falling off in the revenue was due to that cause, but not only did Mr. Gladstone make a large number of speeches himself, which almost every newspaper in the country reported, but he also provoked a large number of replies, which were also reported.[20]

Clearly an MP's position in this league table of speech reporting was of great importance for his reputation: if, at a time when promotion in both Parties was rather slow, he could get from the summary into the 'full' report category he could substantially improve his political position. In this area, the Commons *was* of great significance. The cut and thrust of debate – especially unorthodox *ad hominem* debate – could quickly promote a politician. Randolph Churchill in the 1880s, Lloyd George in the Boer War with his attacks on Chamberlain, are examples of politicians who having promoted themselves into the 'full' report category on a single issue or personal attack, used their ability to widen their oratorical base to keep in the 'full' report category, or even reach the verbatim level, once the original topic was forgotten.

The selection of substantial reporting of extra-parliamentary speeches depended therefore very much on intra-parliamentary manoeuvring between politicians. After the 1886 split the British press became predominantly Unionist, having been overwhelmingly Liberal. In 1884, there were 518 Liberal newspapers to 293 Tory; by 1901 the figures were 403 Liberal, 456 Unionist.[21] This excludes the 'independent' papers: before 1886 these were predominantly Liberal – 'enemies in disguise', as Hartington called them, of the Tory Party. After about 1888 independent papers had on the whole become definitely Unionist in tone. Thus 1886–90 is the period in which the British press became predominantly a Unionist, Conservative press, a tendency reinforced by the growth of *Daily Mail*-type newspapers after 1896 (the *Mail* started as a Liberal Imperialist paper, but was Unionist by the end of the Boer War). In Scotland, for example, both the main dailies, the *Glasgow Herald* and *The Scotsman*, went Unionist in 1886.

Important beyond the extent of their circulation were the London papers. Whereas in the mid-century the brash self-confidence of the new press in the provinces had allowed the development of a regional tone which owed little to London, by the 1870s and 1880s the London press was more dominant. The best known paper was *The Times*, although its circulation was steadily falling (60,000 in 1879; 40,000 in 1890). The most widely-read was the *Daily Telegraph*, the flagship of the Liberals in the 1860s; it turned Conservative over the Liberals' Bulgarian atrocities campaign in the 1870s, but retained its circulation (1880: 250,000). By 1912, the Unionists had thirteen London morning and evening papers to the Liberals' three (*Daily News, Daily Chronicle*, and the evening *Westminster Gazette*).

Getting on the verbatim or full reporting level was thus of particular importance to Liberals, since this was an effective way of achieving publicity in the enemy camp – whose voters had to be won over – for Liberal and Unionist papers tended to report the same people: that is, the market value of verbatim speeches did not vary much from Party to Party or paper to paper at a national or regional level. A four-column Liberal speech in a Unionist paper by a good Liberal speaker was effectively a four-column advertisement. As advertisements, these space-consuming speeches were effective, for they were placed in newspapers which had as yet virtually no illustrations, and whose format was, between the 1860s and the 1900s, almost unchanged.

In the sense of advertisement, therefore, the Boer War, despite its short-term disadvantages to the Liberals, was of long-term help: it promoted to the 'full' level several unknown Liberal politicians, and ensured that when the Tariff Reform campaign began shortly afterwards, there was a much larger body of Liberals well known to readers of both parties than was the case in the late 1890s. Considering that the Party had been out of power for twenty years, and out of office for ten, the Liberal government of 1905 was very familiar to the public, and this was largely an oratorical familiarity.

Thus far I have shown that the need and the conditions for extra-parliamentary speaking, developed with particular enthusiasm by the Liberals but energetically participated in by both parties, were a product of the political structure of the second half of the nineteenth century and of the technical means at the disposal of politicians and journalists. The two together had produced a national debating society inconceivable in the pre-telegraphic days. The nationally integrated reporting system offered the means for a nationally integrated political rhetoric: the same speech reaching the breakfast tables of Wick, Penzance, London and Liverpool on the same morning; the same reply reaching those same breakfast tables the next morning. Linked to this was the local reporting of politicians significant only at a local or regional level – these men offered a coda to the national politicians.

When we come to the content of these speeches we find ourselves faced by two of the quotations with which this essay began: Aristotle's view that rhetoric is a discipline with its own purpose, rules and methodology, and Hobbes' denial of this, and his view that rhetoric is merely part of propaganda: that there are no rules or limitations, but simply the desire to win. A number of recent historians, particularly on the right, but with the cheerful concurrence of certain Labour historians for whom progressivism is deviationalism, have seen oratory of this sort as merely an aspect of a struggle for ascendency within the ruling elite, one weapon among several in a game whose rules are only known to the players at Westminster. The verbatim reporting of speeches poses problems for this view: it is one thing to give a speech in the manner of the 1980s, whose contents are revealed only to those who receive the handouts, and whose significance is confined to the use of certain code words: it is another regularly to produce four columns subject to national public scutiny. On the other hand, it is certainly true that speeches were weapons against colleagues as well as opponents. What is misleading is to see this as a game with secret or closed rules: the extent of open argument created a national rather than an elitist game. Public oratorical accountability was the link between Westminster and a politically fascinated national constituency.

If we look at the two main protagonists in the national debate, we shall see two rather different approaches to content. It is no accident that the first well-remembered Tory speeches were Disraeli's Manchester and Crystal Palace speeches of 1872, given, significantly, to constituency association workers, for it was essentially on organisation rather than speechmaking that the Tories relied. At the Crystal Palace Disraeli made the following claim:

> If you look to the history of this country since the advent of Liberalism – forty years ago – you will find that there has been no effort so continuous, so subtle, supported by so much energy, and carried on with so much ability and acumen, as the attempts of Liberalism to effect the disintegration of the Empire of England.[22]

With these remarks, at a stroke Disraeli seized the wand of patriotism from the dead Palmerston's hand, captured the initiative from the Liberal Party on the dominant theme of late Victorian Britain – imperialism – and effectively wrote the election address of every Tory MP until the 1950s. This extract from the Tory manifesto of 1951 is merely Disraeli without the style:

> Six years ago Britain stood high in fame and greatness. Under Socialism, we have fallen far from those heights of achievement and expectation: to retain and develop the great and unique brotherhood of the British Empire is a first task of British statesmanship. The Conservative party, by long tradition and settled belief, is the Party of the Empire: . . . the socialists should have set country before party, and shown that they were Britons first, and socialists only second.[23]

What Disraeli realised was that in the age of extended electorates rhetoric may be only loosely connected with the realities of policy, that is, that the presentation of politics is distinct, or can be made distinct, from their content. Of course Disraeli did not think the Liberal Cabinet wanted the disintegration of the Empire. Nor was Disraeli himself particularly imperialistic in his *policy* when in office. It was under Gladstone, not Disraeli, that the crucial decisions of the founding of the third British Empire took place. But it was Disraeli, at Victoria's prompting, who made the Queen Empress of India, the greatest symbolic and propagandist act of the nineteenth century. In vain might Liberals protest that Gladstone's interest in the Empire, and in its extension, went back to the days when Disraeli had called colonies 'millstones around our necks': in vain might Liberals point to the reality of their imperial achievements in the Empire of settlement, and in expanding that of the tropics. The Queen, the Church of England and the Empire: these were the three simple, telling cries of Tory rhetoric, with the odd nod to social reform when convenient.

It would be quite misleading to argue that all Tory speeches were non-rational or intended to be so, but it would be fair to say that Tories in general distrusted the concept of politics based on rationality, that they perceived the growing significance of symbol in politics, that they had, especially in the heritage of Disraeli, a clear and early understanding that, as Graham Wallas observed, 'the empirical art of politics consists largely in the creation of opinion by the deliberate exploitation of sub-conscious, non-rational inference'.[24] The themes of monarchy, religion, race and imperialism fell conveniently into this category. Linked to these was the well-known Tory capacity for efficient organisation, by which the potency of slogans could be turned into votes. On the other hand, the reporting verbatim of speeches was a stimulus to rational presentation: to fill four columns required more than mere repetition of stereotypes. But the context of political speechmaking was of Liberal emphasis, and it imposed Liberal restrictions. Thus in the Tariff Reform campaign Joseph Chamberlain was encouraged to present his programme rationalistically and publicly – Liberal exposition of its deficiencies and self-contradictions was therefore possible and prominent as well as the sloganeering of the 'big loaf and the little loaf'. It would be interesting to compare the rationalistic public presentation of the Tariff Reform campaign and its failure with the behind-the-scenes manipulations which were essential to the success of the Common Market initiative.

If Tory politics thus centred around organisational politics and a growing awareness of the potency of images, the position for the Liberals was more complex. Of course the Liberals had their organisations; they had their interest groups, the Celts, the nonconformists, etc.; and they had their slogans. But they also had the need, even the craving, for public discussion of issues, actions and programmes; for Liberals, politics without public discussion and argument lacked their essential ingredients. Liberalism at its most successful involved the combining of various types and levels of political activity. But for Liberal Party workers the rhetorical appeal was not merely the centrepiece but the distinctive characteristic of liberal politics. Liberals persistently gave speeches on the nature of liberalism: the Tories avoided rationalistic articulation of the underpinning of their appeal. That is, the Tories did not depend on rhetoric for the maintenance of party unity, though they used it. The Liberals to some extent did – or thought they did. Gladstone developed the rhetorical idea of the overarching issue: Bulgarian atrocities: Home Rule: the House of Lords: an issue which served as a focus for Liberal rhetoric and which would enable the very different aims of the various Liberal interest groups to unite.

Further, the Liberals were the Party of progress, and thus, at least on paper, the Party of action. Certainly in the 1886–1914 period, when the Tories were in office about sixteen years and the Liberals about eleven, the Liberal legislative proposals – not necessarily achievements – were far more numerous. The Liberals, therefore, while they had their fair share of Tory-baiting, also used their speeches for the ventilation of ideas and for the struggle within the party for legislative priority. Liberals were always ready to spend money on the publication of speeches: the best financed and most carefully organised branch of the National Liberal Federation was the *Liberal Magazine*, most of which was made up of speeches. When the Liberal Imperialists set up the Liberal League in 1902, they spent almost all their income on the distribution of speeches: their publication department was run by Sidney Webb. The Liberals – or at any rate those Liberals who made the sort of speeches which were widely reported – believed that reasonable men, presented with the full case, would naturally vote Liberal: they believed, in other words, that the presentation and quality of political ideas and policies were central to vote-winning. They believed, in fact, that class or personal interest was not the determining factor in voting behaviour. Speechmaking and good coverage by the press were thus absolutely essential to their strategy.

It may be objected that this is a caricature of the Liberal Party in any constituency in which it had a chance of winning. Many examples of efficient Liberal organisations can be cited. Moreover, the reception of these speeches – their incidence in terms of votes – is hard to estimate. There are many interesting questions, of popular assumptions about newspapers, of the general intelligibility of the language used by politicians in their speeches, of the relationship of the newspapers' leaders to the speeches, which unfortunately there is not space to discuss here. That it is hard to estimate and impossible to quantify this incidence should not, however, be a reason for explaining away the phenomenon, especially by reference to the very different political culture of late twentieth-century Britain. The existence of the phenomenon in itself asserts the distinctiveness of the age in which it flourished.

The sort of rhetoric discussed in this essay was that exercised by a political elite which found itself increasingly otherwise isolated from its rank and file. The decline of Whiggery and the loss of Chamberlain meant that the upper levels of the Liberal Party increasingly depended on rhetoric as their link with the party as well as the electorate. Men such as Gladstone, Morley and Asquith had no base for power within their party save their rhetoric and their legislative achievements. They controlled no machine, they spent no money on politics, they had no base in the localities, no real patronage except when in office. Their standing in the Party depended on their success as rhetoricians and legislators, and Liberal governments after 1884 until 1906 could point to few legislative achievements. The absence of a formal party structure allowed them and the policies developed in their rhetoric to become the national focal point, the unifying and determining element in what made up the Liberal Party in the late nineteenth century. Max Weber pointed out the extent to which Gladstone's speeches, belief in 'the ethical substance of his policy' and 'belief in the ethical character of his personality', became fused together: this can be expanded to suggest not the 'Caesaristic plebiscitical element'[25] dominated by one man which Weber sees as characteristic of this period, but rather as the means by which a university-educated, non-industrial, intellectual elite succeeded in coordinating the working of a great political movement in a predominantly industrial and commercial state. They did so by expressing the rationalistic values which the Liberal 'hundreds' regarded as the stuff of national politics.

Changes in the structure of politics and in the structure and techniques of the media drastically altered the forum in which this approach had been effective.

The *Daily Mail* (1896) introduced something of a new style of political reporting, taking up the techniques introduced in the 1880s by W. T. Stead, who was himself mainly inspired by his observation of the American press. The *Mail*'s importance was its size (a circulation of over one million by 1900), its national distribution, which undercut the provincial morning press, and its relative simplicity of presentation and reporting. Appealing to the rapidly expanding service sector of the economy, it was the newspaper of the retailing revolution: the advertisements were much more visual, punchy, and less wordy, and its political reporting mirrored this. We should not exaggerate: the *Mail* maintained a high political content, but it packaged politics in a way that verbatim speech reporting could not do. On the whole, the provincial press did not respond: its techniques began to atrophy: it reflected its Liberal tendency in its reluctance to abandon the importance it gave to what was coming to be seen as 'high-minded' rather than 'normative' political reporting. By 1914 the provincial press and the old metropolitan press was under strong pressure from the *Mail* and its imitators.

The 1918 Representation of the People Act, doubling the male electorate and enfranchising many women, opened a new phase for politicians. The scale of political appeal necessarily had to be much wider: the concept of 'capable citizenship' virtually ceased to exercise any limitation of the electorate. The Tory and Labour Parties both stood to capitalise on these developments; they were both Parties whose appeal was essentially to the 'deliberate exploitation of subconscious, non-rational inference', whether, respectively, of imperialistic nationalism and property or of class, although they both used rationalistic methods when it suited them and speechmaking continued to be of importance in both cases in intra-party debate.

The vast new electorate and the changing structure of the press meant that the complex structure of extra-parliamentary national debate, which had, of course, been largely suspended during the First World War, never recovered its rude, late-Victorian health. Although certain speeches continued to be reported quite fully, gone for good was the notion that at certain times of the year newspapers should report over a period of weeks the verbatim reports of the national debate and the reaction of local politicians to it. Ironically, as the cultural significance of the speeches declined, their cost rose, politicians beginning to hire speechwriters or to allow civil servants to draft their public statements as well as their letters. The age of the 'hand-out' had begun. Political figures continued to speak as if on the platform in Midlothian. Sometimes, as with Ramsay MacDonald's speeches in 1929, something of a similar effect was achieved, at least with the audience actually present. But increasingly politicians' words – or their speech-writers' words – reached only the 'professional' audience: media men, the party faithful and their political opponents. The electorate had not turned to other interests (apart from the freak conditions of 1918, turnout under the universal franchise stayed above 70 per cent), but it no longer met its representatives, except occasionally, through verbatim reporting.

How then was the integration of the new electorate to be achieved? As new techniques of advertising spread, linked to the development of a new popular press, so politics began to be more packaged for consumption by the readership of the newspaper. When speeches had been reported either verbatim or in full, the journalist's views had not come between the politician and the reader in the way we today take for granted, except in the instance of the interview which was used, but not very extensively, from the 1870s: 'It is perhaps this abuse of the interview in many American journals which has retarded its adoption in leading English newspapers . . . The interview is, however, slowly but surely obtaining respectful recognition in this country.'[26]

Kennedy Jones remarked of the *Daily Mail:* 'our influence did more..than anything else..to reduce . . . the speeches of politicians to their right proportions.'[27] This clearly exaggerates the importance of the *Mail*, which was a function of change as much as a cause of it, but it highlights the new role of journalists as political interpreters in addition to their role as leader writers. Although the number of papers with a declared political allegiance fell spectacularly, the partisanship of reporting increased markedly: *Exchange Telegraph* told the Royal Commission on the Press of 1947–48, 'Subscribers to whom the opinions expressed [in a speech] are sympathetic and in line with their own convictions will require perhaps 800 words. Organs with a different frame of mind will require 200 words only.' E. W. Davies of the Press Association told the Commission: 'I may pick up a speech and say "that is what I want to be given" . . . Sir Stafford Cripps . . . sends me his speeches and I mark them myself and my staff knows exactly what I want to go out.'[28] Thus during the inter-war years the chief means of political communication of the late Victorians had become the whim of an agency editor.

This process was speeded on its way by the development of radio, which even in its early days reached huge audiences: George v's broadcast opening the British Empire Exhibition in 1924 was estimated to have been heard by at least 10 million. By 1939, about 75 per cent of households had radio sets. Political broadcasting was from the start a sensitive matter and, partly for this reason, Sir John Reith of the BBC always tried to keep the political broadcasts short, though he encouraged their use in moderation: in the 1924 election all the Party Leaders made political broadcasts. Broadcasting was vital, Lloyd George said, 'to enable the vast mass of the electorate to know what the issues were . . . he did not know of any other way by which [politicians] could get at them.'

There were other ways, but not for Liberals. Nor were the short snaps permitted by the BBC conducive to the exposition of Liberal rationalism, and still less were the image-based media of film and television.

The provincial press, the extensive reporting of extra-parliamentary speeches, the culture of a self-improving, capable citizenship, and a liberal ethos which pervaded one Party and to some extent penetrated the other – all rose and fell together. 'A true Democracy is only possible when Society . . . becomes conscious in its intelligence and will,' wrote J. A. Hobson in 1909.[29] Hobson's statement was intended as an exhortation for the future, but today it reads elegiacally. The peculiar technical and structural conditions of the second half of the nineteenth century had offered one solution, but necessarily one limited to a particular phase, to the problem of 'democracy' in industrial Britain.

## *Notes*

1. R. Whately, *Rhetoric* (B. Fellowes, London, 1841), p. 3. This paper was first given, in an earlier form, to a conference on Rhetoric in the Oxford Union in 1973. A draft of that time shows the benefit of Pat Thompson's trenchant, constructive and sometimes libellous marginalia, which adorn to their advantage almost all my typescripts.
2. *Full and accurate report of Sir Robert Peel's Speeches* (London, 1837); Peel's Rectorial in Glasgow, 11 January 1837.
3. See E. K. Bramsted, *Goebbels and National Socialist Propaganda 1925–45* (The Cresset Press, London, 1965).
4. For a discussion of this, see H. C. G. Matthew, R. I. McKibbin and J. A. Kay, 'The Franchise Factor in the Rise of the Labour Party', *English Historical Review* (1976).
5. Blanchard Jerrold, 'On the manufacture of public opinion', *Nineteenth Century*, xiii, p. 1080 (June 1883); see also D. Read, *England 1868–1914* (Longman, London, 1979), pp. 158–9; and J. Newton, *W. S. Caine, M.P.* (James Nisbet, London, 1907), p. 104.
6. See M. Ostrogorski, *Democracy and the Organisation of Political Parties* (Macmillan, London, 1902), i.416–9.
7. I am obliged to Dr Jeremy Morris for supplying me with a copy of the Croydon local parliament's printed rules.
8. *Synopsis of the Newspapers in the United Kingdom* (London, 1867).
9. G. Scott, *Reporter Anonymous: the Story of the Press Association* (Hutchinson, London, 1968), p. 41. A further problem for parliamentary reporting was 'the midnight portcullis'. Speeches made after

midnight were too late for the morning papers and were not noted by the newspaper stenographers; thus the *Hansard* report was consequently sometimes thin.

10. E. C. F. Collier, *A Victorian Diarist* (John Murray, London, 1944) p. 30.
11. 'Extra-Parliamentary Utterances', *Saturday Review*, 5, December 1863, identified in J. F. A. Mason, 'The 3rd Marquess of Salisbury and the *Saturday Review*', *B.I.H.R.* (1961), xxxiv.36.
12. *The Speeches of Richard Cobden*, ed. J. Bright and J. E. T. Rogers (Macmillan, London, 1870), i.411.
13. 'Secondary Stars', *Saturday Review*, 10 December 1864, identified in Mason, art. cit.
14. *The Biograph and Review* (London, 1879), i.18.
15. J. A. Picton, *Sir James A. Picton* (Isbister, London, 1891), pp. 313–14.
16. For details, see G. Scott, op. cit., *passim* and J. Kieve, *The Electric Telegraph* (David and Charles, Newton Abbot, 1973), ch.11; less useful is J. M. Scott, *Extel 100. The centenary history of the Exchange Telegraph Company* (Ernest Benn, London, 1972).
17. H. C. G. Matthew, *The Gladstone Diaries* (Clarendon Press, Oxford 1986), ix,1xi,ff.; T. H. S. Escott, *Platform, Press, Politics and Play* (J. W. Arrowsmith, Bristol, n.d.[1895?]), pp. 337,353; J. L. Garvin, *The Life of Joseph Chamberlain* (Macmillan, London, 1932), i.245.
18. Cobden quoted in Holyoake, *op. cit.*, ch.2; R. Churchill to Dufferin, 27 October 1885, India Offices MS Eur F 130/3/77; I am obliged to Dr R. Quinault for this quotation.
19. A. Kinnear, 'The trade in great men's speeches', *Contemporary Review* (1899), 1iiv.439 ff. The precise amount according to the Act (31 & 32 Vict. c. 110) was one shilling per 100 words transmitted between 6 p.m. and 9 a.m. for the first report with 2d per hundred words for subsequent reports, or one shilling per 75 words between 9 a.m. and 6 p.m. with 2d per 75 words for further reports, these rates applying to all newspaper material.
20. Scott, op. cit., p. 78.
21. Calculated from C. Mitchell, *The newspaper press directory* (published annually). For the press generally, see A. J. Lee, *The Origins of the Popular Press 1855–1914* (Croom Helm, London, 1976), S. Koss, *The Rise and Fall of the Political Press in Britain* (Hamish Hamilton, London, 1981), vol. i, and A. P. Wadsworth, 'Newspaper circulations, 1800–1954', *Manchester Statistical Society Transactions* (1954–55); Lucy Brown, *Victorian News and Newspapers* (Oxford University Press, 1985).
22. W. F. Monypenny and G. F. Buckle, *Life of Disraeli* (John Murray, London, 1910–20), vol. V, p. 194.
23. Quoted in R. T. McKenzie and A. Silver, *Angels in Marble* (Heinemann, London, 1968).
24. G. Wallas, *Human Nature in Politics* (1908), as quoted in S. Reynolds and B. and T. Woolley, *Seems So!* (Macmillan, London, 1911), p. 130. To this should be added the specific of drink: 'Tory Democ-

racy changed the pump, not the beer'; P. J. Waller, *Democracy and Sectarianism* (Liverpool University Press, Liverpool, 1981), p. 46.

25. H. H. Gerth and C. Wright Mills, *From Max Weber* (Routledge and Kegan Paul, London, 1948), p. 106; see also Matthew, *Gladstone Diaries*, ix,1xii–1xiii.
26. *Pall Mall Magazine* (December 1898), ii.305; see also W. T. Stead's short history of the English interview in the *Idler* (December 1895), vii.495. Another means of communication, from the mid-1880s, was the lobby correspondent; his insidious influence is, by the very nature of his position, impossible to assess.
27. Kennedy Jones, *Fleet Street and Downing Street* (Hutchinson, London, 1920), p. 139.
28. Royal Commission on the Press, *Parliamentary Papers*, 1947–8, xv.146. Davies was describing the editorial excision of the Christian sections of Cripps' speeches: Cripps 'for the last six years emphasised the need of a Christian bias in the post-war world . . . but no one would know that from reading the accounts of his speeches in the newspapers.' The rest of the evidence confirms the general awareness of the decline in the significance and full reporting of the platform. Recently, party bureaucracies have interposed themselves between the politician and the reporter; see J. Prior, *A balance of power* (Hamish Hamilton, London, 1986), p. 152: 'I even had some trouble in getting Central Office to publish my speeches. On one occasion I gave my speech direct to the Press Association, which attracted a lot of publicity.'
29. J. A. Hobson, *The Crisis of Liberalism* (P. S. King, London, 1909), p. 87.

# 3 Style and Substance in Disraelian Social Reform, *c.*1860–80

*P. R. Ghosh*

One approach to the political usages of social reform is via the definition of terms. The primary sense of 'social' was as an antithesis to 'political':[1] consonant with any traditional idea of the state, society was a non-political area, a separate and different sphere. The increasing legislative interventions of Parliament corroded this distinction, and the coining of the term 'social reform' in the later 1860s[2] is a marker as to the time that such interventions were first seen as continuously significant, unlike the dramatic but spasmodic Acts of the 1830s and 1840s.[3] (Orthodox thinkers such as Spencer made the same point theoretically.)[4] But upon this new, and infrequent, coinage the impress of old distinctions remained: Parliament might transgress its traditional functions – the preservation and adjustment of political institutions; finance and foreign policy – but social reform, as the label implied, remained 'social' rather than 'political' in character.[5] Some practical connotations of this terminology were obvious. Social legislation was seen as a distinct sector of public life: not being 'political' meant that it was in principle bipartisan – as in the textbook protestation of W. H. Smith in 1874 on education, 'that he considered all such great social questions should be considered apart from all party feeling . . .'[6] But if such issues were agreed in principle, they were by high political criteria subordinate and often presumed to be insignificant: 'all that which is sober and homely', 'minor measures of practical utility', 'legislation . . . of an unostentatious but thoroughly useful character', 'little' rather than 'large measures'[7] were the terms in which they were described. The value of the work was only matched by its dullness, a feature which moved bored men to eloquence, as in Henry James' famous denunciation of Disraeli's 'policy of sewage' or Thomas Salt's resigned bleat at 'suet-pudding legislation'.[8]

That, none the less, an interest in social questions might carry a political cutting-edge is readily inferred from Disraeli's association with them. Simply as a function of speaking opportunities on the stump, parliamentary time and volume of business, the more energy and attention devoted to the anodyne of social concern, the less there remained for radical, organic innovation in political institutions. The promotion of social reform was thus a natural style for Conservative politicians to adopt. The power of this tactic should not be exaggerated: politically divisive issues could not be wished away by talk of public health, and preoccupation with social topics largely depended on the absence of divisions on first-class topics such as parliamentary reform or the Eastern Question. However, such a preoccupation once established might generate its own momentum, and, at a time of marked class hostility in Europe, a larger number of Conservatives might be led by tactical interest to an appreciation of the fundamental ends served by a classless and conciliatory approach.[9]

Significant preconditions of a distinctively Conservative style in the handling of social reform date from the mid-1860s. The most important, apart from the tendency of social legislation to increase in volume,[10] lay in a long-term shift in Tory strategy. The first two Derby ministries had seen the leadership trying to transcend its minority position by great legislative initiatives, which might win moderate support by providing solutions to outstanding problems. Finance, above all, but also India and administrative reform were chosen, because they largely avoided the sensitive area of the nation's established institutions, protection of which provided the Tory *raison d'être* – though in 1859 they had not been afraid to offer, and to fight upon, a settlement of the vexed reform issue distinctive to themselves. But defeat in the 1850s, and the consequential Liberal and Gladstonian settlement of the issues on which Derby's men had sought to compete, left the strategy of legislative initiative bankrupt and the Tory front bench was thrown rudely back upon the minimal position of constitutional defence[11] – a trend marked by Disraeli's abandonment of the financial reform issue after 1862 and his increasing absorption in the defence of the Church in the years 1860–65. In the absence of any positive programme, the attractions of social legislation as a means of keeping Parliament safely employed were evident. Already in 1864 – though he lacked a term to describe it – Stanley descried 'a vast mass of miscellaneous work on hand quite sufficient to occupy our attention for years to come', if parliamentary reform was left alone; and he was in no doubt that such work was 'quite as much the interest of those classes whose principles and associations make them conservative as any other'.[12]

Meanwhile, an important part of the intellectual framework which came to underlie much Conservative and later 'imperialist' preoccupation with social reform, was supplied by Disraeli in September 1864 when he first advanced the doctrine of an essential connection between the health of the populace and its fortunes as a race:

> The question [of health] is becoming both in town and country one of paramount interest. The greatness of the country depends on the race that fills it, and, whatever our ancestors may have done to make the country great or famous, whatever liberty they may have acquired, whatever wealth they may have accumulated, if the race becomes inferior you lose all these results and all these blessings. It is a question to which we must give our minds.[13]

Physical decline might subvert the moral character of the English people, and once the elements comprising the racial core were corrupt, disaster would strike: the decline of liberty at home, *imperium* abroad, and of economic power and prosperity.[14] It was thus clear how important social questions might become for Disraeli, and it was in this Aylesbury speech, as the result of typically *recherché* reading, he brought to light the motto that was to become famous in 1872, '*Sanitas sanitatum, omnia sanitas.*' But in 1864 these ideas had no legislative application. The context of the speech was a plea to local landlords for greater investment in labourers' cottages(!), and it should be noted that Disraeli's political manipulation of social reform after 1867/68 was preceded by a doctrine worked out years previously on objective, extra-political grounds. The Aylesbury speech, then, was an anticipation, and one which might well lie fallow on other grounds. Reckoning on Palmerston's demise, the dominant Tory concern in 1865 was not to distract but to focus attention on constitutional issues, and so disrupt the Liberal coalition of reformers and proto-Adullamites. Thus significant reference to social topics, either by leaders or backbenchers, was not to be expected in the election campaign of that year.[15]

The mature Tory style on social reform dates not from Disraeli's speeches of 1872, as might be supposed, but from 1868; nor was it a peculiarly Disraelian phenomenon – though his contribution was considerable – but one broadly based, drawing especially on that mass of opinion which had been calling itself Liberal Conservative since the 1830s. Two main sources evoked the increased public awareness of, or agreement upon, the importance of social questions in the late 1860s: education and parliamentary reform. It was in 1865–68 that there arose widespread acceptance that the limits of voluntary expansion in primary schooling had been reached, and that state aid would be required to supplement it. But education was distinct from other topics of Victorian social concern: it had a religious and hence a political tinge, and it was expensive.[16] It was thus important even by traditional criteria and, though a largely bipartisan approach was maintained, its impact on conventionally attuned political sensibilities was proportionately great. To this must be added the double awakening experienced in reforming the borough franchise: the revelation in 1866 of how great the working man's electoral presence already was, and the unfolding drama in 1867 as to how much it was to be enhanced.

The Tory reaction to these changing circumstances now appears as of immense significance for the long-term evolution of British politics, but then the necessary response was as evident to the meanest candidate at the next election as to the high politicians on the front bench. Concerned to defend the Irish Church from Liberal depredations, many protested on the hustings that three years of constitutional crisis were more than enough and 'the important question of Reform having been set to rest, that Parliament will not waste its time in useless recriminations, but devote its energies to useful legislation.'[17] But candidates on both sides felt they must incline more towards new concerns and new voters. Whereas in 1865 relatively few candidates' addresses included 'miscellaneous', non-partisan material – with that largely directed at the concerns of the prosperous, such as legal and bankruptcy reform – in 1868 the volume of matter thereon was largely expanded and its focus shifted towards the supposed needs of the householder – with much reference to education, topical subjects such as trade unions, and the ubiquitous claims of the ratepayer.

Some of this response may have been mechanical, and some must have represented real depth of social experience in the parliamentary class: but undoubtedly Tory tradition, rhetorical or actual, was a principal cause of the smoothness of this momentous phase in the party's evolution. The Tory Party in its 'wilderness years' after 1846 never became diehard; though the Derby–Disraeli leadership differed at points from that of Peel, they were both versions of Liberal Conservatism – a strain of opinion dating back at least to 1832 (*ipsis verbis*) and one more comprehensive than Peelism. The result was that by 1865 the platitudes of reformist Conservatism were more widely diffused than ever. But if these are examined alongside the emergence of social topics, they prove to be curiously malleable in their application, as with routine pledges given in the 1865 election: 'to sudden and organic changes I shall continue to give my steady opposition, while measures of just and enlightened progress will have my continued support', or again: '[I shall] support any improvements in the laws rendered desirable by the growing intelligence and changing circumstances of the country.[18] The original *locus* of the moderate, not to say hypocritical, reformism symbolised by the Tamworth Manifesto had been constitutional or institutional, and in 1865 this was largely still true; but it was now expressed in terms so watered down that it could apply to any sort of moderate reform, including social reform. Thus by a seamless transition the professions of Tory politicians of the 1870s could be expressed in terms reminiscent of the 1830s: 'the Government . . . has passed many measures of unostentatious but great practical usefulness, thus proving their readiness and their capacity, if adequately supported, to advance still further in the course of temperate and national improvement.'[19] But though the words were much the same, there was a difference: that by this time social reform was firmly set alongside institutional reform, and had indeed by 1880 already usurped it, as the focus of moderate progress.[20] Whether one believes in the reality of the reformist tradition or the artificial commitments induced by its rhetoric (or both), its importance in facilitating a continuous and apparently untroubled evolution is apparent.

The Tory leaders of 1868 were neither ahead of, nor behind, their rank and file in demanding a rest from prolonged constitutional agitation, and in proclaiming the need to catch up on 'arrears' of 'neglected' legislation on practical or social topics. The point was made briefly in Disraeli's keynote address published on 3 October[21] in his two principal election speeches, as well as by the departmental ministers most concerned, Cairns and Hardy.[22] However, they did not make too much of this, nor should we:[23] the principal issue was Ireland, and attitudes to social reform depended upon this. Gladstone, like everyone, wanted social reform and said much about it in his address, but for him 'at this time one question, or group of questions, overshadow[ed] all the rest.'[24] Disraeli disagreed with his opponent's Irish premises and thus with the effective postponement of social reform that followed; but it was on Ireland that he too hoped to win the election, and to which he devoted his political energies.

However, the 1868 election did demonstrate that, besides the consideration of political interest outlined, Tories enjoyed a second advantage over Liberals in handling social questions, stemming from financial doctrine. Tory ministries were not extravagant, but they accepted that expenditure might increase within the limits of the 'natural' increment of tax revenue due to economic growth. Gladstone treated their relaxed attitude as the simple subversion of public economy, which was the second principal issue in 1868.[25] Of course, the Tory doctrine conferred greater flexibility in meeting the newly emergent social expenditures – and this point was vividly seized on by Disraeli during the election campaign. In rebutting charges of alleged ministerial extravagance, he gave particular prominence to expenditure on education, justifying it on the fundamental ground that it supplied the basis of effective competition under conditions of increasing political and economic rivalry between great powers, also pointing to the long-term tendency of such social expenditures to increase:

> Among the principal causes of the increased expenditure is this very subject of education, taken in its largest sense. Whether you turn to popular schooling or to technical or reformatory education, all these are policies and progresses which lead necessarily to increased outlay, but the neglect of which would brutalise the people. . . . We have created in this island an immense population, educated and elevated with all those aspirations of freemen that the people of an ancient and famous country will possess, and an expenditure necessary for their education, and for giving them that skill in their industry that will enable them to compete successfully with other nations, is among the requirements which the body of the nation will demand to be satisfied. (Cheers.)[26]

Advancing from the position of 1864, Disraeli had given his ideas about the link between race and social welfare legislative and political application.[27] Elements of this argument, on race and education, derived from his own and other contributions to the 'condition of England' debate in the 1840s; what was new was the legislative centrality allotted to social reform,[28] the emphasis on international competition, and the political position from which he, unlike other intellectuals-cum-prophets, could speak. Moreover, the durability of the argument is indubitable: it anticipated by a generation the *fin de siècle* doctrines of 'national efficiency', and the proposition of a link between education and long-term ability to compete remains relevant to this day. Above all, it exemplified Disraeli's facility in combining the objectively and the politically desirable in one set of policies.

The rapid evolution of the Party's positions on social reform in the 1860s was followed by five years of stagnation during Gladstone's first ministry. This is illustrated by Disraeli's famous speeches of 1872 at Manchester and the Crystal Palace, which even the revisionist historians of the 1960s failed quite to cut down to size.[29] The importance of the great demonstration at Manchester in April 1872 as an unprecedented (nor ever repeated) type of extra-parliamentary movement[30] is unquestioned, but this had no connection with social reform. However, difficulties arose from the exceptional nature of the occasion, which were keenly felt by that earthbound Lancastrian magnifico, Derby, in his position as host:

> Cross talks much with me on the wish of the local Conservatives to have a party meeting some time in the winter. We agree in disliking the idea, partly because for a party in opposition, and likely to continue so, it is disadvantageous to be compelled to announce a policy – their [sic] proper policy being to lie in wait for, and profit by, the mistakes of their oponents: partly also because Disraeli must be invited to make the principal speech, and no one knows, or can guess, what he is likely to say. If he confines himself to criticism on the events of last session, the subject is worn-out: if he lays down a programme for the future, we do not know what we may find ourselves pledged to.[31]

Contrary to Derby's suspicions, Disraeli had some sympathy with these forebodings – he had rebuffed successive invitations from the county over a period of three years[32] – and before his departure for the North he permitted Derby to vet the speech for indiscretions.[33] Knowledge of the genesis of the speech explains its peculiar character: it was not, except in its final pages, a partisan critique,[34] nor did it lay down policy for the future. The normal modes of stump oratory being ruled out, Disraeli supplied instead 'a kind of essay on the British constitution',[35] analogous to his early *Vindication of the English Constitution* or the disquisitions which stud the novels of the 1840s, and arguing that 1867 was a return to the pre-1832 dispensation in its restoration of the class balance of the franchise, thereby illustrating the unchanging nature of the constitution and vindicating his own conduct over Reform. His preparation, the bulk of the speech itself, and the judgement of press and colleagues all centred on these highly individual constitutional doctrines.[36]

Having discussed 'the most important subjects that can interest Englishmen', Disraeli turned to the labouring classes – another topic which, being neither partisan nor dangerously committal, satisfied the negative criteria laid down in advance of the speech. He dwelt on what he knew most, the condition of the agricultural labourer, with allusions to the generally enhanced prosperity of the working classes since the 1830s. His view of the sources of that prosperity was utterly conventional, resting on sympathy and self-help, with judicious legislation 'in the last place'. The one printed page[37] devoted to legislation was about as meagre as it well could be, in that it explicitly echoed Derby's orthodox, *laissez-faire* attack of the previous January on the well-meaning but ill-judged profusion of legislative proposals with the 'New Social Movement'.[38] As *The Times* leader writer sourly observed, 'Sir CHARLES ADDERLEY'S consolidation of all existing sanitary Acts is the single measure to which the Conservative leader is prepared to pledge himself.'[39]

The true Disraelian style on social reform was not to be found in the embarrassing commitments of the 'New Social Movement' (to which none the less a range of eminently sound Tory frontbenchers was prepared to subscribe), but in the piquant epigrams of Manchester, even if piquancy was required to conceal a partly second-hand character: '*sanitas sanitatum*', and again (for they came to the same thing), 'the first consideration of a Minister should be the health of the people'. The context indicates two references in Disraeli's mind when he made these remarks. The first was to 'the health of the people' at large, in the light of his doctrines of race, national efficiency and international rivalry. This was of obvious importance to a minister, because of his general concern with the national welfare, and because at this date he, like all other public men, was deemed to have an important function as a moulder of opinion far beyond his purely political agency.[40] Taking, secondly, a narrow view of Disraeli's words, they may be glossed thus – 'the first [legislative] concern of a Minister should be the health of the people' – and we recognise the familiar calculation of interest: that a Tory ministry committed to constitutional defence could have no interest in legislation, except upon dull, virtuous, bipartisan topics of social concern. This does not mean that Disraeli was insincere. As it transpired,[41] he regarded such statements as pledges to be honoured, but they were pledges only in a general sense – to devote time and attention to social topics – and neither he nor anyone could have predicted the nature and extent of the legislation that might result.

The Manchester speech, unlike the precedent demonstration, was not generally reckoned a success, because it revealed Tory negativism so clearly. Hardy's succinct verdict was, 'No programme, as how could there be?';[42] and in that case, how could they hope to win an election? Social reform would not help. In June 1872 Disraeli gave a little noticed speech to the party faithful at the Crystal Palace,[43] where he attempted *inter alia* to turn Henry James' jeer at a Tory 'policy of sewage' by portraying the Liberals as unfeeling and careless. But the young QC had an easy answer: he himself, he said, ardently supported a policy of sewage; but it became derisory if it was the only policy of a great political party.[44] The solution to the Tories' puzzle was the simple one that negative means would have to suffice to bring victory; not, however, the pseudo-academic and politically inert negativism preached at Manchester, but the type of lacerating, partisan assault in which Disraeli knew no peer. Predictably, therefore, he made no public utterance on social questions of consequence between June 1872 and June 1874; instead his energies went into political criticism of the ministry's foreign policy and its harassment of established institutions. At first this unashamedly partisan posture seemed too violent and unconstructive, but gradually its sense was acknowledged: the most moderate Tories conceded that the criticism was merited, whilst partisans revelled in his exquisite – and brutal – ironies as the old man, Prospero-like, summoned up almost for the last time the spirit of '46.[45]

We cannot know the electoral effect of this, but it did mean that, in the wake of the great victory of January 1874, the Tory Party was more committed than at any time since 1832 to a policy of constitutional resistance. In the resultant legislative vacuum,[46] one symptom of the ministry's lack of initiative on first-class political measures was its unique suggestibility to projects from external sources. Of the three sessions of Disraeli's Commons' leadership 1874–76, two were dominated by Bills of this kind – on Public Worship regulation in 1874 and Royal Titles in 1876[47] – and the phenomenon persisted in milder form until 1880.[48] Though neither Bill originated with government, they were adopted on grounds of general sympathy, as politically important but yet non-partisan in intent. However, they remained highly controversial and consumed large amounts of parliamentary time, even where, as with Public Worship, non-partisan status was conceded by the Opposition. Thus even in a 'do-nothing' ministry social concerns took second place to political and institutional ones. Had there been pressing topics of foreign policy prior to Disraeli's elevation to the Lords, second place would have sunk to third, as may be inferred from his 1874 election call for 'a little more energy in our foreign policy and a little less in our domestic legislation'.[49]

None the less, Disraeli, and hence the ministry, had definite intentions as to social reform, and his recurrence to the ideas voiced in 1867–68 and 1872 was more or less automatic.[50] However, these intentions related to political style and strategy in the first place, and acted only indirectly on specific Bills. In his memoirs R.A. Cross, an untried Home Secretary in 1874 but in the forefront of the legislative implementation of *sanitas*, recalled the Cabinet discussions on the Queen's Speech of that year:

> . . . I was, I confess, disappointed at the want of originality shown by the Prime Minister. From all his speeches, I had quite expected that his mind was full of legislative schemes, but such did not prove to be the case; on the contrary, he had entirely to rely on the various suggestions of his colleagues, and as they themselves had only just come into office, and that suddenly, there was some difficulty in framing the Queen's Speech.[51]

Cross's expectations were unrealistic.[52] It would have been strange if Disraeli had not consulted his colleagues as to proposals on hand for Bills, given the bureaucratic origin of many of these and the fact that the Queen's Speech was the most obviously collective act the Cabinet undertook. But it is also clear that Disraeli controlled the overall structure of the speech, and with it the image and substantive thrust of the legislative programme. Thus in the one year (1875) when social reform was designedly central the first draft of the whole is in his hand, whereas in subsequent years, when domestic legislation was reduced to a tailpiece, he only drafted the principal sections on foreign policy.[53] Again, there was no reason to suppose that Disraeli, whose only official experience was at the Treasury, should be well-informed on the details of politically subordinate social measures. Gladstone's Prime Ministerial style, modelled on Peel's essay at omnicompetence, was fresh in the memory; but, aside from the ever-increasing hopelessness of the attempt, the difficulties they experienced – too much intervention in ministers' affairs leading to friction and divisions, the head of the ministry being excessively compromised over minor slips, the intolerable strain on health – were sufficient to deter all Victoria's other Ministers from following such a course, and political opinion at large acknowledged the rationality of this.[54]

As regards legislative planning for a future government, Disraeli's speeches of 1867–72 will not bear the inference Cross placed on them. They show a clear general grasp of the issues prominent at the time of delivery – education in 1867–68, public health in 1872 – but they betray no sign of legislative plans in embryo. Of course, Disraeli was capable of prospective action on social topics, as, for example, when he asked Hardy in August 1873 for briefing material on trade union law.[55] But this was to prepare his Party's position in case Gladstone's government should introduce a Bill in 1874 – something very different from drafting legislation. The reasons for this apparent lack of ambition are evident: union law was typical of other social topics in its technicality; government had the paid lawyers and draughtsmen to handle it; it was not an issue contested on party lines;[56] and Disraeli was neither a faddist nor an expert, but the leader of a political party more or less continuously in opposition.

Once in government, the absence of legislative preparation was not an embarrassment – quite the reverse. It was, as we have seen, a peculiarly Tory complaint that arrears of social legislation had built up owing to an excessive concentration on unsettling political change. But if its party slant is subtracted, the complaint becomes a commonplace: Parliament had been progressively overloaded with business since the Crimea at least, and its arrears inevitably consisted of social measures, because such topics constituted the bulk of parliamentary business, if that is measured by Bills passed rather than time and attention spent. There was thus a continuous and increasing stream of measures to be considered, and Disraeli could not help but be aware of this:[57] in every session of his second ministry there were complaints that not enough legislation had been carried – not only after 1876 when special causes operated but also in the years before.[58] The problem, then, was not how to generate business, but how to pass a modicum of that which presented itself. In so far as planning amidst the miscellany of social topics was possible, attention to style and overall legislative strategy was the natural and apt function for a Prime Minister to perform. Disraeli was the master of this during his years as leader in the Commons, as Cross in fact recognised: '[his] mind was either above or below (whichever way you like to put it) mere questions of detail . . . but on great questions of principle, and on all questions of high and imperial policy he without doubt asserted his supremacy.'[59]

Disraeli's guiding hand was not strongly in evidence at the opening of his ministry, but for this there were obvious, temporary reasons. The eccentric timing of the January election and the resultant ministerial changeover meant that virtually the first third of the session was lost, which inevitably restricted the amount of work feasible. Moreover, a Cabinet elected on a negative platform, had to finalise its legislative programme in three weeks, a task to which it would normally have devoted some four months of the recess. Not surprisingly, it took the minimal line of framing a Queen's Speech in which 'the measures proposed [were] sufficient to fill up the session',[60] and one can only wonder at Cross expecting more at this stage. The corollary of this rushed opening was that the measures actually pursued by the government diverged more than usual from those outlined in the Speech. This, combined with the Liberals' belief that they were the only competent party of government, occasioned the opening shots in what would prove to be a sustained polemic, typified by Childers' tendentious calculation near the close of the 1874 session that, 'Out of the six measures . . . proposed in Her Majesty's Speech, five had been abandoned, and the sixth had been passed in a very small degree.'[61]

But if circumstances led to a disorganised start in 1874, Disraeli's intention of imposing himself in future was signalled at the end-of-session dinner at the Mansion House, when he laid down the outlines of strategy for 1875.[62] His premise was that, despite the difficulties under which they had laboured that year and a consequent temptation to succumb to 'the delights of a Castle of Indolence', the ministry was committed to legislative activity, and had already achieved results, which if 'not memorable' were at least 'not insignificant'.[63] He reaffirmed the famous *dictum* of Manchester, 'that the condition of the people ought to be the first consideration of English statesmen', and concluded with a pledge for 1875:

> We are now upon the eve of a period when we shall have more time and more leisure to consider the conduct of affairs, and to prepare those measures which we think are necessary and adequate for the opportunities and occasions that await us. [Next year] . . . I trust I shall be able to address you as the representative of a Ministry who have no longer in excuse of their conduct to appeal to the unexpected circumstances under which they accepted office or the want of opportunity to prepare adequate measures for the contingencies they have had to encounter. (Cheers.)

Disraeli's aim over the next twelve months was thus to show by all means, visual and substantial, that a programme of 'necessary and adequate' social measures was being carried out. Already in September he was looking forward to the November planning Cabinets, giving rise to an amusing scene when he encountered Carnarvon while going the country house rounds. The Premier buttonholed the hypersensitive Colonial Secretary,

> saying that it was of no use merely to meet [in November] to ask each other how we had spent the holidays – that it was necessary to have our views as to legislation &c ready. I expected something serious & large after this & remembered the hints as to Reform in '67: but he proceeded to say that Cross, in whom he had got confidence, had promised to consider some scheme as to dwellings for the working classes – that he had not asked him what his plan was but that he believed he was maturing it. And there he stopped adding I think somewhat as to sanitary reform.[64]

The bathetic descent from the great crisis of 1867 to Cross's Artisans' Dwellings Bill, indicates the political status normally enjoyed by social topics; but Carnarvon's alarm was also a measure of the importance Disraeli was now attaching to such questions, and the degree of innovation which, at the ministerial level, he was practising. Of course, fresh Bills proposed at the planning Cabinets would derive from departmental ministers, but the size and direction of the whole programme was in the Premier's hands, and this was reflected in the outcome.[65] He already had a sufficient programme by adding Cross's Bill to the principal remainders from the previous session – land transfer, appellate jurisdiction and trade unions. When the Cabinet met in November, the familiar story of legislative overload was repeated with 'work for several sessions'[66] available, but the final selection was, in business terms, reduced from the impossible to the large, with two more principal items (agricultural tenancy, merchant shipping) and a shoal of lesser ones to add to the previous four.[67] This well suited Disraeli's purpose of a legislative demonstration, as did the omission, so far as possible, of politically controversial proposals touching established institutions – Endowed Schools, Oxbridge revenues, the reform of London government and an ambitious plan by Northcote for the reform of county government[68] – even though reform in the last two cases might have had beneficial consequences for social reform.

The 1875 session records one of Disraeli's most untypical triumphs – the execution according to timetable of his pledge to legislate *en masse* on social topics. The triumph was not unmixed, but it was substantial; it was criticised, but this reflected his success in attaching political significance to his ministry's Acts; and it was achieved in the face of extraordinary difficulty. The difficulty was the first emergence of obstruction in a session where one inescapable political measure was the renewal of Irish coercion – and where the Irish led, Liberals connived or followed. As a result the first half of the session was sluggish in the extreme. By the time the Irish Peace Preservation Bill got through committee on 6 May, three months after the opening of Parliament, it had taken up over a third of all available government time, and only two Bills (Artisans' Dwellings and Regimental Exchanges) had got through the Commons; of these, Regimental Exchanges, a one-clause Bill, had taken up another five government days (out of 26) due to fierce Liberal opposition.[69] That so much legislation ultimately passed indicates that social reform cannot be considered solely with reference to the detail of Bills; it must also include political factors – in Disraeli's case his loyalty to pledges and parliamentary management. The latter normally calls to mind the devilries of 1867, but his skills also found a showcase in the session of 1875.

On 6 May, aware of the imminent departure of the Coercion Bill, he abandoned the stance of the patience-player[70] to deliver a calculatedly violent harangue in which he threatened to keep Parliament sitting for as long as it took to pass the government's Bills.[71] This was a hit at the Liberals as much as the Irish, as Disraeli explained to a confidante: 'The Opposition . . . have a plan to waste time, prevent us passing our measures; & then, in the recess, hold us up to public scorn as incurables who have carried nothing.'[72] He followed up this display on 31 May by calling a party meeting in the afternoon – the first of three that summer – and then trounced Hartington and the Irish in the evening by the swollen majority of 107 on the obstructionist device of 'espial of Strangers'.[73] The measure of the achievement, albeit also of the infancy of Irish tactics, is that this was the only clear parliamentary victory which the Home Rulers ever respected, and for the rest of the session they ceased to feature. Disraeli next cracked the whip over his own Party. The reluctance of his country members to pass legislation (on Agricultural Holdings) enhancing tenants' rights was the perfect foil for the Liberals (many of whom also shared these doubts); to counter Tory apathy, therefore, Disraeli called and harangued two more party meetings, admired by almost silent colleagues.[74]

Largely as a result of these efforts, in late July ministers were pluming themselves on success. In May Disraeli had despaired of fitting the trades union Bills into the timetable and there had been a real danger that Agricultural Holdings would not pass;[75] but by 22 July, the date of the final Party meeting, it was clear that five out of six major items on the legislative programme would be tackled, with Merchant Shipping the exception. The sensations of the next fortnight – Plimsoll's outburst in the House when the Shipping Bill was dropped, the sympathetic upsurge of opinion out of doors, and the rapid passage of a temporary Bill – made little ultimate difference to the statute book, in that the Bill passed was avowedly provisional. Disraeli's final efforts – as principal sponsor[76] of the temporary Bill and then as advocate – were thus mainly presentational, but they were as necessary as those that went before: if the Tory image were tarnished, it would devalue the entire session and with it all Disraeli's pledges. It was symptomatic of their cushioned position that most of the Tory peers – Derby, Salisbury, Carnarvon – were strongly opposed to the new Bill, as legally frivolous and publicly undignified;[77] but they constituted an isolated point in the political spectrum, for this was very much a case of where the Liberals spat, Disraeli polished.

Neither Party distinctly[78] expected the wave of sentiment in Plimsoll's favour, but since a ministerial act occasioned it, the Liberals felt bound to try to exploit it – first by attempting to raise an agitation against ministers for failing to legislate and then, when this was checked by the introduction of the temporary Bill, they accused them of kowtowing to *demos*.[79] Cynical as this was, it was consistent in harping on the apparent divergence between popular sentiment and ministerial actions. To dispel that appearance the decrepit Premier accepted, at the last minute, the invitation to speak at the Mansion House on 4 August,[80] the occasion of his crowning vindication of his involvement with social reform. On Merchant Shipping, he insisted that the government had always wanted to legislate, but had been frustrated by public apathy and the threat of Liberal obstruction; when the public was at last aroused, it enabled the government to pass a new Bill, in accordance with its original intentions: 'We have been successful. (Cheers.) . . . The *vox populi* did not coerce us, but assisted and aided us.'[81] But celebration of the ministry's general commitment to social reform was at once the central theme of the speech and the best defence against 'political sceptics' on the shipping issue:

> . . . it has been a Session in which, as the Ministry, we were called upon to perform that ceremony which, in homely language, but popular phrase is generally described in this country as "redeeming your pledges." During the five years that we spent in Opposition we endeavoured to impress upon the country our sincere convictions that the time had arrived when political change was no longer required, when the distribution of political power was no longer the problem to solve in this country, but that its intelligence and energy should be directed to the improvement and elevation of the condition of the people. (Cheers.) . . . Well, then, when we had acceded to power it became our first duty, and I can say our most ardent desire, to bring into practice that policy . . . And this, among other reasons, is the main reason why the

> Government were obliged to bring forward a greater number of measures than under ordinary circumstances and in an ordinary Session they would have been inclined to produce. It was a crucial Session for a party acceding to power . . .

The pledges given had been redeemed. The Queen's Speech in February had announced eleven government Bills; 'of these 11 measures nine have passed . . . and when the just, and wise, and intelligent people of England look to the great result, they [will] say that the legislative labours of their representatives have added to the great total of national happiness.'

Historians have followed contemporary criticism of these claims half-way. Stung by Disraeli's political and rhetorical *coup*, Hartington presented a contrary view to the Commons 48 hours later, and much of the detail of his assault[82] – emphasising the bipartisan nature of the issues and the limitations of the Acts carried – has passed into modern tradition. But Hartington did not confine himself to detail, nor can we: he advanced general claims that the ministry 'had not solved any problem, nor attempted to battle with any difficulties', and that the session had been 'aimless and purposeless, and barren of all benefit to the country.' Such claims were transparently partisan, and Disraeli scored a fresh triumph in emphasising how much useful legislation had been passed under the aegis of government – a triumph acknowledged as much by the public silence and private confessions of Liberals as by the plaudits of Tories.[83] Yet Hartington's attack was not simply quixotic: if Disraeli's claims were not contested at the general level, then they were not effectively contested at all. So too, we must recognise the fundamental difficulty in detailed modern analysis seeking to demonstrate the supposed unimportance of social reform to an allegedly *bourgeois* party, which can still allow that 'the government of 1874–80 was responsible for one of the most notable instalments of social reform of the century, conspicuously shaming its Liberal predecessors.'[84] What made the social legislation of 1875 remarkable was not its detailed origins, which were technical, bipartisan, and conventional, but a series of political factors – advance pledges, the focusing of legislative strategy, the management of Parliament, and the presentation of the whole. The self-interest of the party and the remarkable gifts of its leader could, and did, make a difference to what was intrinsically bipartisan; political style could react on legislative substance, both in amount and quality passed and in the party attribution it carried in the memory.

The most apt criticism of Disraeli's achievement was provided not by opponents but by himself. In his Mansion House speech he dwelt repeatedly on the session of 1875 as a singular occurence,[85] and gave no promise for the future as in 1874. Since the pledges given were now redeemed, his vindication was also a valediction. There was a personal side to this. Disraeli's health had given way under the burdens of ministerial and Commons' management, and in August-September 1875 he made the first intimations of forthcoming retirement to Derby and Northcote.[86] But political factors were also at work. Given the inherently ordinary nature of social legislation, an extraordinary face could not continually be put upon it. Disraeli's political point had been made – that social reform represented a viable domestic strategy for a Tory ministry under conditions – and it was now only susceptible to the humdrum process of repetition and confirmation.

Planning for the 1876 session exemplified this: 'D. expressed himself as not anxious to have a large programme, but wishing to carry all that we brought in: which was generally agreed to.'[87] The legislative credit of the ministry was to be maintained, but without drama: there were to be no ultimata to the Commons, no party meetings, no rhetorical highlighting, no emergency measures to drive up the legislative product, no risk of failure by aiming high. At the Opening of Parliament, in the Queen's Speech and in Disraeli's comments upon it, the high profile previously allotted to social questions was withdrawn: these were not of 'extreme interest,' the 'great points' were all foreign.[88] The result, once the excitement over Royal Titles had passed off, was the quietest session of the ministry, with a moderate but respectable yield: three principal measures were passed out of five attempted, although two of these (Merchant Shipping and Appellate Jurisdiction) had been largely settled by the conflicts of 1875.

It is important to establish the 'par' position of social legislation in 1876, when foreign questions were already absorbing the Cabinet's energies,[89] in order to show that its subordination after 1875 did not imply the chronic legislative dearth of the three sessions 1877–79. The causes of that dearth were obvious and external – the intense preoccupation of Parliament with foreign affairs (in 1877–78) and the development of Irish obstruction to new extremes (in 1877 and 1879). The latter showed up the weakness of the new Commons leaders, but it was not tacitly convenient to them: in social reform they had something safe and creditable for Parliament to do, and while in public they promised as much for the future as they dared, in private they let slip their frustration.[90]

There is, therefore, no truth in the argument that more deeply-laid causes were at work; that the decline of the ministry's ability to pass social legislation after 1876, allegedly in the exclusive interest of the working class, was a response to the increasingly 'middle-class' composition of the Tory Party, a response aggravated by the defensive reaction of that class to trade depression in 1878–80.[91] The sphere of the 'social' and of social reform was not originally defined along class lines. It included legal reform on behalf of commercial men in the City,[92] agricultural tenancy reform as an aspect of 'the condition of the people',[93] union reform as a vindication of equality before the law and traditional liberties,[94] merchant shipping reform on the moral (or sentimental) ground of putting lives before property, public health measures promoted by the educated classes for the good of the uneducated and unwashed, and environmental Bills in the immediate interest of landowners.[95] Moreover, making all allowance for the influx of property into the Conservative Party, this process operated over a fifty- rather than a five-year timespan. It was far from complete by 1914,[96] and in a European view was striking precisely because it was incomplete, leaving the class catholicity of the Party intact. Examination of Cabinet personnel in this light leaves a predominant impression of continuity, being led throughout by a premier who retained his youthful prejudice against the 'middle class', but suffering the loss of an heir-apparent, Derby, consciously favourable to its aspirations (though also an ardent advocate of social reform).[97]

There was no general connection between the passage of

Bills on social questions and trade depression except in the rare cases where these involved government money. By that criterion almost[98] all the Bills put forward in 1874–76 could as well have been taken up three years later. Depression had a severe impact on government finance – with a sharp fall in revenue in 1877–80 – but none on existing social expenditures. Financial pressures led to a notional attempt to save an odd thousand pounds in the £3.7 million spent on education in 1880, to satisfy complaints by Tory squires at board schools offering the middle classes (*sic*) education on public money.[99] Against this must be set the swingeing economies levied on defence in 1877–80 – a time of sustained foreign crisis – and the £8.1 million effective tax relief granted to all classes in 1878–80 by Beaconsfield's refusal to balance the budget in time of depression and with an election imminent (as Gladstonian canons demanded).[100] Important action was taken in 1879 tending to curb social expenditure, but it was structural, and not linked to the trade-cycle. Gladstonian legislation on education and public health in 1870–73 had permitted a largely unexpected flood of local authority capital expenditure financed by borrowing on cheap government credit. The cost, the anarchy and the feared long-term consequences for public indebtedness led Northcote to take steps to regulate this from 1875 on. In 1879 he took the decisive step of raising government interest rates for local authority borrowers, and though a Bill to this end was rendered nearly toothless, Treasury discretionary power served him just as well.[101] This was undeniably a significant act of reaction, whereby sanitary expenditure thus financed was curtailed, and similar spending under the Artisans' Dwellings Act killed off entirely:[102] but it was in principle no more than a bipartisan restoration of *laissez-faire*, after its unexpected breach. What Northcote objected to was not social expenditure, but its unregulated financing by government agency.

The social consequence of the depression was not the defensive consolidation of the propertied classes under the Tory banner, but the evocation of Beaconsfield's keenest sympathy for the suffering classes based on his memories of the 1840s – a public stance which, as ever, moulded ministerial policy.[103] A humbler symptom of the maintenance of the 'national' or socially comprehensive Tory ideal formulated by Disraeli in the 1830s, was the determination to meet Parliament in 1880, as usual with a sizeable legislative programme, but one which also included significant new proposals on social questions: Cross's Bill for London water purchase, and Cairns' on settled land, in addition to the emergency measures for relieving Irish distress, which occupied the limelight on political grounds.[104] All of these would run second to foreign policy, but they gave the lie to increasingly extreme Liberal accusations that the Tory Parliament had never done any legislative work; that obstruction had been grateful to it; and 'that the Government meant for the future to soar above the details of home reforms and social progress'.[105] The thrust of ministers' proposals was indeed towards the future: most palpably, towards the imminent election, when they and hosts of Tory candidates presented themselves as committed to the enactment of social reforms, just as in 1868 and 1874.[106] In a longer-term view, these proposals were no longer under the aegis of Disraeli, and could not have been, given his elevation to the peerage and concomitant relinquishing of the business management of the Commons.[107] Despite the legislative desert of 1877–79, the rejuvenated programme of 1880 thus illustrated the commitment of the second eleven to continue where Disraeli had left off. Mediocre they may have been, in their attempts to follow a strategy which, as he had shown, was so dependent on political gifts; still, they represent the first link in a party tradition which, though altered and developed, has persisted to the present day.

* * *

The impact of Conservative involvement with social policy must, on its own, have been limited; seen as a supplement to the inherently classless institutional politics dominant in Britain since, say, the 1760s, it becomes significant. The keynotes of that tradition were those of continuous evolution, hence of a striking degree of consensus. The expansion of state activity into new areas carried those same keynotes over with it, and the seamless development of the Conservative reformist tradition from the institutional to the social sphere exemplifies this.[108] In this way the potentially jarring arrival of new issues was dampened in a way markedly different from the post-revolutionary states of continental Europe. There, even if legislative satisfaction was given, as in Germany, its conciliatory effect was nugatory in the absence of political traditions to match. The measure of the success of 'Disraelian' social reform is thus, paradoxically, the *absence* of social policy as a central issue before 1900 and the continued primacy of institutional questions in politics.[109] Correlative aspects of this evolution may be seen in the late founding of a Labour Party, and the extraordinarily indistinct emergence of a class-based element in politics. The Conservative espousal of social reform cannot explain all of this, but it was a central and representative element in an entire tradition of consensual modernisation which largely can.

## *Notes*

1. For this antithesis: e.g. Disraeli at Glasgow, 19 November 1873, pr. *Addresses on Education, Finances and Politics* (1873) p. 11; Derby at Willis's Rooms, 9 May 1873, pr. *Speeches [and Addresses 1854–91* (1894)] i.204, and in *H[ansard*] [218]. 48, 19 March 1874; Shaftesbury to Disraeli, 10 May 1865, [W.F.] M[onypenny & G.E.] B[uckle, *The Life of Benjamin Disraeli* (1929 edn)], ii.145. Neither *OED* nor its *Supplement* are of assistance.
2. Derby's term in 1864 was 'miscellaneous work' (above p. 61); Gladstone described government social expenditure as 'miscellaneous' in the 1880s (e.g. *H* [260].585, 4 April 1881), the formal title, 'Estimates for Civil Services' being another evasion in terms. In the 1868 election we find: Disraeli's 'measures . . . of social amelioration' or Carnarvon's 'social improvements' ([*The] T[imes*], 10 November 1868, p. 3e, 8 October 1868, p. 10b respectively). Reference to individual 'social reforms' can be found, e.g. Beach at Stroud (*T*, 31 October 1868, p. 8a) but not, apparently, 'social reform' as an abstract category, which still struck Hardy as an awkward novelty in 1877 (at Edinburgh, *T*, 13 December 77, p. 6c): 'I now pass . . . to those questions which in the address you allude to under the name of social reform.'
3. The other, principal factor marking out the consideration of social policy after *c.*1860 as distinct from the earlier period, is the altered perception of socio-economic context: Gladstone's celebration of a new social stability in the 1860s is familiar, but the idea was as common to his opponents (e.g. Disraeli at Aylesbury, *T*, 22 September 1864, p. 9d, Northcote at Thelbridge, *T*, 19 October 1868, p. 5a). That there were also continuities is evident, particularly

in Tory exploitation of their 1840s tradition of support for social reform (e.g. Disraeli at Manchester 4 April 1872, in *The Nine Hours Movement . . . Mr. Disraeli's Visit* [Manchester, 1872], pp. 7–8; J. Fielden at Goole, *T*, 24 October 1868, p. 5e; Hicks Beach at Stroud *T*, 31 October 1868, p. 8a).

4. Spencer took 1860 as his marker date – 'The New Toryism', *Contemporary Review* (1884) xlv.153–67, repr. in *The Man versus the State* (1884).
5. The usage exemplified by 'social reform' is close to that of n.1 in that it maintains the 'social'/'political' antithesis, but the 'social' is now brought into the legislative arena; cf. Disraeli, *Speech . . . at the Crystal Palace June 24, 1872* (1872), p. 10, Derby *D[iary]* 7 April 1878, [Derby MSS], Cairns to Disraeli, 24 August 1874 B/XX/Ca/123 [Disraeli MSS].
6. At Westminster, *T*, 29 January 1874, p. 6c; cf. Disraeli at Glasgow 19 November 1873, *Addresses . . .* p. 18; *Daily News*, 25 June 1872, Leader, p. 5b-c; Granville in *H* [218].37, 19 March 1874, etc. It follows that no analysis of social policy can be adequate which looks at one party alone. Lawrence Goldman, 'The Social Science Association 1857–86: a context for mid-Victorian Liberalism', *EHR*, 1986, ci.95–134 is a recent example. By looking only for Liberal ideology he arrives at the position that social policy made an original contribution to party political identity.
7. Respectively: Carnarvon, Presidential Address to the Social Science Congress (*T*, 8 October 1868, p. 10b); Lord R. Montagu, [Election] Address (*T*, 13 October 1868, p. 6e); T.C. Baring, Address (*T*, 12 March 1880, p. 8b); Derby at Edinburgh, 18 December 1875, pr. *Speeches*, i.272.
8. James at Bath, pr. *Pall Mall Gazette*, 7 June 1872, p. 4a; Salt in *H* [225].1064 7 July 1875.
9. Systematic treatment of the interrelations between social policy and class context is omitted here, as a subject in itself; but see pp. 77–81 above.
10. cf. Gladstone, 'The Declining Efficiency of Parliament', *Quarterly Review* (1856), xcix.521–70.
11. See my 'Disraelian Conservatism: a financial approach', *EHR*, xcix.294–6.
12. At King's Lynn, pr. *T*, 20 October 1864, p. 8f.
13. To the Bucks. Agricultural Association, pr. *T*, 22 September 1864, p. 9f.
14. The association of social reform and maintenance of empire was thus natural to Disraeli, as in the *Speech . . . at the Crystal Palace June 24, 1872*, pp. 8–9, but it was not the only possible linkage. For that between social reform and economic welfare, see above p. 65.
15. e.g. Disraeli, Address to Bucks. electors, pr. *T*, 22 May 1865, p. 5e; at Aylesbury, *T*, 14 July 1865, p. 6a-f; Stanley at Lynn, *T*, 10 July 1865, p. 6a-b. For the general elections 1865–80 I have used the sample represented by such candidates' addresses as were printed in

*The Times*. The electoral address is of particular use in studying of social reform, since the latter was not much politically contested, but was still part of the overall make-up of both parties: the address provides the best synopsis of that overall image. I omit here source evaluation, but the sample may be considered useful as to the broad lie of candidates' commonplaces, as at p. 63 above.

16. The cost was primarily marginal: thus in 1869–80 the public education votes rose by as much as those for defence expenditure (£2.51 m: 2.51 m), but the absolute proportions in 1880 were £3.72 m: 26.03 m: *P[arliamentary] P[apers]*, Estimates' Series, as corrected by S. Buxton, *Finance and Politics 1783–1885* (1888), ii.345.
17. A Walsh, Address (Radnorshire), *T*, 10 October 1868 p. 5d; cf. Addresses of (e.g.) Lord R. Montagu (Hunts.), T. Baring (Huntingdon), Alderman Gibbons (City) in *T*, 13 October, p. 6e, 20 October, p. 6a, 27 October, p. 5a.
18. Addresses of Sir M. Farquhar (Hertford), G. Cubitt (Surrey W.) in *T*, 3 July, p. 5b, 1 July 1865, p. 5a.
19. Address of Loyd Lindsay (Berks.), *T*, 17 March 1880, p. 10c; emphasis on the amount of legislation passed was, of course, different from the 1830s.
20. For a precise discussion: Northcote at Plymouth, *T*, 28 August 1877, p. 4c. On the primacy of social reform by 1880: see addresses, e.g. Truscott (Gravesend), Smith (Herts.), Boord (Greenwich) *T*, 10 March, p. 10d, 13 March, p. 10c, 10f.
21. The relevant sentence was inserted at the instance of Hardy (to Disraeli, 24 September 1868, B/XX/Ha/42; amended draft [29 September 1868], B/1/D/94). Significance should not be attached to the omission: Hardy did not, and Disraeli was aware of the idea: Hardy, *[The] D[iary of Gathorne Hardy, 1866–92* (Oxford, 1981) ed. N.E. Johnson] 28 September 1868; Disraeli at Edinburgh, 30 October 1867, *The Chancellor of the Exchequer in Scotland. Two Speeches . . . in Edinburgh* (1867), p. 32.
22. Disraeli, Cairns at the Guildhall, *T*, 10 November 1868, p. 3d-e; Disraeli at Aylesbury, *T*, 20 November 1868, p. 5d; Hardy at Rye, *T*, 4 November 1868; etc.
23. For a contrary view, Paul Smith, *Disraelian Conservatism and Social Reform* (1967), p. 121. This is an example of his systematic assumption that social reform could be used to win (working-class) votes in the same way as ordinary political issues.
24. Address to Lancs. Electors, *T*, 10 October 1868, p. 9f.
25. The average increment was *c.*£1½ millions p.a. in a total revenue of *c.*£70 millions: 'Disraelian Conservatism: a financial approach', *EHR*, xcix, 287–8.
26. At Aylesbury, *T*, 20 November 1868, p. 5d-e.
27. He first made the point at Edinburgh, 29 October 1867, *The Chancellor of the Exchequer in Scotland . . .* pp. 25–6; that he would react in this way to the expanded suffrage was evident in 1866, *H* [183], 108–110, 27 April 1866.
28. Disraeli's well-known 1840s references to 'the social WELFARE of

the people' (*Sybil*, IV.xiv), allude rather to political institutions and the church, than to social legislation, cf. Smith *op.cit.*, pp. 16, 18.

29. Smith, *op.cit.*, pp. 158–61; R. Blake, *Disraeli* (1966), pp. 522–4.
30. The Manchester demonstration was a specifically personal tribute to Disraeli by all the (200+) Lancashire Conservative organisations. Its nearest precedent was the Liverpool banquet given for Derby in 1859.
31. Derby *D*, 7 October 1871; the date of the speech was later put back.
32. Beginning with Stanley to Disraeli, 2 February 1869, B/XX/S/846; Disraeli to Stanley [3–4 February 1869], cit. *M & B*, ii.443.
33. Derby to Disraeli, 28 March 1872, no.1, B/XX/S/880, Derby *D*, 30 March 1872. This is not to subscribe to the erroneous notion that Disraeli was hostile to platform speaking; cf. H.J. Hanham, *Elections and Party Management. Politics in the Time of Gladstone and Disraeli* (1959), pp. 206–8.
34. See *Speech . . . at the Free Trade Hall, Manchester, April 3, 1872* (1872), pp. 15,20. Unattributed references in the text are to this version.
35. Derby *D*, 3 April 1872; Disraeli's saying he had 'not come . . . to deliver an essay on the English Constitution' but only to offer 'practical remarks' upon it, suggests his sensitivity on the subject: *loc.cit.*, p. 4.
36. Those who approved were partisans, constitutional reactionaries or both: Cairns to Disraeli, 6 April 1872, B/XX/Ca/89; Hardy *D*, 5 April 1872; Derby *D*, 16 April 72 (reporting Carnarvon). For Disraeli's preparation, Derby *D*, 30 March 1872.
37. *loc.cit.*, p. 19; the proportions of the speech were as follows: 12pp. on the Constitution; 3pp. on the labouring classes; 7pp. critique of current events.
38. cf. Derby at Liverpool, 9 January 1872, pr. *Speeches*, i.170–1. Disraeli had previously written to Derby approving this speech, Derby *D*, 12 January 1872.
39. *T*, 4 April 1872 p. 9a.
40. See e.g. pp. 61–2 above & n.103.
41. Above pp. 75–6.
42. *D*, 5 April 1872; cf. Derby *D*, 6 April 1872, *T*, Leader, 4 April 1872, p. 9a.
43. *Speech . . . at the Banquet of N.U.C.C.A. at the Crystal Palace, June 24, 1872* (1872). To my knowledge there is no Cabinet-rank correspondence relating to this speech, and the only diary reference is belated and dismissive (Derby *D*, 4 July 1872). There are several reasons for this: a speech to the fledgling NUCCA did not carry the same weight as those to independent electors; this was not offset by opportune timing, since it occurred in mid-session, or by content, since, suiting his style to his audience, Disraeli delivered a textbook homily on the Tory creed, a stale précis of the Manchester speech lacking even its academic ornament. But what made it tedious to contemporaries (Leaders in *T*, *Daily News*, 25 June 1872 p. 9a,

5b), made it suitable for the propagation of Disraelian tradition, hence its disproportionate importance in subsequent Conservative histories.

44. James at Taunton, n.d., pr. [G.R.] Askwith, *Lord James of Hereford* (1930), pp. 43–4.
45. For critical reactions in 1873: e.g. Hardy *D*, 20 March; Derby *D*, 9 October; Smith to Ford, 11 October, PS3/173 Hambleden MSS; for a more favourable response: Derby *D*, 27 November, 2 February 1874; Hardy *D*, 25 November 1873, Cairns to Disraeli, 3,6 February 1874, B/XX/Ca/109,110.
46. There were legislative remainders from Gladstone's ministry: notably Endowed Schools, the amendment of army purchase, and, in the 'social' sphere, the settlement of the appellate jurisdiction.
47. Disraeli sympathised with the principle of the Royal Titles Bill, but would not have proposed it *sua sponte* for the 1876 session: *M & B*, ii.796–8 exaggerates this sympathy only slightly.
48. Particularly the County Boards Bills of 1878–79, provoked by C.S. Read's resolution of 9 March 1877, and the Irish University Act of 1879 triggered by the Bills of the O'Conor Don in 1878–79.
49. Address to Bucks. Electors, *T*, 26 January 1874 p. 8a. This was a constant theme after 1870 even before the Eastern Question became critical: Disraeli to Derby, 25 January 1871, 10 March 1874, 25 January 1876 in *M & B*, ii.472, Derby MSS 16/2/1,2 respectively.
50. See n.62 below.
51. R.A. Cross, *A Political History* (priv. pr.1903), p. 25; cf. Smith, *op.cit.*, pp. 199f, who greatly depends on taking passages of this sort at face value.
52. Attention should also be directed to the obvious weaknesses of a source written *c*.25 years after the event. On 1874, above p. 72–3.
53. For Disraeli's 1875 draft, B/XII/H, QS1875(O) n.d. [18–25 January 1875], accepted with only verbal alteration in Cabinet: Derby *D*, 29 January 1875.
54. See *T*, 7 August 1874, p. 8e, 'The Past Session', for a balanced comparison between the leadership styles of Disraeli and Gladstone.
55. Disraeli to Hardy, 10 August 1873, pr. *Gathorne Hardy . . . A Memoir* (1910) ed. A.E. Gathorne Hardy i.329; Hardy to Disraeli, 19 September 1873, B/XX/Ha/67. Neither the January dissolution, nor Cross's subsequent insertion at the Home Office was anticipated.
56. An important revision of the traditional view that the ministries in 1871 and 1875 had different views on union legislation is introduced in *The Gladstone Diaries* (1982), ed. H.C.G. Matthew vii.1xxvi, based on the unpublished work of Mark Curthoys, to whom I too am indebted; cf. *H* [218].78–9, 19 March 1874 (Gladstone), [226].653–4, 6 August 1875 (Hartington).
57. Disraeli, *Speech at . . . Manchester April 3, 1872*, p. 7; cf. n.10 above.
58. e.g. above pp. 71, 76.
59. *A Political History*, p. 44; cf. Carnarvon *D*, 30 September, 15

November 1874, Add. MS 60906. The more plausible criticism which emerges here is Disraeli's fallibility as to detail, a point conceded in the text so as not to cloud the argument; in fact a contemporary stereotype of Disraeli is here mistaken for the man. cf. p. 76 above, n.78 below.

60. Derby *D*, 12 March 1874; cf. Cairns to Disraeli, 7 March 1874, B/XX/Ca/114.
61. *H* [221].635, 24 July 1874 (Childers); cf. c.628 (Gladstone).
62. *T*, 23 July 1874, p. 8b-c. Disraeli's view forward to 1875 is anticipated in his speech at the Merchant Taylors, *T*, 25 June 1874, p. 8b; this may in turn be linked back to a reference to his social reform pledges in his election address, *T*, 26 January 1874, p. 8a.
63. This was contentious and provoked Childers' remarks two days later – n.61. Intermittent guerrilla warfare ensued, via an inflated closing Queen's Speech, Disraeli's November Guildhall address, and Hartington's counter at the 1875 Opening of Parliament, providing an *hors d'oeuvre* to the main action of that session: *H* [221].1418–20, 7 August 1874, Hardy *D*, 4 August 1874; *T*, 10 November 1874 p. 6c; *H* [222].58–60, 5 February 1875.
64. Carnarvon *D*, 26 September 1874, Add. MS 60906.
65. While Disraeli was Leader in the Commons, he customarily began the autumn Cabinet with a strategic survey of the legislative and sessional prospects: Disraeli to the Queen, 10 November 1874, no.2, 6 November 1875, PRO CAB 41/6/15,31; cf. p. 69 and n.53 above.
66. Derby *D*, 11 November 1874.
67. For the planning Cabinets: Derby, Carnarvon and Hardy, *D;* and Disraeli to the Queen in PRO CAB41 for 10–20 November 1874, 12–30 January 1875, *passim*.
68. On the exlusion of political topics, see also Disraeli to Cross, 12 October 1874, Add. MS 51265 ff.10–11; Cross to Disraeli, 21 October 1874, B/XX/Cr/9; Derby *D*, 13 February 1875. Compulsory education, with a strongly partisan dimension to it, was also staved off for this year, Derby *D*, 19 November 1874, 10 February 1875. The Regimental Exchanges Bill, touching the charged subject of army purchase, could not be excluded, but it was omitted from the Speech and hence the debate upon it – a typical stylistic device.
69. Derived from *H* [224].165–7, 6 May 1875 (Disraeli) and analysis of the sessional calendar.
70. Disraeli to Lady Bradford, 5 May 1875, pr. [*The Letters of Disraeli to Lady Bradford and Lady Chesterfield* (1929) edn], Z[etland], i.237.
71. *H* [224].165–8; cf. cc.168–73 (Hartington, Gladstone), Hardy *D*, 7 May; Derby *D*, 6 May 1875 for reactions. In fact the session was extended by a week over the norm for a quiet session – a moderate execution of the threat.
72. To Lady Bradford, 31 May 1875, *Z* i.250; cf. Derby *D*, 6 May 1875.
73. *H* [224].1136–85; the 'par' government majority was 45:50. This complex dispute (the key sessional trial of party strength) was also

about parliamentary reporting, with major consequences for press sources.

74. Hardy *D*, 22 June, 23 July; Derby *D*, 22 July 1875; Cairns and Salisbury spoke briefly at the second meeting. On the collusive nature of Liberal and Tory backbench delay on Agricultural Holdings, e.g. Hardy *D*, 21,22,30 July.
75. On ministerial fears, Derby *D*, 29 May, 26 July 1875; on their success, Derby *D*, 17 July; Disraeli to Lady Chesterfield, 20 July 1875; *Z* i.262–3.
76. He had allies: Cairns to Disraeli, 26 July 1875, B/XX/Ca/155; on Hardy, n.78.
77. Disraeli to Lady Bradford, 27 July 1875, *Z*, i.265–6; Carnarvon *D*, 26,27,30 July 1875, Add. MS 60907.
78. Disraeli and Hardy had opposed dropping Merchant Shipping in favour of Agricultural Holdings, for fear of a sentimental, naval agitation, but yielded to the argument that, in that case, *both* Bills would be lost due to Adderley's incompetent management of the former: Derby, Carnarvon *D*, Add. MS 60907, 21 July 1875; Hardy *D*, 27 July. This is an important, detailed case where Disraeli's social sympathies and political awareness prove to be more soundly based than he is given credit for, cf. Smith, *op.cit.*, pp. 235–6.
79. The Liberal leaders met at 12.15 on Monday, 26 July, prompting the 2 p.m. meeting of the Cabinet which resolved to introduce the temporary Bill: *The Gladstone Diaries*, vol.ix (1986), ed. Matthew, Derby *D*, both 26 July 1875; cf. Disraeli to Lady Bradford, 26,29,30 July; *Z* i.265–71. On the kowtow, *H* [226].150–1,661 (Goschen, Hartington) 28,30 July, 6 August 1875.
80. Cairns to Disraeli, 2 August 1875, B/XX/Ca/156, Disraeli to Lady Chesterfield, 4 August 1875; *Z* i.272. If the speech had not come in August, it would have been made at the November dinner under the same auspices.
81. *T*, 5 August 1875, p. 8b-d, here cc.c-d.
82. *H* [226].652–67; subsequent quotations at cc.661,667.
83. Speech, *loc.cit.*, cc.667–79; reactions: Gladstone in *Diaries*, 6 August 1875; Disraeli to Lady Bradford, 7 August, *Z* i.272; Derby, Hardy *D*, 7 August; *Daily Telegraph*, 7 August, Leader, p. 4e-f. Overall sessional verdicts in similar vein: Hardy *D*, 3 August 1875, Derby *D*, 17 August, 10 September (reporting Disraeli).
84. Smith, *op.cit.*, p. 322; cf. p. 202.
85. Quotation above p. 75.
86. Disraeli to Northcote, 3 August 1875, B/Box 296 (Copy); Derby *D*, 10 September 1875.
87. Derby *D*, 5 November 1875, cf. Disraeli to the Queen, 6 November, PRO CAB 41/6/31; Derby, Disraeli in *H* [227].33,89, 8 February 1876.
88. *H, loc.cit.*, c.92; cf. Disraeli to Derby, 25 January 1876, Derby MSS 16/2/2.
89. The crucial triggers of foreign policy involvement occurred in the autumn of 1875 – Turkish bankruptcy, imminent Egyptian bank-

ruptcy, Northbrook's resignation as Indian Viceroy. For a contrary argument, and different foreign policy chronology, Smith, *op.cit.*, pp. 266–7.

90. In public, Northcote at Plymouth, *T*, 28 August 1877, p. 4c-d; Hardy at Edinburgh, *T*, 13 December 1877, p. 6c; Salisbury, *Speech delivered at Bradford . . . October 11, 1877* (1877), pp. 8–12; cf. Beaconsfield at Victoria Dwellings Association, *T*, 25 June 1877, p. 12b. In private, e.g. Cross to Derby, 23 October 1877, Derby MSS 16/2/5; Northcote to Cross, 17 November 1878, 8 January 1879, Add. MS 51265 ff.147–b, 153b–154.
91. Smith, *op.cit.*, pp. 272–4, 299, etc. One of the most serious weaknesses of his book is its failure to define 'social reform', resulting in the assumption that it was directed solely at the working classes (e.g. p. 4); topics are then selected on this basis, which in turn leads to the interpretative conclusion. The element of circularity is apparent. cf.n.23.
92. e.g. Cairns, Disraeli at the Guildhall, *T*, 10 November 1868, p. 3d,e.
93. *H* [222].40–1, 5 February 1875 (Stanhope).
94. e.g. Disraeli at the Mansion House, *T*, 10 November 1874, p. 6c, 5 August 1875, p. 8c; *H* [225].651–86, 28 June 1875; cf. M. Curthoys, 'The Home Office and Trades Union legislation 1866–76' (unpublished seminar paper).
95. On Salisbury and rivers' pollution, Smith, *op.cit.*, pp. 224–6. Alkali fumes from a works adjacent to the Knowsley estate caused both the 14th and 15th Earls of Derby to take leading roles in promoting, respectively, the pioneering Alkali Regulation Act of 1863 and the Amendment Act of 1874: on the latter, Derby *D*, 22 August 1871, 4 July 1873, *H* [216].1778–9, 4 July 1873.
96. In 1910 the Liberals still commanded 30–40 per cent of the propertied plural votes cast: N. Blewett, *The Peers, the Parties and the People* (1972), p. 363.
97. For Derby's and Disraeli's opposing views of 'the middle classes', Derby *D*, 4 March 1875, 30 June, 2 October 1877. Disraeli's snobbery should not be exaggerated, but it indicates little enthusiasm for a strategy of consolidation of property, whereas paeans to the working classes were loud and frequent, e.g. *T*, 10 November 1874 p. 6c, an important statement. Paul Smith points to the rise of Cross, Smith and Sandon into the Tory Cabinet in 1874–8 as evidence of increased 'middle-class' presence: but since each of these men was an ardent proponent of social legislation, the moral lies in the impossibility of arguing from social class to social policy (*op.cit.*, p. 272).
98. An exception is the Factory Hours Act of 1874, given the link between the Nine Hours agitation and the boom conditions of 1871–73: cf. Derby *D*, 25 December 1874.
99. For the complaints, Yorke, in *H* [246].1608–11, 10 June 1879. The ministry made cuts in grant under the Education Code for 1880, which were never implemented due to the change of government,

but their estimated financial impact was nil: estimates in *PP* (1880), XLV.306 & XLVI.306.

100. On the deficit, Northcote in *H* [251].829, 11 March 1880; for Beaconsfield's role in enforcing this policy, letter to the Queen, 27 July, 5 November 1879, PRO CAB 41/13/5,13, etc.; for its electoral presentation, Addresses of Northcote, Cross, *T*, 11 March 1880 p. 13c, 13 March p. 8c. £1.5 m is a crude counterfactual estimate of the saving on ordinary defence expenditure.

101. On 1875: e.g. Northcote in *H* [222].217–29, 11 February, [223].1045–9, 15 April; on 1879: *H* [249].601–47, 743–800, 1033–4 *passim*, 9,11,15 August; Treasury minute raising interest rates 16 August 1879, PRO T250/4:I f.420.

102. *PP* 1881 XXVIII.686–90, 1884–85 XX.527–30, 6th & 10th Reports of the Public Works Loans Board. J.L. Garvin, *Life of Joseph Chamberlain* (1932), i.273 supposed Chamberlain won; Smith, *op.cit.*, pp. 267–8 reached no decision.

103. Apart from financial policy, note Beaconsfield's preoccupation with the subject in speeches, the Royal Commission on Agricultural Depression of July 1879, and the consideration of a national subscription to relieve distress, led by the Crown and ministers in their capacity as social leaders, see e.g. Beaconsfield to Northcote, 22 December 1878, B/Box 297 (Copy).

104. Queen's Speech in *H* [250].1–6, 5 February 1880. Cross also had long-term plans for Ireland, which look forward to constructive Unionism after 1886: to Beaconsfield, 13 December 1879, B/XX/Cr/85. On the credit accruing from successful handling of London water, Northcote to Cross, 25 October 1879, Add. MS 51265 f.161b, Derby *D*, 3 March 1880, etc.

105. Granville, in *H* [251].989, 15 March 1880; cf. Hartington, in *H* [250].99 (5 February 1880), Gladstone to Cowan, 30 January 1879, pr. *T*, 3 February p. 10c, etc.

106. The proposition is that the tradition of Tory commitment to social reform in 1880 was unbroken (cf. Smith, *op.cit.*, pp. 269, 310 *per contra*); but not that social reform was a significant contested issue: see the formulation n.15 above. Addresses in *T*, e.g. Northcote, T.C. Baring, W.H. Smith, Cross, Sclater Booth, Loyd Lindsay, etc. On the electoral factor in planning for 1880, e.g. Hardy *D*, 5 November 1879, 9 February 1880.

107. On vital home questions he ruled supreme (the Irish Bills of 1880; nn.100, 103); and he intervened in individual items of interest (Cairns to Beaconsfield, 7 January 1880, B/XX/Ca/260, on settled land; education). There is thus no truth in the notion that in old age he succumbed to the fascination of foreign at the expense of domestic policy (cf. Smith, *op.cit.*, pp. 267, 289, etc; Blake, *op.cit.*, pp. 570,719). But subject to political priority, Northcote was the business manager, who undertook detailed planning (e.g. Northcote to Cross 8,10 January 1879, Add. MS 51265 ff.153–6; memo. on '*Cabinet Business*' 12 November 1879, Add. MS 50018 ff. 173–4b).

108. Above pp. 63–4.

109. However, this peculiar evolution was profoundly double-edged, A. Fox, *History and Heritage* (1985), cc.4–6.

# 4 The Movement for the Higher Education of Women: its social and intellectual context in England, *c.* 1840–80[1]

*Gillian Sutherland*

I have . . . no practical connexion with the proposed college, beyond subscribing to it, and occasionally answering questions which Miss Davies has put to me about the curriculum which would be desirable. I feel too deeply the difficult complications that beset every measure likely to affect the position of women and also I feel too imperfect a sympathy with many women who have put themselves forward in connexion with such measures, to give any practical adhesion to them. There is no subject on which I am more inclined to hold my peace and learn, than on the 'Women Question'. . . .

But on one point I have a strong conviction, and I feel bound to act on it, so far as my retired way of life allows of public action. And that is, that women ought to have the same fund of truth placed within their reach as men have; that their lives (i.e. the lives of men and women) ought to be passed together under the hallowing influence of a common faith as to their duty and its basis. And this unity in their faith can only be produced by their having each the same store of fundamental knowledge. It is not likely that any perfect plan for educating women can soon be found, for we are very far from having a perfect plan for educating men. But it will not do to wait for perfection.

(George Eliot to Mrs Nassau Senior, 4 October 1869, concerning the foundation of Girton College, *Letters*, V, p. 58)

There is a temptation to sub-title this essay 'If Emily Davies had not existed, she would have needed to be invented'. For the historiography of women's secondary and higher education in England has been one of the last bastions of heroic fairy-tale, a story of great women battling against all obstacles, Jill the Giant-killer.[2] Whatever the inspirational force of such writing, it does not answer the two basic questions about any new departure: Why them, and why then? We should try to put the founder of Girton, Emily Davies, and the rest back among their peers; to talk about the group photograph rather than the single portrait; to see what kind of collective social and intellectual profile might be constructed of the women – and the men – who wrote and spoke, organised and raised money, and created and served institutions for the secondary and higher education of women in nineteenth-century England. Such a profile might help us towards explanations.

When were the principal institutions founded and what was new about them? In the early nineteenth century, day and boarding schools for girls, whether they resembled Miss Pinkerton's Academy for Young Ladies, graced by Becky Sharp and Amelia Sedley, or the Misses Franklins' school at Coventry attended by the young Marian Evans,[3] were not unknown. But they were short-lived, private ventures dependent upon the energy of their founders and their success in the market. The mid-nineteenth century saw the foundation of institutions intended to be more durable, taking the form either of limited companies or charitable trusts, needing not to make a profit but simply to break even. First, in 1848, came Queen's College, in Harley Street, London, a secondary school, followed in 1849 by Bedford College, also in London, which eventually divided into a school and a university college. In 1850 another school was opened in Camden, which became the North London Collegiate School and in 1854 a 'Ladies College', another school, was opened in Cheltenham. In 1865 the Cambridge Local Examinations Syndicate was persuaded to admit girls to the secondary school examinations originally devised to raise the standards in boys' schools.

The eleven years 1869–80 saw activity more intense than at any other time in the century. Successive commissions, charged under the Endowed Schools Act 1869 with the remodelling of educational endowments, made schemes which led to the establishment of 61 schools for girls. In 1872 a Girls' Public Day School Company was formed, which by 1880 had opened eleven schools in London and eleven elsewhere – at Bath, Brighton, Gateshead, Ipswich, Liverpool, Norwich, Nottingham, Oxford, Sheffield, Weymouth and York.[4] In 1869 a women's university college was established at Hitchin, moving to Girton on the outskirts of Cambridge in 1871. Likewise in 1871, a second residential establishment for women was created in Cambridge, moving in 1875 to the site at Newnham which it has occupied ever since. In February 1869 the London Ladies' Educational Association, based at University College, had begun a series of classes designed 'to place within the reach of ladies (not under 17) a course of higher instruction similar to that offered to the students of the College': and when in 1878 the University of London opened all its degrees except medicine to women, 288 women promptly registered as full students at UCL.[5] Then in 1879 two women's colleges, Somerville and Lady Margaret Hall, were founded at Oxford. In the 1880s more schools were to follow and three more colleges: St Hugh's in Oxford and Westfield and Royal Holloway in London. In the 1890s the Charity Commissioners commented that the period had proved as important for the education of girls as the Reformation had been for boys.[6] There was something approaching a system where, hitherto, there had been nothing.

Who were the system builders: founders and benefactors, teachers and lecturers, pupils and students? There is much work that could be done on this, although the sources are inevitably uneven in their distribution. What follows is in the nature of a pilot, an attempt to show how a systematic analysis of the finances and registers of the first four women's colleges at Oxford and Cambridge in their earliest years can help fill out the picture presented by existing secondary sources.[7]

Certain outlines are already clear, notably those of class. Education then was stratified not in terms of age but of class. The categories familiar to twentieth-century England – 'primary', 'secondary', 'tertiary' – relate to age groups and most children proceed from the first to the second, if not to the third. The categories familiar to the nineteenth century were 'elementary', 'secondary' and 'higher'; and despite the inclusion of 'secondary' in both groups – and, indeed, the survival of 'elementary' and 'higher' as terms well into the twentieth century – the two groups are not interchangeable. Elementary education was that provided for the labouring poor. Elementary schools could and did include children as old as fourteen. The teaching provided in Mechanics' Institutes and night schools for adult members of the working classes was also deemed elementary and could earn grants under the government's Elementary Education Code until 1893.[8] Secondary schools were those provided for the middle classes and could and did take children of all ages from 7 to 20. From such schools a handful of children might go on to the higher education of the universities.[9]

The great divide was thus between elementary and secondary schools; and the controversies and campaigns about education for girls all related to secondary and higher education. From the beginning of the century it had been taken for granted that elementary education included girls as well as boys. They sat side by side in the same buildings. The only acknowledgement of difference was the inclusion of needlework in the girls' timetable and the expectation that because of the time taken by this, they were likely to do less well than the boys in the annual arithmetic examination.[10]

The debate about women's education was, therefore, a debate about what was appropriate for 'ladies', the women of the middle and upper classes. Those pioneer institutions were supported by and housed their daughters. We can, indeed, go further and claim that predominantly women's education was an affair of the middle rather than the upper classes. It worked very hard to become respectable,[11] but smart it never was. Queen's College, Harley Street boasted royal patronage; but its initial objective was to provide training for governesses, those unfortunates driven to seek employment by fathers' or husbands' economic collapse.[12] Queen Victoria's sixth child, Princess Louise, Marchioness of Lorne, became President of the 'National Union for the Education of Girls of All Classes above the Elementary' (as the parent body of the Girls' Public Day School Company was called) and subsequently patron of the Company.[13] But no royal daughter or grand-daughter attended any of their schools.

Both Cambridge colleges had aristocratic links, but of an idiosyncratic kind. Among Girton's major benefactors – and a key figure in the National Union – was the widowed Lady Stanley of Alderley, whose daughters included Kate, Lady Amberley, the mother of Bertrand Russell and Rosalind, later Countess of Carlisle, the fanatical temperance campaigner.[14] Girton, Newnham and Lady Margaret Hall benefited also from the Lyttelton connection, the single most crucial network of associations for the education of women in the whole period. The fourth Lord Lyttelton was at Eton and Christ Church with W. E. Gladstone and in a double ceremony they married respectively Mary and Catherine, the daughters of Sir Stephen Glynne, in 1840. The Gladstones had eight children, the Lytteltons twelve; and when Mary Lyttelton died prematurely in 1857, Catherine Gladstone became surrogate parent, a role extended after George Lyttelton took his own life in 1876. Their family circle drew in also the Balfours, nephews and nieces of the third Marquess of Salisbury, and the High Anglican Talbots.[15]

Lyttelton had helped bring girls' schools within the orbit of the Royal Commission of Inquiry into Endowed Schools – the Taunton Commission – and as a Commissioner under the resulting Endowed Schools Act of 1869, worked devotedly to secure money for girls. He contributed both advice and money in the early days of Girton.[16] To Newnham in 1877 came his niece, Helen Gladstone. Her family had consented in part because Arthur Balfour's sister Eleanor, now married to Henry Sidgwick, the philosopher and founder-organiser of the Cambridge Lectures for Women, was Treasurer of the college.[17] Meanwhile in Oxford in 1878 the first effective steps towards what became Lady Margaret Hall were taken by Edward Talbot, Warden of Keble College, and his wife Lavinia, née Lyttelton. The High Anglican activism here exemplified proved of great importance in the next two decades, both in shaping LMH and in founding the third college, St Hugh's.[18]

The Balfours and Henry Sidgwick were among Newnham's greatest benefactors materially and spiritually in the early years.[19] They were much the most affluent members of this network. The others gave infinitely of their time and counsel but could give little money. George Lyttelton, for example, gave only ten guineas to Girton; and the 'Glynnese Glossary', the key to the language of the family circle, illustrated the term 'false flash' as follows: 'Lady Glynne applied it to her daughter's marriage with Lord Lyttelton, alluding to the combination in that nobleman's circumstances of respectable rank with comparative poverty, "quite a false flash".'[20] Overall, none of the aristocratic benefactors of these first four Oxbridge women's colleges was of the sort characterised by David Cannadine as 'super-powers', or close, indeed, to the second rank.[21]

Super-powers were super-powers often because they diversified from a landed base; and the absence of aristocratic connections need not mean an absence of wealth.[22] But all four colleges were financially very modest enterprises and those benefactors they did attract, did not come from the wealthiest sectors of the industrial and commercial classes. The extreme example of a modest foundation was Lady Margaret Hall, because Miss Wordsworth, the first Principal, and its Council wished it to retain the character of a private household. The cost of purchasing and refitting the house in Norham Gardens where they began, seems to have come out of the Council's own pockets; and when in 1886 Miss Wordsworth received a windfall of £600, she used it not for the benefit of her own establishment, but for founding another – St Hugh's.[23]

Similarly, the Somerville Council found the £600 needed to purchase the lease of Walton Hall out of their own pockets. But once St John's College offered the freehold at market price, they began to see the uses of a public appeal and by 1881 were setting a target of £10,000.[24] The founders of Newnham behaved in the same way. In 1871 they began in a private house, but by 1875 they were wanting their own site and building. Just over £5000 was raised for the building of South (now Old) Hall, a further £9000 in 1880 for North (subsequently Sidgwick) Hall; and further unspecified sums for a laboratory and gymnasium in 1877–8. In addition, over £3000 was donated for scholarships, fellowships and prizes in the same period.[25]

Girton, chronologically the first, was also, thanks to Emily Davies, the most ambitious in fund-raising. By the summer of 1874 almost £12,500 were subscribed, aside from £3250 for presentations and scholarships. The college was then breaking even in terms of meeting running expenses from fee income;

but a debt of £5000 was outstanding from the purchase of the site and building work.[26] These were significant sums for the worried pioneers, although paltry by comparison with the resources of most of the established men's colleges, even in the depths of agricultural depression; small, too, by comparison with the money raised for Nathaniel Woodward's middle-class Anglican boarding schools.[27] Martha Vicinus scolds 'an almost excessive amateurism about finances and administration' in the early women's colleges,[28] but chronic poverty precluded more than hand-to-mouth operations.

W. D. Rubinstein has divided the wealthy Victorian middle classes into metropolitan-banking-commercial and provincial-industrial sets. It is notable that the women's colleges did not benefit greatly from the former, more affluent group. Of the forty largest personal fortunes in the period 1809–1914, only three of the family names turn up on a subscription list, that of Girton. Up to 1880, members of the Goldsmid family gave £1075, Crawshays £200 and Baron and Baroness Lionel de Rothschild £110.[29]

In so far as groups are identifiable among the early benefactors, there are the Lancashire-Liverpool manufacturing and commercial group, the liberal intelligentsia and, in the case of Somerville, the party-political connections of J. G. Shaw-Lefevre, Postmaster General in Gladstone's 1880–85 ministry and brother of the first Principal.[30] Foremost in the Lancashire-Liverpool group was Mary Ewart, the unmarried daughter of William Ewart, the advanced Liberal MP for Dumfries Burghs, and grand-daughter of John Gladstone's friend and rival in the Liverpool shipping world. She was Newnham's second largest benefactor, giving £4700 during her lifetime, inaugurating the Teachers' Education Loan Fund and bequeathing £20,000 for scholarships on her death. She gave on a similarly generous scale to the Camden and North London Collegiate Schools, to Bedford College and bequeathed a further £10,000 to Somerville.[31]

Miss Ewart, a single benefactor – and a woman – with this kind of money, was really a special case.[32] More typical were the family clusters. Among the most beneficent was another Liverpool commercial family, the Aikins, who gave just over £1000 to Newnham in 1871–80;[33] and a major Unitarian group, the Winkworths, Thomassons, Penningtons and Shaens, much of whose money came from textile manufacture around Bolton. They gave £1275 to Newnham and £300 to Girton in the 1870s, and £900 to Somerville's Building Fund between 1882 and 1886. William Shaen was solicitor to the Girls' Public Day School Co., a member of Bedford College Council and draughtsman of Somerville's Articles of Association.[34] This Unitarian contribution is comparable in importance to the Anglican impetus mentioned above and had manifested itself earlier. Unitarians were prominent in the governance and support of Bedford College from Elizabeth Jesser Reid, the founder, onwards.[35]

The Liverpool-Lancashire connection was particularly in evidence among Newnham's early benefactors, who included also the Booth and Rathbone families. Almost certainly the entrepreneur, as it were, was Anne Jemima Clough. The daughter of a Liverpool cotton merchant, she founded in 1867 the North of England Society for Promoting the Higher Education of Women. Her brother, the poet and civil servant Arthur Hugh Clough, married Florence Nightingale's cousin Blanche Smith and, like Sidney Herbert, was absorbed, exhausted and ultimately died in Miss Nightingale's service. It was at her sister-in-law's house in London that Miss Clough made the acquaintance of Henry Sidgwick, who in 1871 persuaded her to take charge of the house for women students which became Newnham.[36]

Miss Clough was thus a pivot between the provincial supporters and the liberal intelligentsia, those 'lights of liberalism' whom Matthew Arnold had exhorted to 'work inwardly upon the predominant force in our politics – the great middle class – and to cure its spirit'. As Christopher Harvie has shown, it was in this period, *c.* 1860–86, that they were at their most self-conscious and distinct, but also at their most outward-looking.[37] They were there *en masse* among the earliest supporters of the women's colleges. The list was headed in Cambridge by Henry Sidgwick, Henry Fawcett and Alfred Marshall, followed by Benjamin Hall Kennedy, W. H. Bateson and John Neville Keynes; in Oxford by T. H. Green, Arthur Sidgwick, Arnold Toynbee and A. V. Dicey.[38] Like George Lyttelton, they could give more advice, support and labour than cash. But the teaching they provided, the advocacy within the University as a whole and the unpaid labour of their wives were all indispensable.

The wives merit separate mention. The efflorescence of English liberalism has been treated too much as a male affair. Yet Eleanor Sidgwick, Millicent Garrett Fawcett, Mary Paley Marshall, Charlotte Green (née Addington Symonds), Charlotte Toynbee (née Atwood) and Elinor Dicey (née Bonham Carter) contributed both ability and connections.[39] Anne Jemima Clough belongs here, as does Emily Davies. Through her brother Llewelyn Davies, Rector of Christ Church, Marylebone, Emily Davies met F. D. Maurice and approved of his work for women's education. She supported Elizabeth Garrett through her battles to secure a medical qualification in the 1860s; and in 1858 she formed a firm friendship with Barbara Bodichon. Barbara in turn introduced Emily to George Eliot; and in due course the Girton subscription list included £50 'from the author of *Romola*'. George Eliot and George Henry Lewes visited both Girton and Newnham; and after George Eliot's death, J. W. Cross gave both advice and money to Newnham.[40]

Barbara Bodichon, even more than George Eliot, represents the exotic fringe of these circles. Her father never married her mother, and for much of her childhood she and her brothers and sisters were known as 'the taboo'd family'. Like George Eliot, she was involved at one point with John Chapman the publisher; then in 1857 she married a French doctor practising in Algiers, with whom she subsequently spent six months of each year, spending the remainder in London. But her father was Benjamin Leigh Smith, the wealthy Unitarian Radical MP for Norwich, linking her thus with the cousinage of Cloughs, Nightingales and Bonham Carters. She led the Girton subscription list in 1869 with £1000, gave a further £5000 in 1884, and on her death in 1891 bequeathed £10,000 to Girton and £1000 to Bedford College.[41]

Beyond these groups and the party political contacts of J. G. Shaw-Lefevre, who, he told his sister, were good for one approach but no more,[42] there was a host of other subscribers, contributing sums occasionally in the hundreds, more often in the tens. They include Joseph Chamberlain, Samuel Courtauld III, the Russell Gurneys, John Stuart Mill and Helen Taylor. It is appropriate to find the author of *The Subjection of Women* and his stepdaughter here. But in general these subscribers appear as a mass of individuals. There may be more connections to find: it is tempting, for example, to link Samuel Courtauld III, the textile magnate and prominent Unitarian, with the Winkworth family cluster. Chamberlain, too, was brought up a Unitarian. But more is needed to establish links beyond coincidence.[43]

The picture, thus, is of enterprises attracting the support of the 'middling' middle class, affluent and comfortable, with continuing provincial links, rather than rich, smart and metropolitan. That hypersensitive social observer, and considerable snob, A. C. Benson, Henry Sidgwick's nephew and son of the Archbishop of Canterbury, observed mournfully, 'We have got a middle-class taint about us. We are none of us aristocrats in any way.' But he admitted, 'It is an interesting record intellectually';[44] and the founders and benefactors of the four colleges lacked neither cultivation nor status.

The picture can be filled out by analysing the social backgrounds of the first students at the four colleges. This cannot be definitive. The biographical registers, although full by comparison with those of many men's colleges, are not complete.[45] Impressions can be formed, however, and supplemented with evidence on fee levels, scholarships and subsequent employment.

The data about father's occupation can most tidily be presented in tabular form (see Table 4.1). The prominence of the professional middle classes – clergy, lawyers, doctors and teachers – is striking: Emily Davies' own family background – daughter of an Evangelical clergyman who was also a schoolmaster, sister of a clergyman – begins to look typical. But there are too many unknowns to do more than form an impression. In the case of Newnham in particular, it could be argued that material about only one-sixth of the students is no basis on which to form even an impression. For all we know, the fathers of the remainder may have been landed gentry, with no occupation to speak of.

On the other hand, the absence of occupational description could have been the consequence of obscurity; for Newnham was further down-market than Girton. Oral tradition, no

*Table 4.1: Social Background of Oxbridge Women Students, 1869–80*

| College | Total | Father's occupation /source income unknown | Anglican, clergy | Noncon. clergy | Father's occupation/source of income<br>Academics /school-masters | Lawyers | Doctors | Com-merce | Indus-try | Land | Other | Total known |
|---|---|---|---|---|---|---|---|---|---|---|---|---|
| | (1) | (2) | (3) | (4) | (5) | (6) | (7) | (8) | (9) | (10) | (11) | (12)* |
| Girton 1869–80 | 113 | 64 | 11 | 4 | 7 | 5 | 5 | 7 | 5 | 6 | 6(a) | 49 |
| Newnham 1871–80 | 258 | 216 | 11 | 1 | 6 | 2 | 3 | 12 | 5 | 0 | 5(b) | 42 |
| Somerville 1879–80 | 20 | 5 | 5 | 0 | 2 | 1 | 0 | 3 | 1 | 0 | 3(c) | 15 |
| LMH 1879–80 | 15 | 9 | 5 | 0 | 1 | 0 | 0 | 0 | 0 | 1 | 0 | 6 |
| Total | 406 | 294 | 32 | 5 | 16 | 8 | 8 | 22 | 11 | 7 | 14 | 112 |

* the sum of cols.(3)-(11) may sometimes total more than col. (12) as occasionally more than one occupation is recorded – e.g. a number of the Anglican clergymen are also academics or schoolmasters.

(a) This total is comprised of 2 actuaries, 1 publisher, 1 sculptor and 2 military men.

(b) This total is comprised of 1 publisher, 1 dispensing chemist, 1 clerk to a Board of Guardians and Mr Gladstone.

(c) This total is comprised of 1 land agent, 1 Inland Revenue chief clerk and 1 local government auditor.

*Sources:* the *Registers* of Girton, Newnham, Somerville and Lady Margaret Hall, supplemented in the case of Somerville by additional material from their archives most generously provided by Mrs Janet Howarth.

less to be neglected in a Cambridge college than in an African village, has it that Newnham was for governesses while Girton was for ladies. Girton students were provided with both bedrooms and sitting-rooms, while Newnham students had only single bed-sitting rooms. Newnham, moreover, did not insist upon all students taking the equivalent of a Tripos examination, entailing three years' work. Hence the far higher turnover: 95 of the 258 students in 1871–80 came for three terms or less. The Newnham fees were also lower than those at Girton. In 1875 the maintenance charges were £20 a term, totalling £60 a year, with a maximum additional twelve guineas a year for tuition. Those intending to become teachers, however, were charged £45 p.a. for maintenance and a maximum six guineas p.a. for tuition. At Girton the all-inclusive charge was £35 per term or £105 p.a. At Oxford similar differences prevailed. The Lady Margaret Hall fees were £75 p.a., while Somerville fixed theirs at £60 p.a.[46]

These were still considerable sums for a family on £300 a year, especially one with sons to educate as well; and this was the argument used by Elizabeth Wordsworth for founding St Hugh's in 1886 with fees of £45 a year.[47] But a proportion of the earliest students were women in their twenties, a few even in their thirties, who may have had some savings on which to draw, or who could call on family resources at last freed from the burden of brothers' education, and whose education might finally enable *them* to cease being a charge upon the family income. Janet Howarth has argued that

> for many girls from genteel or middle-class families college education was not a means of moving up in the social scale but an insurance against downward mobility. It opened the way to professional or quasi-professional employment for single women whose fathers could not make adequate long-term provision for their support.

She calculates that 'about one in five of the women at Oxford before 1914 were orphans or the daughters of widows when they first came into residence.'[48] Likewise, among the first 28 students who came into residence at Royal Holloway College in October 1887, five were either the daughters or wards of widows and a sixth, aged 24, paid for herself.[49] The early Cambridge data are not full enough to permit a systematic search for orphans or the daughters of widows;

but the information about age on entry to college, in Table 4.2, is suggestive.

*Table 4.2. Age on entry to college of Oxbridge women students 1869–80, where known*

| College | 15–20 yrs | 21–25 yrs | 26–30 yrs | 31+ yrs | Total | Total number students |
|---|---|---|---|---|---|---|
| Girton 1869–80 | 38 | 11 | 6 | 2 | 57 | 113 |
| Newnham 1871–80 | 54 | 28 | 17 | 7 | 106 | 258 |
| Somerville 1879–80 | 9 | 2 | 1 | 1 | 13 | 20 |
| Total | 101 | 41 | 24 | 10 | 176 | 391 |

*Sources:* Newnham, Girton and Somerville *Registers*. The early LMH *Register* does not give dates of birth.

The importance attached by the institutions to scholarships and loan funds heightens the impression. Mary Ewart had established a Teachers' Education Loan Fund, 'by the help of which, many women too poor to provide for their own education were enabled to qualify themselves for teaching', and in 1894 this was amalgamated with the Newnham College Loan Fund. This Fund, which lent without charging interest and also made small grants, had been started in 1875 by Mrs Adams, Mrs Aikin, Miss Alice Bonham-Carter, Thomas Paley and Henry Sidgwick and was administered by Mrs Aikin's daughter, Mrs Bateson. Newnham scholarships were inaugurated in 1871 with a gift of £40 a year for two years from John Stuart Mill and Helen Taylor; and between then and 1880 a further £2065 was given for scholarships. Comparable sums were given to Girton;[50] and scholarships were particularly mentioned in the Somerville fund-raising prospectus of 1881.

Finally, the majority of these students went into paid employment at some point after college (see Table 4.3).

Mrs Howarth's systematic study of the Oxford women students to 1914 will show to what extent this, like other patterns, was an enduring one. But what evidence there is already available points to its continuance. In founding a

*Table 4.3. Oxbridge women students known to have entered paid employment at some point after college, 1869–80*

| College | Total nos. of students | Total known to have been employed | Teachers, at all levels from university to private governesses |
|---|---|---|---|
| Girton | | | |
| 1869–80 | 113 | 71 | 63 |
| Newnham | | | |
| 1871–80 | 258 | 171 | 167 |
| Somerville | | | |
| 1879–80 | 20 | 17 | 15 |
| LMH | | | |
| 1879–80 | 15 | 8 | 3 |
| Total | 406 | 267 | 248 |

*Sources:* Girton, Newnham, Somerville and LMH *Registers.*

college 'to afford the best education suitable for women of the middle and upper classes' Thomas Holloway had declared it his 'express and earnest desire . . . that the College shall neither be considered nor conducted as a mere training college for teachers and governesses.' Perhaps, as the biographer of Ivy Compton-Burnett suggests, he was reacting against what he had observed of the early Oxbridge women. Whatever the founder's intentions, the majority of Ivy Compton-Burnett's peers at Royal Holloway 1902–6 expected to work, probably in teaching.[51] The pattern seems similar at Miss Wordsworth's cut-price institution, St Hugh's, and at Westfield.[52]

For some of these women employment may have been a choice rather than a necessity. Even so, the fragments of information about jobs, age, loans and scholarships, family background and fathers' occupations combine to emphasise the middle-class nature of the demand for higher education for women. The prominence of the professional middle classes among students' fathers is unsurprising. These families naturally appreciated the uses of formal education; and many professional fathers may have resembled Colonel Campbell in Jane Austen's *Emma:* 'though his income, by pay and appointments, was handsome, his fortune was moderate.' The best the Campbells could do for their ward, Jane Fairfax, was to give her a superior education, to equip her, if she failed to marry money, to become a superior governess. It looks as though some professional families in the 1870s, aware by now of the 'surplus women' problem, were beginning to search more systematically for sources of income other than marriage for their daughters.

It remains to be seen to what extent this sense of their social location can function also as an explanation of the activities of the early supporters of women's education. Probably some parents and their daughters were beginning to see education as a form of investment. But economic self-interest was clearly not a factor for all involved – for example, the more substantial benefactors – and it would not on its own have sustained the pioneers against the difficulties they encountered. Simple self-interest, indeed, might dictate retreat, whether back to the bosom of the family, into marriage or even governessing; and parents could always be ostrich-like about the fate of daughters. Self-interest can be but one strand in a complex tangle.

Richard Evans has proposed an increased professionalisation of occupations such as teaching, nursing, business and law, a process which extruded women, who then fought back.[53] Certainly we need to ask about the relationship between women's education and the rise of the professions; but it may be that in seizing the right bundle, Evans has started to unravel it at the wrong point. Of the four occupations that he offers as examples of ones from which women were extruded, there is no evidence that women occupied a significant place in either law or business at the beginning of the nineteenth century – aside from the thorny question of *when* business in England became professionalised. The other two occupations he names are nursing and teaching. The interesting questions about professionalisation in nursing relate to its process and timing in an exclusively female occupation. Teaching is different again: in the nineteenth century the elementary/secondary divide was as powerful among teachers as among pupils. Elementary teachers were recruited from the working classes of both sexes and the proportion of women grew steadily throughout the century. In secondary teaching there was no question of the extrusion of women. Schools were single-sex: men taught boys and women taught girls.[54]

Professionalisation was in no sense gender-specific in nineteenth-century England. It was a process to be observed in a variety of occupations, old and new. It did indeed entail either the raising or the creation of formal educational standards for entry. And it is on aspects of the process as such, rather than on particular occupations, that we should focus in attempting to answer the original questions, 'Why them, and why then?' The century 1780–1880 saw a transformation of attitudes to educational qualifications and to schooling *as a whole*. It was only then that education became a formal institutionalised process, its stages marked by competitions and prizes. The enthusiasts for women's education find places naturally, both in terms of interests and ideals, in this larger development.

Among the first signals of the transformation were the Trinity College, Cambridge Fellowship competition in 1786 and the Oxford Examination Statute of 1800. From the end of the 1830s came the great waves of proprietary boys' boarding schools. Only two were founded in each of the decades 1800–9, 1810–19, 1820–29 and 1830–39. But thirteen were founded in 1840–49, five more in 1850–59 and another thirteen in 1860–69. In 1845 Stanley's *Life of Arnold* presented to the world the ideal-type of a public school headmaster; and between 1859 and 1869 the Clarendon and Taunton Commissions reviewed the whole field of secondary education and provided a blue-print for its articulation into a system.[55]

Between 1850 and 1852 Oxford and Cambridge were at last investigated by Royal Commissions and the Acts of 1854 (Oxford) and 1856 (Cambridge) began the process of translating into institutional form that which recent writers on Oxford have discreetly called 'reform' and which, in Cambridge, Professor Rothblatt has labelled 'the revolution of the dons'.[56] By 1871 most religious tests had gone. In 1872 appeared the first married Fellows of colleges. The central organs of university government were strengthened, new courses devised, the status of both scholarship and teaching enhanced and the latter activity drawn back into the hands of the colleges. Henry Sidgwick told Oscar Browning in 1866: 'We ought to be more, not less, strictly educational than we are. If ever I become a power in my College a considerable increase in work (at least of teachers) will take place.'[57] This belief became increasingly widely shared.

University teachers now worked harder but had gained a career structure. The transition 'from clergyman to don' formed an important part of these institutional changes; and by the end of the 1870s the professionalisation of university teaching was well advanced. Professor Engel notes that this was essentially a male phenomenon; it has taken considerably longer for female university teachers to establish themselves in a professional framework.[58] Even so, amongst the men experiencing and benefiting from this process were some who began to address the question of formal education for their wives and daughters.

The movement for the higher education of women phased into this wider process and its central preoccupations were the preoccupations of the activists as a whole. External examinations were weapons to improve standards in girls' schools as well as in boys'.[59] Concern for religious freedom made Newnham the first non-denominational college – it has never had a chapel – and brought about the separation among the Oxford enthusiasts between non-denominational Somerville and Lady Margaret Hall, with its explicit Anglican connection.[60]

From the start, for reasons of social propriety, the women's colleges retained tight control of teaching; and paradoxically, because poverty and vulnerability drove them to rely heavily upon the free or underpaid services of so many distinguished and senior male academics, their students may have received better teaching than some in men's colleges. Those colleges begun as women's colleges still benefit from the fact that their long exclusion from central university facilities led them to allot a proportionately larger share of their resources to their libraries than did some men's colleges.

Debates about curricula and courses in the Cambridge women's colleges also belong within this framework. Newnham's initial policy of allowing students to pursue a variety of courses at a variety of levels and at a variety of paces is sometimes presented as a decision, in part, out of weakness. In the earliest days it was difficult for girls to gain access to the systematic teaching at the secondary level needed as a foundation for a full university course. Certainly some of the early students could not have coped with its demands. The Newnham policy can also be construed as an episode in the perennial debate among feminists as to whether there is such a state as 'equal but different'. Equality for Emily Davies and Girton meant identity; and all Girton students had to pursue courses of study and take examinations identical to those for men.[61] The entry in the *Girton Register* for Agnes Amy Bulley reads: 'The College, Hitchin and Girton L. 1871–3; Newnham 1873–4; Moral Sciences Tripos Class I, 1874 from Newnham, whither she had migrated because Miss Emily Davies would not consent to her postponing her Tripos for a 4th year.'

But there is a third construction to be placed on Newnham's early policy which need not exclude these other two. That is, the flexibility favoured in Newnham was as much a commitment to the cause of educational reform as to the cause of higher education for women. In August 1870 the Regius Professor of History, J. R. Seeley, had withdrawn his teaching support from Girton so long as they insisted upon 'stationary' education: 'I cannot take any pleasure in attending to the details of a College where the old and to me obsolete routine goes on. I do not cease to wish it success. . . . I hope for times when you may feel able to be bolder and more progressive.'[62] Henry Sidgwick did not go that far. He continued to teach Girton students despite his disagreements with Miss Davies. But he was unconvinced of the educational uses of some of the Cambridge examination requirements, especially compulsory Greek, to *any* students, male or female, and was unable to see why they should be inflicted on the women. Newnham provided an admirable opportunity to devise alternative, more satisfactory schemes – which eventually were to become the rule in the University at large, rather than the exception.[63]

The campaign for the higher education of women thus takes its place alongside the campaign for university reform and the broader issues of social and political change which preoccupied the 'lights of liberalism'. To see it simply – even primarily – as a unique, *sui generis* feminist campaign is to take too narrow a view, to separate it from some of its roots and to mishear or to ignore some of its most characteristic tones. George Eliot supported Emily Davies in the foundation of Girton; but on the 'Women Question' she was inclined to hold her peace. In that letter of 1869, quoted as epigraph to this essay, she described one of the objectives of education for both women and men as 'a common faith as to their duty and its basis'. Such language was common currency in the circles we have been exploring.

Many of the future 'lights of liberalism' came together in the Oxford Essay Society in the 1850s and Christopher Harvie chose that Society's statement of objectives as one of the earliest, yet most characteristic utterances of these self-conscious and energetic progressives:

> As members of a Society, we are anxious to put on record the reasons which have induced us to unite together, the obligations to which we have pledged ourselves, and our general principles of action. Our object is to impress ourselves more effectually with a sense of the duties entailed upon the educated classes by the present state of society in this country and by every means in our power to prepare ourselves for combined action, wherever it may seem likely to have any useful result. We feel that in a transitional period like the present, intermediate between an old order and a new the formation of such a society may be of the greatest use to ourselves and to those whom we may induce to join us, if it led us to increased thought on the questions of the day, a keener sense of our own duties and larger and more active sympathies with the interests which surround us. Especially we believe in the possibility of in this turning to good account much of that irresolute energy, and sincere though indefinite desire to do good, which no one connected with the Universities can fail to recognise as characteristic of many of our contemporaries there.[64]

Beside this we may juxtapose a private statement very different in tone and made in circumstances not far short of tragedy, yet articulating essentially the same objectives. In November 1885 Winnie Seebohm, whose asthma had limited her activities at Newnham and was now forcing her home, wrote in her private memorandum book:

> In case I should ever be tempted to regret my desire to come to Newnham and doubt my motives, I want to write them down as I honestly conceive them.
>
> My first object was to learn history well and thoroughly, that I might be able (should I prove capable later) to write it for the working classes.
>
> Secondly, I thought after a year or two here I should be better able to judge whether I was likely to be capable of any work of this sort.

> Thirdly, I hoped to learn here self-reliance, judgment and self-confidence.
>
> I am quite sure that I never cared a bit about the examinations, and I do not think I ever counted much upon the enjoyments here – certainly not when I actually came. I looked upon the life here as the best preparation within my reach for the work which I hoped someday to spend my life over. And I thought it was perhaps as well that the enjoyment should be put out of my reach, for fear I might forget the definite purposes for which I came.[65]

Winnie Seebohm was grieving for what she could not now achieve and shortly after returning home she died. The Young Turks of the Essay Society were preparing to sally forth to change the world. Both, however, were preoccupied with their duty: both saw the privileges of their education as entailing responsibility.

* * *

It may be objected that the foregoing paragraphs bring us no nearer *real* explanation of either timing or personnel. To suggest that the movement for women's education was part of a wholesale shift in the society towards formal, institutionalised schooling, a movement spearheaded by the bourgeoisie and owing many of its peculiarities of form and detail to the activities of a self-consciously liberal intelligentsia, is at one level simply to offer an extended description. But it does decisively affect the kinds of explanations subsequently to be sought. We become less concerned with women reacting to changes imposed on them and more concerned with the response of a whole society to industrialisation and resultant changes in the patterns of socialisation. At this level, description is probably at present the nearest we can get to explanation. But the exercise protects us from seeing the enthusiasts for women's education in nineteenth-century England as lone figures out of time, battling heroically against the forces of reaction, or huddled in a ghetto, acted upon, sinned against, but seldom active participants in the wider life of a thrusting and energetic middle-class society.

# *Notes*

1. A version of this essay was first delivered to the George Eliot Centennial Conference at Rutgers University in November 1980. Successive versions have been given at seminars in Oxford, Cambridge and London and read and criticised by many friends and colleagues. I must also acknowledge the especial help of the historians, archivists and library staff of the first four Oxford and Cambridge women's colleges. I hope all those whose comments have helped improve the essay will forgive me for not listing them by name.
2. E.g. the works of Josephine Kamm, *Hope Deferred: Girls' Education in English History* (London, 1965), *How Different From Us: a Biography of Miss Buss and Miss Beale* (London, 1959), *Rapiers and Battleaxes: the Women's Movement and its aftermath* (London, 1966), *Indicative Past: A Hundred Years of the Girls' Public Day School Trust* (London, 1971); and Margaret Bryant, *The Unexpected Revolution: a study in the history of the education of women and girls in the nineteenth century* (London, 1980), esp. pp. 60–1.
3. W. M. Thackeray, *Vanity Fair* (first published 1847–8), ch.1; Gordon S. Haight, *George Eliot. A Biography* (Oxford, 1968), ch.1.
4. Sheila Fletcher, *Feminists and Bureaucrats. A study in the development of girls' education in the nineteenth century* (Cambridge, 1980), Appendix 3; Kamm, *Indicative Past*, Appendix.
5. N. B. Harte, *The Admission of Women to University College, London. A Centenary Lecture* (London, University College, 1979), pp. 11,21.
6. *Report of the Royal Commission on Secondary Education* (Bryce), P.P.(1895) xliii, p. 76.
7. Such an analysis is now being developed further for the Oxford women by Janet Howarth and Mark Curthoys, as part of work on the History of the University of Oxford: see their article, 'The political economy of women's higher education in late nineteenth- and early twentieth-century Britain', forthcoming in *Historical Research* in 1987. I am indebted to them for allowing me to read this in draft and to Janet Howarth for fruitful exchanges over several years.
8. *Special Reports on Educational Subjects in England, Wales, Ireland and Scotland*, vol. I, P.P.(1897), xxv, pp. 54–5.
9. For fuller discussion, see Gillian Sutherland, 'Secondary Education: The Education of the Middle Classes', in *Government and Society in Nineteenth century Britain: Commentaries on British Parliamentary Papers: Education*, ed. Gillian Sutherland (Dublin, 1977), pp. 137–66.
10. See the comments scattered throughout the reports of the School Inspectors in the *Annual Reports of the Committee of Council on Education;* those of Fraser and Moncrieff in 1873 – P.P.(1874), xviii, pp. 101,124 – are typical. On the social composition of girls' secondary schools, see Fletcher, *Feminists and Bureaucrats*, ch.6 and

Appendices 1–4; and Carol Dyhouse, *Girls Growing Up in Late Victorian and Edwardian England* (London, 1981), chs. 2 and 3.

11. See e.g. Emily Davies' observation on the first Girton Committee: 'the list includes no one specially known as advocating the Rights of women. It was felt to be important to put forward only such names as would be likely to win the confidence of ordinary people.' Barbara Bodichon's name (on whom, see above, p. 99) was therefore not included. Barbara Stephen, *Emily Davies and Girton College* (London, 1927), p. 162.
12. M. Jeanne Peterson, 'The Victorian Governess: Status Incongruence in Family and Society', in *Suffer and be Still* ed. Martha Vicinus (Bloomington, 1972), pp. 3–19, esp. pp. 11, 17–18.
13. Kamm, *Indicative Past*, pp. 42–5.
14. Ibid.pp. 19–23; Bertrand and Patricia Russell (eds.), *The Amberley Papers. The Letters and Diaries of Lord and Lady Amberley* (London, 1937), 2 vols., esp. ch.1. In the period 1869–80 Lady Stanley gave over £2000 to Girton – Girton Archives, *Girton Reports*, vol. I (1869–90), Reports 1874/5–80, my calculations. In the 1880s she was to give the Library, the Chemical Laboratory, a gardener's lodge and many other smaller gifts – Stephen, *Emily Davies*, p. 314.
15. Mary Gladstone, *Diaries and Letters*, ed. Lucy Masterman (London, 1930); Georgina Battiscombe, *Mrs Gladstone* (London, 1956); Betty Askwith, *The Lytteltons* (London, 1975).
16. Fletcher, *Feminists and Bureaucrats*, esp. ch.2; *Girton Report 1874/5*, p. 19.
17. Battiscombe, *Mrs Gladstone*, p. 73. *Pace* Mrs Battiscombe, Mrs Sidgwick did not become Principal of Newnham until 1892.
18. Vera Brittain, *The Women at Oxford* (London, 1960), p. 49; Georgina Battiscombe, *Reluctant Pioneer: A Life of Elizabeth Wordsworth* (London, 1978); Betty Kemp, 'The Early History of St Hugh's College', esp. pp. 15–17 in *St Hugh's: One Hundred Years of Women's Education in Oxford* (London, 1986), ed. Penny Griffin. I am grateful to Janet Howarth for underlining the importance of this – see her review of Griffin forthcoming in the *Oxford Review of Education*. Anglican activism, although of a more Evangelical cast, also provided the main impetus behind the foundation of Westfield College in London, in 1882 – see Janet Sondheimer, *Castle Adamant in Hampstead. A History of Westfield College: 1882–1982* (London, Westfield College, 1983), ch.1.
19. Between 1871 and 1880 alone, they contributed just under £3500 with further unspecified amounts for the Laboratory and Loan Fund – my calculations from the *Newnham College Record of Benefactors, made in the Jubilee Year of the College, 1921* (Cambridge, privately printed, 1921) (henceforward *Newnham Benefactors' Book*).
20. *Girton Report 1874/5*, p. 19; Battiscombe, *Mrs Gladstone*, p. 79.
21. David Cannadine, 'Aristocratic Indebtedness in the Nineteenth Century: the Case Re-opened', *Economic History Review* 2nd series, vol. xxx (November 1977), pp. 624–50.

22. See W. D. Rubinstein, 'The Victorian Middle Classes: Wealth, Occupation and Geography', ibid, pp. 602–23.
23. Battiscombe, *Reluctant Pioneer*, pp. 73, 121–2.
24. Brittain, *The Women at Oxford*, p. 59; Somerville Archives, Appeal Prospectus 1881.
25. My calculations from the *Newnham Benefactors' Book*.
26. *Girton Report 1874/5*, pp. 7–8, 22–4. The sums given for scholarships are not recorded in such a way as to enable one to be precise about the absolute totals involved. A presentation or nomination was a kind of closed scholarship, soon discontinued. On Emily Davies' ambition and determination, see Stephen, *Emily Davies, passim*, but esp. ch.X and p. 163.
27. J. P. D. Dunbabin, 'Oxford and Cambridge College Finances 1871–1913', *Economic History Review* 2nd series, vol. xxviii (November 1975), pp. 631–47, also the exchange between Dunbabin and Engel, ibid.,vol. xxxi (August 1978), pp. 437–49. Brian Heeney, *Mission to the Middle Classes: the Woodard Schools 1848–1891* (London, 1969), ch.2.
28. Martha Vicinus, *Independent Women. Work and Community for Single Women 1850–1920* (London, 1985), p. 130.
29. W. D. Rubinstein, 'Wealth, Elites and the Class Structure of Modern Britain', *Past & Present* no. 76 (August 1977), pp. 99–126; and 'The Victorian Middle Classes', p. 614. *Girton Reports 1874/5, 1876, 1878, 1880*, lists of contributions to the Capital Fund.
30. Information from the Somerville Archives provided by Lady de Villiers.
31. W. A. Munford, *William Ewart MP 1798–1869. Portrait of a Radical* (London, 1960); and S. G. Checkland, *The Gladstones. A Family Biography 1764–1861* (Cambridge, 1971); Newnham Archives, *Newnham College Letter 1911* (printed for private circulation by the Newnham College Club, i.e. the association of old students), pp. 41–5; B. A. Clough, 'In Memoriam: Miss Mary Ewart'.
32. Most nearly comparable are Lady Stanley and Barbara Bodichon at Girton, for whom see above, n. 14 and pp. 95, 99; Ann Dudin Brown, who gave £10,000 to launch Westfield College in 1882 – Sondheimer, *Castle Adamant*, p. 22; and Clara Evelyn Mordan, who gave of the order of £20,000 to St Hugh's between 1901 and 1915 – Kemp, 'Early History', pp. 31–3, and Brittain, *The Women at Oxford*, pp. 140–1. All pale in comparison with Thomas Holloway, who spent over £600,000 on his college – Chrys Salt and Liz Bennett, *College Lives. Royal Holloway and Bedford New College, University of London* (London, n.d. [1986]), pp. 3, 7.
33. Besides the £1175 specified in the *Newnham Benefactors' Book*, a further contribution of an unspecified amount to the Loan Fund is also recorded. On James Aikin, see the obituary notices in the Liverpool journals *The Porcupine* and *The Liberal Review* for 13 July 1878. His daughter Anna married W. H. Bateson, later Master of St John's College, thereby launching a distinguished Cambridge

dynasty. I am indebted for information about the Aikins to Mrs Ann Richards.

34. *Newnham Benefactors' Book, Girton Reports 1874/5–80*, lists of contributions to the Capital Fund; *Newnham College Register 1871–1971* 3 vols. (Cambridge 1979–) (henceforward *Newnham Register*), I, p. 69, entry for Mabel Winkworth; Somerville Archives, List of Donations to the Building Fund 1882 and 1886; entry for William Shaen in the Biographical Appendix to Margaret J. Tuke, *A History of Bedford College for Women 1849–1937* (London, 1939); information from Lady de Villiers.
35. Tuke, *Bedford College*, ch.1, also pp. 55–60 and Biographical Appendix. See also Clyde Binfield, *Belmont's Portias: Victorian Nonconformists and Middle-Class Education for Girls*, Friends of Dr Williams's Library 35th Lecture, 1981 (London, 1981).
36. B. A. Clough, *A Memoir of Anne Jemima Clough* (London, 1897); Cecil Woodham-Smith, *Florence Nightingale 1820–1911* (London, 1950); A[rthur] S[idgwick] and E. M. S[idgwick], *Henry Sidgwick: A Memoir* (London, 1906), p. 207.
37. Quoted in Christopher Harvie, *The Lights of Liberalism. University Liberals and the Challenge of Democracy 1860–86* (London 1976), p. 9.
38. See the roll-call of benefactors, teachers and members of the early Councils in the *Newnham Benefactors' Book*, the *Newnham Register* I, pp.v-vi and the *Girton Reports 1874/5–80*. For Oxford, see Batti-scombe, *Reluctant Pioneer;* Brittain, *The Women at Oxford*, chs. 3 and 4; Somerville Archives, Appeal Prospectus 1881 and List of Subscribers, 1879–86.
39. See e.g. B. A. Clough, *Memoir of Anne Jemima Clough;* Woodham Smith, *Florence Nightingale*; Ray Strachey, *Millicent Garrett Fawcett* (London, 1931); R. S. Rait, *Memorials of Albert Venn Dicey, being chiefly Letters and Diaries* (London, 1925), esp. pp. 76–8; Victor Bonham Carter, *In a Liberal Tradition. A Social Biography 1700–1950* (London, 1960); and Brittain, *The Women at Oxford*, pp. 41–7.
40. Stephen, *Emily Davies*, esp. chs. 2 and 4; Haight, *George Eliot; The George Eliot Letters*, ed. Gordon S. Haight, 9 vols. (Yale, 1954–78) IV, pp. 399, 401 and 467–8, V, p. 58 and VIII, pp. 409 and 414; *Newnham Register* I, p.v.; and *Newnham Benefactors' Book*, pp. 9, 12.
41. Stephen, *Emily Davies*, esp. ch.3; Hester Burton, *Barbara Bodichon 1827–1891* (London, 1949) – both of which suppress the fact of her illegitimacy – and Haight, *Eliot*.
42. Information from Lady de Villiers.
43. See above n.38. For Samuel Courtauld III, see D. C. Coleman, *Courtaulds: An Economic and Social History* 3 vols. (Oxford, 1969–80) I, esp. ch.x.
44. David Newsome, *On the Edge of Paradise: A. C. Benson the Diarist* (London, 1980), pp. 110–11.
45. *Somerville College Register 1879–1971* (Oxford, privately printed

n.d. [1979]); *Girton College Register 1869–1946* (Cambridge, privately printed, 1948). The *Lady Margaret Hall Register 1879–1966* (Oxford, privately printed, 1970) is more difficult to use than either these or the *Newnham Register* since, unlike them, it does not reprint material from earlier editions. Those working on the earliest LMH students need the second and third editions of the *Register* (1947) which are now rare.

46. Newnham Archives, *Newnham Hall Report 1875; Girton Report 1874/5*, p. 8; Battiscombe, *Reluctant Pioneer*, pp. 120–1; Somerville Appeal Prospectus, 1881.
47. Kemp, 'Early History', pp. 15–17. On the problems of defining an average middle-class income, see Patricia Branca, *Silent Sisterhood. Middle-Class Women in the Victorian Home* (London, 1975), ch.3.
48. Janet Howarth, 'Public Schools, Safety-Nets and Educational Ladders: the classification of girls' secondary schools 1880–1914', *Oxford Review of Education* xi (1985), pp. 59–71.
49. Caroline Bingham, *Social Life in a Women's College. Royal Holloway College, the first 50 Years 1887–1937*, Centenary Lecture n. 4, delivered at Royal Holloway and Bedford New College, 29 January 1986. I am indebted to Mrs Bingham for permission to read and cite this.
50. *Newnham College Letter 1911*, p. 43, *Newnham Benefactors' Book*, pp. 18–19, 27; for Girton, see above, p. 101.
51. Thomas Holloway quoted in Caroline Bingham, ' "Doing Something for Women": Matthew Vassar and Thomas Holloway', *History Today*, June 1986, pp. 46–51, p. 50; Hilary Spurling, *Ivy When Young: The Early Life of I. Compton-Burnett* (first published 1974, revised edition London, 1983), p. 145.
52. Kemp, 'Early History', pp. 28–30; Sondheimer, *Castle Adamant*, p. 42.
53. Richard J. Evans, *The Feminists* (London, 1977), pp. 28–30.
54. Brian Abel-Smith, *A History of the Nursing Profession* (London, 1960); also Jean Donnison, *Midwives and Medical Men* (London, 1977), pp. 66–9. In midwifery Dr Donnison sees a process not unlike that described by Richard Evans, i.e. an occupation dominated by women having its status and responsibilities progressively eroded and diminished by the imperialism of male doctors. But she sees this as largely complete by the end of the *eighteenth* century and in the nineteenth century a struggle by *both* groups for an assured professional status. A. Tropp, *The School Teachers* (London, 1957); for an account of attempts made to recruit middle-class women to elementary school teaching, see Frances Widdowson, *Going Up Into the Next Class. Women and elementary teacher training 1840–1914* (London, 1980, 1983).
55. On the passion for the mechanism of examination, see Gillian Sutherland, *Ability, Merit and Measurement. Mental Testing and English Education 1880–1940* (Oxford, 1984), pp. 96–111. T. W. Bamford, *The Rise of the Public Schools* (London, 1967), p. 18.
56. E. G. W. Bill and J. F. A. Mason, *Christ Church and Reform 1850–1867* (Oxford, 1970); E. G. W. Bill, *University Reform in*

*Nineteenth Century Oxford. A Study of Henry Halford Vaughan 1811–1885* (Oxford, 1973); Sheldon Rothblatt, *The Revolution of the Dons* (London, 1968).

57. *Henry Sidgwick: A Memoir*, pp. 158–9.
58. A. J. Engel, *From Clergyman to Don. The Rise of the Academic Profession in Nineteenth Century Oxford* (Oxford, 1983), p. 5, n.5.
59. Fletcher, *Feminists and Bureaucrats*, ch.1.
60. *Memoir of A. J. Clough*, p. 154; Brittain, *The Woman at Oxford*, p. 49.
61. Rita McWilliams-Tullberg, *Women at Cambridge* (London, 1975), ch.4, esp. p. 58.
62. Quoted ibid., p. 65. See also Deborah Wormell, *Sir John Seeley and the Uses of History* (Cambridge, 1980) pp. 58–60.
63. *Henry Sidgwick: A Memoir*, pp. 265–7, 509–11; McWilliams-Tullberg, *Women at Cambridge*, pp. 58, 78–9, Appendix A.
63. Harvie, *The Lights of Liberalism*, p. 65.
65. Victoria Glendinning, *A Suppressed Cry. Life and Death of a Quaker Daughter* (London, 1969), pp. 86–7.

# 5 Conflicts and Change in Liberal Theory and Practice, 1890–1918: the case of Bertrand Russell

*Richard A. Rempel*

Debates about the fall of the Liberal Party and its eclipse by Labour risk preoccupying modern historians as debates about the rise of the gentry once absorbed Tudor and Stuart historians.[1] Two of the most persistent controversies revolve around the questions of when to assign an obituary notice to the Liberal Party and, if not a death certificate, when at least to pronounce a judgement upon the degree of illness afflicting Liberal Britain. An answer to the first is difficult enough. But a resolution to the second is even more vexatious, since many values of late Victorian and Edwardian Liberalism did not perish with the attenuation of the Liberal Party but had been adopted by the Labour Party before 1914 and were consolidated and expanded after the Great War. An evaluation of Bertrand Russell's political thought after 1890 and his subsequent political career, however erratic, sheds some light on these questions.

Three clearly demarcated phases in Liberal Party fortunes curiously parallel similar episodes in Russell's life. First, from 1890 to 1903, the Party experienced sharp electoral fluctuations and underwent substantial ideological re-examination. There followed from 1903 to 1914 a period of great achievement – electoral triumphs and legislative enactments – but also of continued questioning. Finally, the war years 1914–18 saw a serious challenge to Liberal values, and schism in the Liberal Party leading to minor party status. In each phase, Russell reflected upon and, in turn, rejected, central aspects of Liberalism. During the first stage, when at Pembroke Lodge and at Cambridge, Russell both personified the Liberal heritage and epitomised its search for a new identity; through the Edwardian years he manifested the strengths and limitations characteristic of the Liberal apotheosis; and during the war he became an implacable foe of the Party his ancestors had helped to create.

Recent historical debates about the nature and impact of Liberal theory and practice have focused on the Edwardian and Great War phases. Essentially, there are three interpretations. Peter Clarke and Michael Freeden, for example, argue that New Liberal ideas and policies came to dominate prewar Liberalism. Within the 'Progressive' alliance of the Liberal Party and the small Labour Party, the direct taxation doctrines of J. A. Hobson and the philosophical justification for state action of L. T. Hobhouse had directed Liberalism away from primary attention to middle-class concerns. Instead, the New Liberalism emphasised the interests of working men, thereby inaugurating modern class politics.[2] Secondly, historians such as Kenneth Wald and G. L. Bernstein contend that traditional nonconformist and Radical issues were still pre-eminent in the Edwardian Liberal Party. For them, the fundamental shift to class politics occurred only during and after the war, in conjunction with the rising power of the Labour Party and the fall of the Liberals.[3]. Thirdly, there is Ross McKibbin's thesis, shared in part by Bernstein, that, while the prewar Liberal Party enacted some New Liberal-inspired policies, such legislation failed to satisfy workers and could not arrest the growing class-consciousness of the labour movement even in the immediate prewar years.[4] Indeed, regardless of the effects of the war, the Labour Party eventually would have replaced the Liberals.

Why should the political writings and activities of Bertrand Russell, which were sporadic up to 1914 though voluminous during the war, shed new understanding on the two questions posed at the outset of this essay? From 1896 to 1900 Russell was engaged principally in becoming a logician. From 1903 to 1910 he collaborated with Alfred North Whitehead in producing their *magnum opus, Principia Mathematica:* Volume 1. By 1914 Russell was on his way to warrant the accolade later bestowed by Lord Annan, that he was the greatest British philosopher since Hume, and the greatest English logician since Occam.[5] His importance arises partly because, unlike any other significant British philosopher, he was intensively, if intermittently, active in political thought and action from 1890 to 1914, and almost exlusively so from 1914 to 1918. He was certainly no rank-and-file Liberal, he was never an MP, much less a Cabinet minister; nor can he be ranked as a major political theorist. Moreover, Russell recognised that, by temperament and intellectual ambitions, he could never be an effective day-to-day politician. None the less, Russell's writings on Liberalism and on forms of socialism make him a barometer of the degree to which New Liberal thought permeated the Party. Moreover, his political statements and wartime peace campaigns give some insight into the debate as to when class questions supplanted traditional Liberal issues.

Russell matured intellectually while arguments over New Liberal theory and practice took shape. After 1902, parallel with the resurgence of the political fortunes of Liberalism, Russell's philosophical talent developed dramatically and was recognised when he became a Fellow of the Royal Society in 1908. During these years he frequented the Liberal intellectual worlds of London, Cambridge and Oxford. Liberal politicians often took note of his political comments, for Russell belonged to that progressive elite whose allegiance Liberalism had to retain or be diminished.

As a Russell, he came from one of the great Liberal families. His grandfather, Lord John Russell, was a prime architect of the Great Reform Act of 1832. Orphaned before he was four, young Bertrand was raised at Pembroke Lodge, the home of his paternal grandparents, whither the great men of Victorian Liberalism made pilgrimages. Here, Russell's education in history, literature and almost all of John Stuart Mill gave him a firm base in classical Liberal theory. From his grandmother, who supported Irish Home Rule and dismissed the House of Lords as 'injurious to the best interests of the nation', Russell, ironically, gained an appreciation of the evils of a privileged landed class. He manifested that hostility to aristocratic power in 1906, when he wrote to the French historian of England, Elie Halévy: 'I wish the Lords would reject the Trade [*sic*] Dispute Bill; that might give a real chance for getting them abolished . . .'[6] Russell's antipathy to the economic power of the landed classes, as well as his belief that comprehensive social reforms could be financed primarily by taxing land values, were developed at Pembroke Lodge. His Aunt Agatha gave him Henry George's *Progress and Poverty* (1879), advocating a single tax on land. Arguably, attachment to the doctrine of Henry George arrested Russell's development in financial theory. He later confessed to believing 'that land nationalisation would secure all the benefits that Socialists hoped to obtain from Socialism, and continued to hold this view until the war . . .'[7] His unwillingness in the Edwardian years to advocate direct taxation of the industrial capitalist or the financier displays a surprising limitation, but by then he had absorbed at Cambridge the orthodoxy of the high priest of neoclassical economics, Alfred Marshall. Russell read Hobson before 1895 but rejected his thesis.

It was in 1894, over the question of women, that Russell made the first of his many testimonials in favour of socialism, as the best means of improving 'the condition of the great mass of women'.[8] Russell's lifelong commitment to women's rights was rooted both in the example of his parents and in his readings of Mill. His upbringing also developed a reverence for the anti-war Radicals and free-traders, Richard Cobden and John Bright. This admiration was particularly evident during the Great War, when he looked for leaders who would play the role the two Radicals had played during the Crimean War. Primarily, however, he learned discipline and independence at Pembroke Lodge. These helped shape the intellect which co-authored *Principia Mathematica* and the character who 'would not follow a multitude to do evil'. By 1890 Bertrand was the only Russell who could be expected to attain high Liberal office, and indeed, Countess Russell ceaselessly groomed him for the premiership.[9] All the other Russell males were either incapable or unacceptable.

Cambridge revealed what Russell had not grasped before – the extraordinary range, depth and quickness of his intellect. Those student years, 1890–94, coincided with the emergence of the New Liberalism, at the time often labelled 'progressivism'. Progressivist ideas and controversies involving Fabians, Radicals and Labour men were given an impetus by the legislative disappointments of the Gladstone-Rosebery administrations of 1892–95. Russell, however, was not especially concerned with politics at the time. Delight in the society of the Apostles and his growing interest in philosophy absorbed him, as did his attachment to the expatriate American Quaker, Alys Pearsall Smith. Despite his family's determined opposition, Russell married her in December 1894. Alys shared Russell's moral earnestness and possessed a greater concern for the plight of the working classes, for the advancement of women's rights, and for the spread of temperance. They spent their honeymoon in Berlin early in 1895. He returned to apply, successfully, for a Cambridge Fellowship to study the foundations of geometry. With Alys, Russell then revisited members of the German Social Democratic Party and worked on economics at the University of Berlin. Even when he received news of a Fellowship, he was still determined to prepare a study on German Social Democracy. From his correspondence with Alys, it is clear that, however vaguely, Russell then viewed himself as a socialist.

Russell's research produced six lectures for the Fabian Society at the London School of Economics and their subsequent publication as his first book, *German Social Democracy* (1896). Like many Liberal Progressives, Russell was attracted to Fabianism. He joined the Society in March 1897, having been courted by Beatrice Webb as one of a vanguard of collectivists whom she was assembling to transform public policy and to supplant the old guard of the Liberal Party. Russell was pleased to be wooed by the Fabians who, by the 1890s, had 'cornered the market in collectivism'.[10] He felt sufficiently committed to Fabianism to assign the whole of his Trinity Prize Fellowship honorarium to the new London School of Economics for the provision of research studentships. Russell's lectures at the LSE contained sharp criticisms of Marxism which were consistent with Fabianism. For instance, he damned the Marxist focus on the class war for the hatred such a policy engendered, and rejected the labour theory of value and Marxist determinism. Indeed, with slight variations, Russell assessed Marxism all his life in this limited, incomplete manner. By implication too, he urged British Labour supporters to work with the Liberal Party. This was at variance with Fabian advice, since in 1893 George Bernard Shaw and Sidney and Beatrice Webb had despaired of the Gladstonian Liberals though they were also sceptical of Keir Hardie's Independent Labour Party. From 1896 they were increasingly drawn to flirtations with the Conservative Party through Arthur Balfour and then to links with the Liberal Imperialists. In this last, Russell joined them, perhaps influenced by W. A. S. Hewins, the LSE's first Director.

There was no precedent in Russell's background for his brief encounter with Liberal Imperialism, but initially he supported the South African War. His support opened a gulf between Russell, the old Radicals such as Leonard Courtney, young Radicals, notably David Lloyd George, and New Liberals such as Hobhouse, who claimed that the Boer War was 'the test issue of this generation'.[11] The war broke the Progressive alliance of the 1890s, separating the Fabians from the New Liberals who were opposed to the war. The Liberal Party itself was split into what appeared to be three irreconcilable factions. Russell's belligerence erupted in bitter correspondence throughout 1900 with the French logician, Louis Couturat. To the appalled Frenchman, Russell explained his intense feelings as stemming 'from a stupid and instinctive patriotism'. His imperialism he justified as 'inspired by the idea of Rome, the history of Mommsen . . . from Carlyle and from Nietzsche, and finally from Darwin and evolution.' Russell expressed his ethnocentric belief that he 'desired that every part of the world should be governed by some European power or another.'[12]

Early in 1901, Russell's conceptions of imperialism and international relations were altered dramatically by an experience he described subsequently as a conversion. When drafting in 1931 what came to be the first volume of his autobiography, Russell claimed simplistically that the 'conversion' established the psychological and ethical imperatives for his later pacifism. He wrote ruefully to Couturat in June 1902: 'The concentration camps disgusted me . . . and I find myself less imperialist than formerly.'[13] In May 1911, Russell recalled the impact of these events to Lady Ottoline Morrell, reflecting that until the South African War aroused his compassion for the tragedies of other people he had been 'hard and intellectual'.[14]

The resurrection of his earlier Radical beliefs deepened with Joseph Chamberlain's proclamation of the Tariff Reform campaign on 15 May 1903, which involved Russell in his first public political endeavour. Coupled with nonconformist hostility to the 1902 Education Act, the challenge to free trade reunited the divided Liberal Party. Conflict over these issues anticipated the major disputes between the Liberals and their Unionist opponents during the Liberal administrations from 1906 to 1914. Indeed, the fundamental Edwardian terms of political debate revolved around free trade, the grievances of the nonconformists, the privileges of the House of Lords and the Anglican Church, and the landlords as a class. Whether to finance social reform by direct taxation, as the Liberals wanted, or whether to follow the Unionist argument for indirect taxation also divided the major parties. Especially after 1910, women's suffrage and Home Rule were also problems.

In defence of free trade, Russell, through numerous papers and speeches, dissected the flaws in Chamberlain's appeal for protection and imperial preference. Russell's correspondence is suffused with the morality he believed to be associated with free trade. To his American friend from Bryn Mawr, Lucy Donnelly, he wrote: 'We are all wildly excited about Free Trade; it is to me the last piece of sane internationalism left, and if it went I would feel inclined to cut my throat.'[15] To Halévy, Russell interjected moral considerations into theoretical expositions, declaring that he 'sympathised with all internationalism; and my *enthusiasm* for Free Trade is derived from this; not from economics.'[16] His advocacy of free trade deepened his 1901 conversion to pacifism, reawakening his admiration for Richard Cobden's hostility to economic nationalism. Through this campaign Russell returned to the Liberal fold. In July 1903, in opposition to the Webbs' imperialism, he resigned from the Co-Efficients, their interparty dining club, and in December 1903 Russell left the Fabian Society.

The tenacity with which Liberals such as Russell supported free trade was seen by the Webbs and many Liberal Imperialists as 'the rehabilitation' of *laissez-faire*.[17] Clarke has challenged this interpretation of the Liberal revival, but accepts that Russell's position was paradigmatic of the Liberalism Mrs Webb deplored. For Clarke, Russell's Liberalism was an amalgam of commitments to classical economics, Mill's civil liberties and the traditional reformism of nineteenth-century Radicalism.[18] For example, Russell's second Edwardian campaign, the struggle for women's suffrage, harked backed to his parents' Radicalism. He wrote many serious papers on the subject and, however frivolously he may have perceived the contest, in 1907 he was the first man to run officially as a candidate for the National Union of Women's Suffrage Societies.

Russell was the most scathing critic of the philosophical doctrines of New Liberalism, the teleology of evolutionary ethics as expounded by Hobhouse. By 1903 G. E. Moore and Russell had rejected neo-idealism and replaced it by a philosophy of objectivist ethics. Hence, Russell accused Hobhouse, essentially, of arguing the tautology that 'the more evolved is the more evolved.'[19] Moreover, Hobhouse's belief in a beneficent natural order conducive to human progress affronted Russell, for in one of his most famous essays, 'The Free Man's Worship' (1903), he contended that the universe was indifferent to man's fate.

Clarke shows that Russell was virtually silent on Hobson's advocacy of higher direct taxation and only addressed himself marginally, if positively, to such reform measures as pensions and sickness and unemployment insurance. In so far as Russell was typical of many prewar Liberals, his relative silence about social reform measures supports the judgement that Edwardian political debate on domestic issues was not focused on 'the "progressivism" of the *Guardian* circle'.[20] (Almost all the leading New Liberal theorists at one time or another wrote for *The Manchester Guardian*, a paper whose national influence has been shown to be limited in comparison with the major Liberal London dailies.)[21]

As the policy proposals in Russell's May 1910 'Addresss to the Bedford Liberal Association' reveal, he was in the mainstream of those Liberals who were determined to curb or even to abolish the powers of the House of Lords.[22] Such an attack was designed mainly to accommodate the Edwardian middle classes, rather than the working classes with whom the New Liberals were attempting to forge a political alliance. Indeed, with the exception of pensions, many in the working classes were apprehensive about much of the Liberals' social legislation because of the prying nature of the bureaucracy which implemented the measures.[23]

Tactically then, Russell seemed right in addressing the sins of landlordism and aristocratic institutions. Two historians have recently emphasised about the 1909 Budget that 'all the leading Liberals, including businessmen disadvantaged by the land monopoly', supported a 'pan-class alliance' against aristocratic privilege.[24] Representing the Labour movement, MacDonald wrote 'bravo' about the Budget.[25] To win the Edwardian elections, the Liberals needed as many middle-class votes as working-class votes on what was still a restricted franchise. The 1910 election victories and the subsequent passage of the Parliament Act opened the way for a wider Liberal assault on privilege.

Between 1911 and 1914 the Liberal momentum met serious resistance on two fronts. On one side, the Liberal attack on privileged institutions, of which the Unionist Ascendancy in Ireland was one part, drove many leading Unionists to contemplate civil war. It was not social reform, whether inspired by New Liberal theory, administrative pragmatism, or fiscal necessity, which drove many Unionists to contemplate treason. The other challenge was labour unrest, which raised class tensions and threatened the shaky Liberal-Labour 'Progressive' alliance. More instalments of 'New Liberal' social reform would not, in all probability, have reduced tension, even if a capitalist-dominated Liberal Party could have been persuaded to advance them. Russell railed against what he viewed as ministerial discrimination against the workers. Hence, when Asquith's government appeared insensitive to the miners' strike in 1912, Russell contemplated joining the Labour Party. Along with other prominent Edwardians, notably the historian G. M. Trevelyan and the classicist Gilbert Murray, Russell signed a letter protesting against the imprisonment of the syndicalist leader, Tom Mann, who had allowed a letter to be published in the paper he edited urging soldiers not to fire on strikers. These incidents caused Russell to explore ideas which during the war led to his advocacy of Guild Socialism.

Despite his irritation with the Liberal government, Russell remained loyal – partly out of admiration for Lloyd George, partly to see that Home Rule was passed and, crucially, because he viewed Liberalism as the only bulwark against the xenophobic Right. In June 1914, he rebuked his close friend, Margaret Llewelyn Davies, for celebrating C. F. G. Masterman's defeat at a by-election. Was she now

> praying for 20 years of Tory government, War with Germany, food taxes and conscription? Or are you still prepared to support the wicked Government in spite of all their sins?[26]

The outbreak of war on 4 August 1914 none the less took Russell, like the vast majority of Britons, by surprise. Russell was convinced that the Liberal Party had betrayed its most fundamental principles. The depth of his anger is conveyed in a letter to Miss Davies on the day Britain declared war:

> You were right about the Liberals. I have done with them. I had never believed anything so frightful could happen. I *feel* as if it meant the end of all happiness for the rest of our lives. . . . Anyhow everything has to be begun afresh – old fixed points are gone. I feel it *utter madness* for us to join the war.[27]

While Russell's objection was primarily moral, arising from his 1901 conversion, and was accentuated by emotional outrage at the Liberals' 'betrayal', there was also a practical element. As 'The Ethics of War' reveals, he was a confirmed believer in Norman Angell's doctrine that wars were economically irrational – for the victors as well as for the vanquished. Moreover, recent scholarship notwithstanding, this essay and his debates with the Harvard philosopher, Ralph Barton Perry, demonstrate that Russell had confronted the possibility of a successful German invasion. Russell's strategy for such an eventuality was passive non-resistance, which he only rejected in 1940 when the murderous nature of Nazism caused him to resort to his 'just war' contingency as outlined in 'The Ethics of War'.[28] During the Great War, however, Russell viewed the possibility of a German victory as of little consequence when weighed against the death of millions of soldiers and the irreparable damage to western civilisation which would result from a prolonged conflict.

Even after German ruthlessness mounted, and was blatantly displayed by the sinking of the *Lusitania* in May 1915, Russell and other anti-war activists continued to argue that only a negotiated peace could preserve civilisation and avert future war.

The Liberals' conduct of the war compounded Russell's disillusionment. First alone, and then in coalitions with the Unionists and the Labour Party, the Liberal government systematically resorted to policies which were patently illiberal. Liberalism was compromised by the authoritarian character of the Defence of the Realm Act and its various amendments, by Lloyd George's assertion of September 1916 that Britain would fight to the 'knock-out blow'; most of all by the enactment of conscription, and by the subsequent harassment of the conscientious objectors. The Liberal Party and many Liberal values of prewar Britain had been eroded by 1914, but it was the war which was the decisive factor in the decline and fall of the Liberal Party. Liberal values, already deeply embedded in the labour movement's tradition by 1914, became more firmly anchored in the post–1918 Labour Party. The attacks of disillusioned Liberals such as Hobson, Russell and Morel on their Party's rejection of Liberal principles deepened the alienation of many former Liberal stalwarts. The end of the war saw the Party bitterly divided, and its most dynamic leader, Lloyd George, dangerously dependent upon the Conservatives. Allies of the Liberals disappeared offstage, notably the Irish Nationalists, or, like the nonconformists, shrunk dramatically in influence. Moreover, the Reform Act 1918 gave the vote to 8½ million men and women whose party allegiances were undeclared. The war accelerated the development of the Labour Party, characterised mainly by class-conscious but non-ideological trade union leaders allied with organisationally-minded politicians, notably Arthur Henderson. They were determined to replace Liberals on the Left by absorption or by political destruction. The passage of important Liberal politicians to the Labour Party during and after the war has been clearly documented.[29] Most Liberals who opposed the war from the outset were Radicals fundamentally critical of Grey's prewar foreign policy. By contrast, with the exception of Hobson, most New Liberals staunchly supported the war, until the enactment of conscription in 1916 caused some to doubt their commitment. Russell had not been closely associated with either group before the war. He had been an intermittent supporter of the anti-Grey Radicals, particularly in his repugnance towards the Anglo-Russian Convention of 1907. But from the outbreak of the war few Liberal dissenters were as remorseless as Russell in opposition to government policy, although the administrations could afford to ignore him until the spring of 1916, when he became committed to the No-Conscription Fellowship.

Russell initially wrote and acted without any clear idea of how to end the war. Certain political realities, however, very soon became evident. In his first protest against the war, written for August 1914, Russell called for a party of anti-war Radicals and Labour. He was disconcerted when Norman Angell, the peace advocate he most admired in 1914, rejected his plea to lead 'young men' in a 'great anti-war movement'.[30] Such a rejection, coupled with overwhelming trade union support for the war, forced Russell to recognise just how isolated the anti-war Left was in the face of the Liberal government's success in mobilising the deep reserves of patriotism within the country. Only sustained propaganda could possibly cause the masses to desert the 'war front' – that combination of official Liberalism in alliance with most of the Labour movement and the Unionist Party.

Russell joined the fledgling Union of Democratic Control immediately after the war broke out. Although he gave dozens of speeches for the UDC, Russell soon became impatient with many of the Liberal and Labour politicians who led the organisation. His dismissal of them in August 1914 as 'eight fleas talking of building a pyramid' had shifted to irritated tolerance by June 1916:

> The UDC will be all right *after* the war . . . but for the moment they are tumbling over each other in their eagerness to disclaim any lack of patriotism or of determination that victory must be ours. This puts such restraint upon what one can say that it half paralyzes one.[31]

He found traditional pacifists, often Quakers, even more unsatisfactory: 'they don't know the volcanic side of human nature.' With self-awareness, he wrote that it was 'the violent side of my nature [which] makes it possible for me to appeal to people who are not temperamentally pacifist.' Indeed, he later claimed melodramatically that he had feared a chance encounter with Asquith or Grey, for he might have committed homicide.[32] Russell's capacity for hostility was recognised by Beatrice Webb as early as July 1901, when she described him as 'a good hater'.[33] His impatience with many anti-war politicians and prewar pacifists included academic friends who made up what was to become the Bryce Group, founded to create a new international basis for a stable postwar world. Russell complained about the first meeting:

> Almost all were just as happy as if there were no war, and enjoyed themselves re-making the map of Europe. I had not realized such people were so totally heartless. Goldie [Dickinson] spoke well and movingly; J. A. Hobson was good; Keynes sensible but cold; the rest dreadful.[34]

Russell did not eschew all intellectuals, nor did he oppose the concept of a League of Nations. Men and women dedicated to ending the war as rapidly as possible, without victory to either side, had his complete allegiance, especially Clifford Allen, Edward Grubb and E. D. Morel. Collaboration was essential because

> The ILP will not be powerful alone, for lack of brains and education; it will need reinforcement by the remnant of Liberals who do not admire the Government.[35]

To become a leader of working-class men and women as well as intellectuals, Russell recognised the need to develop a new approach and new talents. He had to abandon philosophy, at least temporarily, to gain time for extensive research into the origins of the war – a war which he believed arose from the machinations of privileged diplomats who were isolated from democratic control. Also, he needed to construct a coherent political position and to develop a forthright style to appeal to a wide audience. Throughout 1915 and 1916 he attempted to achieve these objectives.

Setting aside his work in logic was not difficult, for Russell found his work for peace 'more continuous and more appealing to my whole nature than philosophy. I am happier than I have been for a long time.'[36] His study of prewar foreign policy emerged in December 1915 as a lengthy pamphlet, *The Policy of the Entente. A Reply to Professor Gilbert Murray*. In collaboration with the Foreign Office, his old friend Gilbert Murray had published a defence of Sir Edward Grey. Russell and the prominent dissenter, Henry Noel Brailsford, were accused of presenting misleading, essentially pro-German views. With his anti-Grey tract, Russell became involved in a pamphlet war he had not anticipated when he had begun his research on the origins of the war months before Murray's attack actually appeared. With C. K. Ogden of *The Cambridge Magazine*, Russell was the most conspicuous of the anti-war activists at Cambridge. The pro-war salvoes from Oxford, however, were far more numerous. Murray's pamphlet was only one of 87 such pamphlets by prominent academics published by the Clarendon Press.[37] Nevertheless, Russell's attack on Grey received a good deal of attention in 1916: and later A. J. P. Taylor described it as 'one of the best statements of the Dissenting position'.

From mid–1915 Russell also worked out a system of socialism which incorporated his political values, economic and social theories, and psychological insights. These ideas were contained in *Principles of Social Reconstruction* (1916). This comprehensive statement went far beyond his rhetorical assertion of November 1914 that 'Socialists are the hope of the world' and that he would 'swallow socialism for the sake of peace'.[38] As late as July 1915 he had declined an ILP attempt to recruit UDC members, claiming that while he thought he might be a syndicalist, he could not yet give a commitment to the ILP. (In fact, he had only resigned from the Liberal Party in April 1915.)[39]

*Principles of Social Reconstruction* represents Russell's most substantial attempt to replace what he viewed as an inadequate Liberal theory. Before the war he had been impressed by the ideas of William James and Graham Wallas about the dangers of thwarted impulses.[40] Certainly his emphasis on impulse was strengthened by his stormy year-long association with D. H. Lawrence. Russell was discouraged by the apparent popular enthusiasm for the war, witnessed by the demonstrations in London. Shock at this perception led him to revise his view of human nature, downgrading the role played by reason. He developed a theory of politics and social behaviour based on nurturing creative as opposed to possessive impulses. The synthesis was presented as a series of eight lectures in London between January and March 1916. In an introduction which was omitted from the book, he asserted that traditional Liberalism was 'dead'. Indeed, after Mill 'no political theorist of any importance' had 'arisen in England'. Implicit in this paper was Russell's assumption that he would be the pioneering left-wing political theorist of the twentieth century.[41]

Despite the book's limitations, particularly in its imprecise definition of 'impulse' and in its neglect of any institutional context, *Principles of Social Reconstruction* reveals how far Russell had moved from his Edwardian Liberalism. The industrial capitalist was seen as almost as pernicious as the landlord in producing neurasthenia, alienation and class conflict in the workplace. Only workers' democracy could give a sense of purpose, dignity and creativity to the masses. Russell's Guild Socialism was developed more fully in *Roads to Freedom* (1918) where the psychological elements were played down. The war instilled an emphasis on class politics in Russell. In July 1916 he wrote to Lady Ottoline.

> I see my career after the war quite clearly now. . . . [I] will try to teach men what they should know to be politically effective. . . . One would preach the abolition of the whole wages system . . . no more slavery to capitalists or Government officials.[42]

Such statements, particularly as developed in the *Principles*, reveal vestiges of aristocratic paternalism combined with ILP democratic socialism. Through his individualistic variant of Guild Socialism, Russell also tried to retain certain core ideals of Liberalism, especially its inherent suspicion of state bureaucracy. His emphasis on class issues paralleled a broad realignment in British politics, accentuated by the war, which swung many voters to the Labour Party in 1918 and afterwards.

Russell's belief that society could be radically reformed was inextricably bound up with his struggle against conscription. When the Asquith government enacted conscription in January 1916, Russell found a focus for his anti-war protests.

He embraced the No-Conscription Fellowship, an organisation which finally allowed him to devote his entire energies to peace. Russell was convinced by the indefatigable persistence of Catherine Marshall and the heroic idealism of Clifford Allen. These two in particular gave Russell the support he found essential when so many of his pro-war friends deserted him. The NCF in turn gained from Russell's aristocratic connections and speaking ability, as well as from his contumacious defiance of authority and his gleeful participation in their activities against conscription. These last two characteristics, and the often satanic cast to his countenance, earned him the sobriquet 'Mephisto'[43] The steadiness and hard work which Russell contributed to the NCF contrast with the alternating moods of exaltation and despair revealed in his letters to Lady Ottoline and, from the autumn of 1916, to Lady Constance Malleson.

In April 1916 Russell attempted to persuade other anti-war organisations to join the NCF in a massive campaign to force the government to seek a negotiated peace. The moral example of the conscientious objectors was to be the inspiration for unity. Russell's enthusiasm led him into public controversy when he claimed that they were 'performing a national service' which demanded 'a higher order of courage, than that of men who fight for their country'.[44] Such praise of the COs was almost certainly deliberate strategy and not emotional aberration, for Russell wanted to convince potential conscriptees and the general public that refusal to fight was the nobler cause. Other apparently puzzling aspects of his wartime writing may also be construed as deliberate. For example, until the United States entered the war in April 1917, Russell's numerous essays for Americans applauded their pacific character, contrasting the morality of their neutrality with the 'barbarism of all the belligerents'.[45] Yet Russell had written to Lucy Donnelly in 1902 that many Americans were not only politically corrupt but also superficial and pusillanimous. It was probably by design that Russell scarcely mentioned the terrible details of particular campaigns, and only alluded to alleged German atrocities. He hoped to elevate his readers' thoughts and emotions to consider the ideals of a fair, negotiated peace dictated not by hatred, which a litany of seemingly endless published casualty lists threatened to accomplish. He agreed with his research assistant and UDC associate, Irene Cooper Willis, who claimed that the atrocity stories and the harsh treatment of German aliens were the direct result of the Liberal government's need to present the struggle as a crusade against evil.[46] His main object, however, was not to eulogise the COs or to protect their rights. Primarily, he reasoned that the war could be stopped by compelling the Asquith coalition to abandon conscription, thereby forcing the administration to negotiate an immediate, fair peace.

In July 1916 he became the first national anti-war figure to embark on an extended peace campaign. He made close to 40 speeches in South Wales trying to link workers and peace activists in an effort to push the government towards peace negotiations. A successful miners' strike the preceding July, and growing popular anger about the carnage, led the ILP and the NCF to send Russell to that volatile area.[47] Russell thus escaped from the constraints placed upon him by the government and the press, which had conspired to restrict his publications. In the autumn, he undertook another speaking tour, but was restricted to Manchester and Birmingham. The impact of Russell's July speeches in Wales disturbed the government. They were not in the least concerned about the pacifist message of his pamphlet 'The Ethics of War' (1915), to which they calculated few would respond. They were, however, worried about the effect he might have on workers by his mockery of the government's conflicting statements, his emphasis upon war-weariness and his encouragement of growing aspirations for peace.

In Parliament, the former New Liberal, Herbert Samuel, now Home Secretary, denounced Russell's Cardiff speech of 6 July as 'vehemently anti-British'.[48] Foreign Office officials had been opposed to allowing Russell to go to America, while the Home Office officials seemed more concerned about Russell's capacity to incite conscientious objectors to reject alternative service.[49] Both ministries, however, proceeded cautiously, no doubt because of Russell's international intellectual eminence. Only when the debate reached MI5 was the decision taken to restrict his activities within the country. Colonel Vernon Kell, first head of MI5, warned the government that he and other War Office officials could not allow Russell to subvert the war effort by proclaiming 'his vicious tenets amongst dockers, miners and transport workers'.[50]

Russell paid heavily for his often reckless attempts to stop the war, and for his defence of the conscientious objectors. In July 1916 he was prosecuted and found guilty of writing a pamphlet which deplored the harsh treatment of the conscientious objectors. This verdict allowed the government to deny him a passport to America, fearing, correctly, that Russell would not restrict himself to logic but would urge Americans to cease giving aid to the Allies. Lloyd George supported the decision, asserting bluntly in Parliament that speeches by him in America would 'undoubtedly interfere with the prosecution of the war'.[51] The next blow fell on 11 July, when the governing council of Trinity College used Russell's conviction as a subterfuge to dismiss him from his lectureship. Then, the War Office banned him from all prohibited regions in Britain on 1 September, an area covering roughly one-third of the country. Lastly, in January 1918, Russell was sentenced to six months in prison for having written a pamphlet which was seen as prejudicial to Britain's relations with its ally, America. Other dissenters, especially Clifford Allen and E. D. Morel, suffered much worse emotional and physical injury because of harsher prison sentences. Indeed, Russell's punishment must be considered mild. Moreover, Russell was certainly not a passive victim. He had deliberately courted official reprisals by baiting government officials whose view of patriotism was profoundly at odds with his own. Yet no British intellectual since the French Revolution had experienced such combined governmental and university censures. Many of Russell's countrymen as well as the government viewed him virtually as a traitor. He found this obloquy deeply wounding, reflecting in old age that love of England was almost his strongest emotion. But when war came he had to resist, for the inner summons was as if he had heard 'the voice of God'.[52]

The government's concern over Russell's potential to endanger the war effort was arguably greater than that caused by any other intellectuals, Morel and Allen included. Unlike them, Russell was an aristocrat, a Fellow of the Royal

Society, and his writings were admired by many other intellectuals, particularly in Bloomsbury, for whom Russell remained the touchstone of humane liberalism.[53] He was also highly regarded in progressive circles in America, particularly at the eastern universities and by readers of such periodicals as *The Atlantic Monthly*.[54]

The government's constraints arrested Russell's impact. In a letter smuggled to America in January 1917, Russell claimed the contrary, boasting that he had gained influence 'by the Government's blundering attempts of suppression'.[55] He was wrong in his cocksure defiance. Governments which could contain and defuse dangerous outbreaks of labour militancy, especially on the Clyde, were not going to let Russell arrest their purpose.[56] Russell made other miscalculations, for he had grossly overestimated both the number of men who would become conscientious objectors and their ability to have any effect on policy. He had realised that the trade union leaders and most of the membership were patriotic, but the attrition and mismanagement of 1916 convinced him that NCF agitation, combined with a campaign by Labour leader Philip Snowden, would persuade the working class to revolt. Russell was profoundly mistaken for, on the whole, 'the working class was quite as military-minded as the bourgeoisie: within the labour movement perhaps more so'.[57] Also, by aligning himself with the NCF, he placed himself on the extreme of the anti-war spectrum. Such prominent critics of the war as Swanwick and Brailsford rejected the NCF as too confrontational to be effective against the government or to win popular support.[58] At the international level, Russell's many appeals to America to remain entirely neutral reveal his economic naivety, for the British blockade and its military needs dictated that many Americans could make great profits only through dealing with the Allied Powers. Indeed, by the spring of 1917, 'Britain's only chance was now to throw herself on the mercy of the American Treasury . . .'.[59]

The Russian revolutions of 1917 temporarily encouraged Russell, for he believed the crisis would compel the Allies to seek peace. Again he miscalculated. Ultimately, he was disillusioned by the government's resourcefulness in sustaining the war effort. Shortly after he resigned as Acting

Chairman of the NCF, and largely withdrew from pacifist agitation, he was sent to prison for alleging that American troops in Britain could be used to break up strikes – a task they performed at home.[60] Russell's prewar cynicism about America thus reasserted itself. When the war ended, as he related in his *Autobiography*, he felt no sense of relief or personal achievement. All his life he believed that his pacifist activities in the Great War had been in vain.

What was Bertrand Russell's impact on the Liberal Party and on Liberal values? His anti-war writings, notably over 100,000 copies of *Principles of Social Reconstruction*, reached a sizeable audience, not just among intellectuals but also among many workers whose correspondence survives in the Russell Archives. His agitation, particularly his speaking tour of 1916, forced the government into policies which made Liberal leaders appear to be profoundly illiberal. Many approved of the attempts to silence Russell, but they were precisely those Conservatives to whom the war gave an added lease on power. Many Liberals, on the other hand, were upset by the government's and still more by Trinity College's actions. As Freeden has observed, Russell's dismissal from Trinity alarmed Liberals and Social Democrats whose livelihood depended upon their liberty to criticise. Russell's case, for them, revealed the Liberal Party as enemies of free thought.[61] His work in holding the No-Conscription Fellowship together during 1916 and 1917, when tension within the organisation almost caused it to collapse, meant that the treatment of conscientious objectors continued to be publicised as an indictment of Liberal morality. Moreover, statements in *Principles of Social Reconstruction*, that 'the Labour movement was morally irresistible', gave added confidence to Labour leaders and supporters. Thus, he assisted in discrediting the Liberals and replacing them after 1918 by a genuinely independent alternative to Conservatism. His libertarian statements, whether made personally or read by proxy, as in Glasgow in October 1916 by the miners' leader, Robert Smillie, gave an intellectual and moral dimension to the Labour Party, and when he was sent to prison in spring 1918 a memorial from trade union organisations all over the country was sent to Lloyd George protesting against the government's action.[62]

Russell did not provide Labour with a prescriptive political and economic ideology like Sidney Webb or, later, John Maynard Keynes. Russell's individualistic version of Guild Socialism was anathema to the trade union and Labour movements. Yet along with Hobson, Morel and other essentially Radical activists, Russell was instrumental in transferring to Labour much that was healthy in the British Liberal tradition – namely faith in liberty, free speech and suspicion of privileged elites. As for the individual reckoning, his First World War protests transformed him from a reclusive don into a public personage, a controversialist who wrote for ordinary people right up to his death in 1970.

## Notes

1. The controversy historians have had in assigning an 'obituary' notice to the Liberal Party is succinctly conveyed in P. J. Waller's review of P.F. Clarke, *Lancashire and the New Liberalism* (Cambridge, 1971) in the *Eng. Hist. Rev.*, 87 (October 1972), pp. 843–6.
2. *Lancashire and the New Liberalism* (Cambridge, 1971); *Liberals and Social Democrats* (Cambridge, 1978); *The New Liberalism* (Oxford, 1978).
3. *Crosses on the Ballot* (Princeton, NJ 1983); and *Liberalism and Liberal Politics in Edwardian England* (New York, 1986).
4. *The Evolution of the Labour Party* (Oxford, 1974).
5. *Leslie Stephen* (1984), p. 347.
6. Russell to Halévy, 11 October 1906. BRA, McMaster University. (Photocopy; original presumably in the possession of the Halévy Estate.)
7. *The Autobiography of Bertrand Russell*, 3 volumes (1967–69), Vol. I (1967), p. 46.
8. Russell to Alys Pearsall Smith, 21 September 1894. BRA. (Photocopy; courtesy of Barbara Halpern Strachey.)
9. George Santayana perceived Countess Russell's aspiration for Bertrand. See *My Host the World* (1953), p. 44.
10 Clarke, *Liberals and Social Democrats*, p. 44.
11. Quoted in Stefan Collini, *Liberalism and Sociology* (1979), p. 82.
12. Russell to Couturat, 18 December 1899, Couturat Papers. BRA. (Photocopy; original in Bibliothèque de la Ville, La Chaux-de-Fonds, Switzerland.) My translation.
13. Russell to Couturat, 25 June 1902.
14. Russell to Lady Ottoline Morrell, No. 72, 18 May 1911. (Photocopy; original in the Harry Ransom Humanities Research Center, University of Texas, Austin).

15. Russell to Lucy Donnelly, 29 July 1903. BRA.
16. Russell to Halévy, 3 November 1903.
17. Beatrice Webb Diary, 1 March 1904, p. 317 in *The Diary of Beatrice Webb*, Vol. 2 (1892–1905), ed. N. and J. MacKenzie (Harvard, 1983).
18. See P. F. Clarke, 'Bertrand Russell and the Dimensions of Edwardian Liberalism', pp. 209–19, in *Intellect and Social Conscience*, ed. M. Moran and C. Spadoni (Hamilton, Ont., 1984).
19. Collini, *Liberalism*, pp. 230–1.
20. Waller, *op. cit.*, p. 843.
21. A. J. A. Morris, *The Scaremongers* (1984), p. 384.
22. See *The Collected Papers of Bertrand Russell* (1985), Vol. 12. pp. 297–303.
23. See Standish Meacham, *A Life Apart* (Harvard, 1977), pp. 206–13.
24. G. R. Searle, 'The Edwardian Liberal Party and Business', *Eng. Hist. Rev.*, 88 (January 1983), p. 47; and Bruce Murray, *The People's Budget* (Oxford, 1980).
25. David Marquand, *Ramsay MacDonald* (1977), p. 116.
26. Russell to Davies, 9 June 1914. BRA.
27. Ibid., 4 August 1914. BRA.
28. See *The International Journal of Ethics*, 25 (January 1915). pp. 127–42. When his argument for passive or non-resistance was attacked cogently late in March 1915, Russell temporarily modified his advocacy of the policy on the grounds that the Liberals had made too many commitments to France in 1914 and that the British were not yet morally ready. But he did assent that passive resistance was essential in the future, 'even to the point of enduring death' (*The Westminster Gazette* 27 March 1915, p. 2). By the time of his last retort to Prof. Perry in October 1915 Russell had reasserted his belief in non-resistance, claiming the 'present war was all . . . in the nature of pretexts' (*International Journal of Ethics*, 26 October 1915), p. 27. See Trevor Wilson's critique of Russell's anti-war stand in *The Myriad Faces of War* (New York, 1986), p. 26.
29. See Marvin Swartz, *The Union of Democratic Control in British Politics during the First World War* (1971).
30. Norman Angell, *After All* (1951), p. 215.
31. Russell to Lady Ottoline, No. 1069, 10 August 1914 and No. 1240, 8 June 1915.
32. Russell to Lady Ottoline, No. 1214, 30 January 1915; and see *Autobiography*, Vol. 2 (1968), pp. 6–7.
33. Webb, *Diary*, Vol. 2, p. 210.
34. Russell to Lady Ottoline, No. 1130, 18 October 1914.
35. Russell to Lady Ottoline, No. 1108, 14 September 1914.
36. Russell to Lady Ottoline, No. 1110, 10 September, 1914.
37. P. H. Sutcliffe, *The Oxford University Press* (Oxford, 1978), pp. 172–4. Despite the professorial imbalance for and against the war, the casualty rates of Oxford and Cambridge men were virtually the same. See J. M. Winter, *The Great War and the British People* (Macmillan, London 1986), pp. 96–8. See also *The Troublemakers* (1985 edn). p. 171n.
38. Russell to Lady Ottoline, No. 1147 [11 November 1914].

39. Russell to G. Turner, 26 April 1915, BRA.
40. See *C.P.B.R.* Vol. 12, pp. 376–7 regarding Russell's debt to James and his letter of 19 January 1916 on his debt to Wallas. Copy of Wallas letter in BRA.
41. Unpublished paper entitled 'Disintegration and the Principle of Growth', probably written late in 1915 or early in 1916, BRA.
42. Russell to Lady Ottoline, No. 1391 [17 July 1916].
43. Alan Wood, *The Passionate Sceptic* (1957), p. 110.
44. See 'Liberty of Conscience', *The Cambridge Magazine*, 5 (27 May 1916), p. 505.
45. Margaret Moran, ' "The World As It Can Be Made": Bertrand Russell's Protests During the First World War', *Prose Studies*, 8 (December 1985), p. 56.
46. *England's Holy War* (New York, 1929).
47. K. Morgan, *Rebirth of a Nation: Wales 1880–1980* (Oxford, 1981), p. 163.
48. *H. C. Deb.* (5), 86 (1916), col. 880, 18 October 1916.
49. See Jo Vellacott's excellent study, *Bertrand Russell and the Pacifists in the First World War* (New York, 1980). pp. 79–93.
50. See copies of correspondence in PRO, 80 45/110112/3141670, quoted in Vellacott p. 93 and 273 n. I emphasise slightly more than Vellacott the determination by which Kell overcame any Home Office scruples. Government concern over Russell's potentially disruptive influence on workers is also demonstrated in the Home Secretary's Cabinet reports to the King during 1916. Herbert Samuel's Papers record that Russell was the only antiwar activist discussed not merely once but twice (A152/267). The Administration's fears about Russell's impact on neutral opinion in the United States are reflected in Gilbert Murray's confidential report to Grey on the *Special Case of Bertrand Russell (Cab 37/153/36).*
51. H. C. Deb. (5), 86 (1916), col. 533, 18 October 1916.
52. *Autobiography*, Vol. 2 (1968), pp. 17–18.
53. See S. P. Rosenbaum, 'Bertrand Russell in Bloomsbury', *Intellect and Social Conscience*, p. 19.
54. See Julian Bell, *We Did Not Fight* (1935), p. 117.
55. See 'For Conscience Sake', *The Independent*, New York, 89 (15 January 1907), p. 101.
56. James Hinton, *The First Shop Stewards' Movement* (1973), ch. 10.
57. Ross McKibbin, 'Arthur Henderson as Labour Leader', *Inter. Rev. Soc. Hist.*, 23 (1978), p. 86.
58. Swanwick to Russell, 26 June 1916, copy, BRA and Brailsford to Marshall, Marshall Papers, 15 January 1917. Marshall Papers in Cumbria County Record Office, and copies of relevant correspondence in BRA.
59. Kathleen Burk, *Britain, America and the Sinews of War 1914–1918* (Boston, 1985), p. 8.
60. See R. Clark, *The Life of Bertrand Russell* (1976), pp. 338–40.
61. Michael Freeden, *Liberalism Divided* (Oxford, 1986), p. 25.
62. Accounts of the memorial are contained in a number of Liberal and Labour newspapers, and there was an editorial praising Russell's 'national importance' in *The Manchester Guardian*, 4 May 1918.

# 6 The Labour Party, Capitalism and the National Debt, 1918–24

*R. C. Whiting*

The high cost of winning the First World War and the enormous increase in the national debt which resulted, raised significant questions about the distribution and functions of different sorts of wealth in postwar Britain. The national debt had its impact on the economy through the interest payments which had to be made to its holders. The debt had increased roughly ten times as a result of the war, and in March 1920 stood at £7830 million, £1230 million of which was owed to other countries, principally the United States.[1] The annual interest payments rose to over 40 per cent of the budget in the 1920s. War loan had proved to be a popular investment, and its share of private property increased sharply.[2] It was plausible to argue that, as a result of the increase of the debt, active producers in the population were handing over, through their income tax payments, substantial sums to the *rentier* or passive capitalist.[3]

The central question was this: should the main tax burden to meet the debt fall on current income or accumulated wealth? Current income (profits of companies, salaries of businessmen) was widely regarded as the worthy reward of the most dynamic and strategic economic groups; accumulated wealth, on the other hand, did not have such a clear economic function and, if it was in the form of paper titles, not such a powerful moral claim. In so far as the orthodoxy of return to gold at the prewar parity involved deflation, the real burden of the debt increased. Who was to pay the cost of this political virtue? This essay will examine one solution, the capital levy, proposed by the Labour Party. Although the idea for such a levy was not confined to Labour, it was the Party's policy between 1918 and 1924, and it is arguable that, as Snowden grappled in the summer of 1931 with the consequences of the May Committee report, which wanted the Labour budget to meet the claims both of the sinking fund and of the unemployed, Labour suffered more severely than other political parties from the failure to deal with the debt under conditions of monetary orthodoxy.

Edwin Cannan, Professor of Economics at the LSE, linked the debt and a levy when writing to Reginald McKenna, Chancellor of the Exchequer in 1916:

> It may be that the burden of debt will be no greater at the end of the war than it was at the end of the war in 1815 but the bearers are very different, more intelligent and less patient than their predecessors. The huge incubus will not be tolerated for long, and the best that the propertied classes can look forward to is that it will be got rid of by a levy on all capital, such as Ricardo always advocated, the fundholder of course contributing to his own extinction along with the rest.[4]

The case for a levy was made under two markedly different conditions, under inflation immediately after the war, and then under deflation during the 1920s. From 1918–20 anxiety about inflation and the need to contain the floating debt, and doubts about the effectiveness of currency restraint in controlling prices, encouraged interest in a capital levy from groups and institutions in no sense socialist.[5] Those on the Labour side also wanted to use a levy to cancel the currency notes which had been issued during the war and which were not backed by gold.[6] At this point the levy scheme ran parallel with a more modest proposal to tax gains in wealth made during the war, to deal specifically with the floating debt. Although the Pearce Committee reported that a war wealth tax would work, the scheme was defeated in Cabinet.[7] After 1920, when inflation had eased, the attention shifted to the increasing real burden of interest payments under falling prices. There was, of course, no levy, but the importance of the problem which it addressed cannot be denied. In 1922 Keynes suggested that the burden of the debt was near to being insupportable, and was aware that 'we are in danger of being the only country which will have a very heavy internal debt in relation to its resources.'[8] By 1930 this had become true; Britain had a higher indebtedness in relation to national income than any other country. Although an internal debt did not directly mean a diminution of aggregate wealth (unlike an externally owed one) it was none the less widely regarded as involving undesirable transfers of wealth from active producers to *rentier* capitalists which impeded economic efficiency.[9]

The Labour Party grew in political presence during the 1920s and within that Party there were those who saw the virtues of attacking accumulated wealth and the value of liberating the budget from interest payments on the debt. In the end the Labour leadership thought that the benefits of leaving alone the debt and property were greater than the costs, a calculation which depended a great deal on seeing how opinion ebbed and flowed outside the Party. And so in this essay there will be two main sections: first an examination of the proposals for a capital levy generated within the Labour Party and the principles on which they were based; second, a consideration of the views held by others whose opinions had some weight – principally the tax economist, J. C. Stamp, and J. M. Keynes. The main conclusion is that the levy was never resorted to because of the highly developed nature of the British tax system and the view that British business could sustain a high incidence of taxation. In other words, there was a great deal of timidity shown to accumulated wealth and not towards current income, even though the latter was arguably more strategic.[10]

* * *

Because the budget was burdened by interest charges on the debt, a scaling-down of it would have eased the pressure on income tax (after the war it was feared it might rise to 7s 6d [37½p] in the £) and provided scope for social spending. Such a diminution of the debt could have been achieved either by depreciating the value of interest payments through inflation or by redeeming the debt in whole or in part. Both courses of action, in attempting to deal with the holders of war loan, affected much wider constituencies. Inflation would have penalised the small saver relying on fixed interest investments. Repayment, if this involved a tax on wealth, affected property in general. With a large debt

> the *rentier* will be the subject of perpetual jealousy and perpetual attack; the owners of other forms of capital wealth whose property could, at any rate in the opinion of a large section of the public, be appropriated to meet the *rentier*'s claims, will be in a position scarcely less vulnerable.[11]

Inflation was socially unjust, repayment, if it meant a capital levy, politically adventurous. The Labour Party was not willing to pursue inflation, and the degree to which it actually supported deflation increased the necessity of doing something about the debt, and therefore of exploring the idea of a levy.

Hugh Dalton, who along with F. W. Pethick-Lawrence was one of the main protagonists for a levy, was in favour of a sharp dose of deflation after the war because he felt that inflation was far more conducive to social tension. Pethick-Lawrence argued that individual wealth ought to be written down after the war by the whole amount of the state debt, since war loan had no relation to any productive assets.[12] For wider reasons too there was little possibility that Labour would turn to inflation to ease the problem of the debt. If Labour were to gain any confidence among non-working-class voters it had to be hostile to inflation. Even sympathetic opinion thought that the main danger posed by the first Labour government was a rise in prices; 'though quite well intentioned now, it would probably lose its head more easily when once started upon the slippery slope [of inflation] than either of the other two parties.'[13] But to fall in with conventional wisdom and support deflation and stabilisation of the £ at the prewar parity increased the real burden of the debt. Yet, as *The Economist* pointed out, 'the key to Labour policy, as to that of any party which holds out hopes of social improvement, is the budget.'[14] In avoiding one politically provocative policy (inflation), they were pushed back onto another (taxation of capital). This dilemma was well expressed by Keynes:

> I think those people suffer from a certain confusion of mind who simultaneously hold we must indubitably restore sterling to par, in all circumstances we must respect contract, and in no circumstances must we have a capital levy.[15]

The alternative was to do nothing, and this was the route

which Labour took under MacDonald. But political moderation had a high price, for it proved impossible in 1931 for a Labour government to meet the claims of the war loan-holders on the one hand and the unemployed on the other and still maintain credibility in its budget. While the levy was part of the Labour Party's programme the support it received from MacDonald and Snowden was always half-hearted. It proved far from easy to handle at election time, when they tried to drain it of any socialist content, and MacDonald decided to bury the issue during the first Labour government. The nails were hammered into the coffin by the Colwyn Committee on the National Debt and Taxation, which MacDonald and Snowden appointed to 'strengthen themselves against their extremists'. By 1928 the levy idea was 'as dead as Queen Anne'.[16]

The energy for a levy had come from outside the leadership of the Party. During the war Sidney Webb had drafted a conscription of riches policy as part of the War Emergency National Workers' Committee's opposition to conscription, and in 1920 F. W. Pethick-Lawrence produced a pamphlet on the levy.[17] Further discussions took place in the Party's Advisory Committee on Trade Policy and Finance. There had been parallel interest from outside the party, Sidney Arnold, a Liberal MP, speaking in favour of a levy in April 1918.[18] The Labour Party's advisory committee was peeved in 1919 to find that the parliamentary group favoured a scheme less radical than Arnold's in its trawl of capital wealth.[19] The intention was to tax personal wealth (not corporate assets) to raise £3000 million, to pay off roughly half of the debt and so save about £140 million from expenditure on interest payments.[20]

Labour's proposals sustained three main emphases. The first was to alleviate the burden of debt interest payments on the budget, and so allow income taxpayers to commute future income tax payments with a once-and-for-all payment under the levy. This was closest to views outside the Left, which saw the levy as a politically neutral choice between different forms, but not levels, of taxation.[21] The second emphasis saw the levy as a way of providing scope for social spending in place of interest payments to war loan holders, so that there would not be a commensurate fall in income tax following a levy. At this point non-Labour writers had severe reservations about the levy. A third emphasis suggested that if the government retained the securities surrendered as part of the levy, it would acquire control over the companies to which they related. While this was played up by some of the opposition to the levy it was never a central feature of the Labour scheme and was dropped fairly smartly.[22] When the chief proponents of the scheme felt themselves to be on the defensive, as they were before the Colwyn Committee, the greater emphasis was placed on 'pure' debt redemption, and the degree to which subsequent social spending would be discretionary was underlined.[23]

A capital levy was, by its very title, politically provocative. The tax expert J.C. Stamp recognised this when he envisaged businessmen saying: 'we must compound in some way for our income tax burden by redeeming the National Debt on a large scale, but we must not call it a capital levy, we must call it something different.'[24] But although the idea of taxing wealth fitted in closely with the views of some on the Labour side – principally Dalton – the arguments in favour stressed how little the levy would interfere with the essentials of production. Those subjected to the levy would either pay in war loan, which would be torn up, in cash, or in kind, with securities. Securities surrendered in payment would be taken up by those anxious to find new sources of investment for their newly redeemed war loan. The levy would involve the transfer of titles to wealth, not the break-up of physical assets. As Dalton argued, 'It is of course real capital – the concrete means of production – which is fundamentally important, not script and bonds, bank balances and cheques.'[25]

It was further argued that a levy would actually increase the level of savings in the community, for while taxpayers reacted to a high income tax by maintaining consumption at the expense of savings, those with capital in their hands from newly-redeemed war loan were more likely to invest than to spend it; in addition levels of saving might increase further under the stimulus of lowering of income tax following reduction of the debt.[26] In its combination of an assault upon large aggregations of wealth and an anxiety to protect savings the levy was right in line with the welfare economics of the Marshall-Pigou tradition which had been forged in the Edwardian period.[27] It was in this tradition that both Pethick-Lawrence and Dalton had been trained. Lawrence had taken a double first in Mathematics and Natural Sciences at Cambridge in 1894 and then attended lectures by Marshall in 1896 which 'were not only illuminating but inspiring',[28] and it was to Marshall that he dedicated his short book on the levy, published in 1918. Dalton acknowledged that Pigou's *Wealth and Welfare* had a great influence upon him when he was at Cambridge, and later at the LSE he worked on the distribution of wealth under the supervision of Edwin Cannan.[29]

While the arguments for the levy on the Labour side were detached from socialist economics they also had little connection with the class struggle in industry which seemed so threatening after 1918. In its most moderate guise a levy was a commutation of future income tax and therefore entirely a decision for middle-class taxpayers. According to Sidney Webb: 'it is proposed as a substitute for a crushingly heavy Income Tax on the whole body of professional and businessmen' and was 'the alternative for the doctor, teacher or minister of religion to consider'[30]. The working class had largely solved their problems about taxation without a capital levy, and despite the debt. Although some workers had become income taxpayers during the war as a result of wage increases, it was thought politically impossible to make any demands upon the working class after 1918 in view of the strong opposition to income tax, particularly in South Wales.[31] Further, improved real wages, shorter hours of work, and a greater share of national income indicated that, as far as indirect taxes were concerned,

> labour has been successful . . . in throwing back onto profits a considerable proportion, though not the whole, of the additional taxation imposed during the war, which, it was intended, the working classes should bear.[32]

Even though the TUC claimed that the debt aroused a strong sense of injustice among the working class, there was little sign that it took a close interest in the levy. The TUC had to be led by the Labour representatives on the committee in drawing out the wider implications – how a levy would hit accumulations of wealth without diminishing incentives – and was at sea over the important question of the yield of a levy. The TUC had not read Dalton's book on the levy which gave the clearest picture of its technical ramifications from the Labour side, and it admitted: 'we approached the matter *de novo* as a representative body of working people. We did not study anyone else's theories at all; we came straight to it ourselves in our own way.'[33] The Labour Party, therefore, was not leading a great working-class crusade over the debt (even though the workers would have benefited from increased social service expenditure); and to try to remove the partisan element MacDonald was fond of claiming that the levy idea 'had come from businessmen and economists like Cambridge professors'.[34]



* * *

If the Labour Party's views on the levy lay within traditional economic thought, how helpful were the economists who stood outside the Party? At the heart of the debate lay the role of savings and incentives in capitalism and the effect of taxation upon them. The main line of argument here will be that while economists had a pretty robust view about the level of taxation which the economy could sustain, this was in the end unhelpful to the specific case for a capital levy. Two economists come into view, J. M. Keynes and J. C. Stamp. Keynes needs no introduction; Stamp had entered the civil service in 1896 and served on the Board of Inland Revenue until 1919 when he left to become Secretary of Nobel Industries. He was a key figure in the Dawes Commission which dealt with Inter-Allied debts, and was described by the Cambridge economist, D. H. Robertson, as a 'theorist, practician, savant and man of affairs' who gave 'what most people will probably now be content to regard as the last word on the most important aspects of the Capital Levy.'[35] It was Stamp's technical expertise in the field of taxation which gave him authority, an ability in statistical matters rather than in economic theory which led both sides in the levy debate to claim his views in support of their arguments. Yet the general ideas which Stamp brought to his work on taxation lay within the same framework as those used by Labour's economists, and in some respects he was willing to take a more radical perspective. Of the Marshall-Pigou tradition within which Dalton and Pethick-Lawrence had been raised he wrote that 'There is no nobler writing in any books on the whole aims of life and the realm of ends than the opening chapters of the treatises by Marshall and Pigou.'[36] Where Stamp went further than the Labour side was in his application of J.A. Hobson's views about taxation to company profits. In 1919 Stamp proposed a continuation of excess profits tax on the American model to generate extra revenue and act 'as a brake upon those dynamic elements of the present and the future in our social system which we are anxious to see brought under control'. This scheme, which taxed profits if they exceeded a certain percentage of a firm's capital, was seen by Stamp as a specific application of Hobson's ideas about taxing surplus wealth.[37] But this was not a path which Labour wished to follow, and the Party's advisory committee deliberately turned its back on current and future business income, and did not want to touch corporate assets at all.[38]

Most economists found little to object to in the mechanics of a capital levy as proposed by the Labour Party. The Labour Party publicists insisted that physical assets would be untouched; all that was involved was a transfer of paper titles to wealth. Railway securities (for example) surrendered by A as part of his contribution to the levy would be taken up by B, anxious to re-invest funds released by redemption of his war loan; for every seller there would be a buyer, and the danger of a fall in share values for this reason was illusory.[39] Economists interested in the utilitarian functions of private property had little to quarrel with in such a transfer, but it left opponents of the levy exposed. They tried to argue for the economic importance of the undisturbed ownership of personal property. When A.C. Pigou pointed out that the 'real stuff', factories and materials, would be undamaged by a levy, *The Economist* replied that 'these things are financed by complicated arrangements in which ownership is an important factor'.[40]

The point was argued most closely between J.C. Stamp and W.W. Paine, of Lloyd's Bank. Two specific questions arose: the degree of confiscation involved in a levy, and its effect on credit. Paine argued that a levy involved a greater degree of confiscation than a high income tax because it would hit accumulated wealth. Stamp could not see the distinction. A wealthy man might quite rationally make one payment under a capital levy on all his property and get relief from subsequent annual taxation on income, because the only value from capital was the income deriving from it. When Paine argued that 'That is a very narrow view of capital. Some people regard capital as a trust possession which they are bound to turn to the best advantage of the community', Stamp thought this to be 'a purely psychological' view.[41]

The question of ownership was further drawn out over the effect of a levy on credit and employment. The point at issue was not only the fairly technical one of how much wealth subject to the levy would be acting as collateral for credit, but whether change of title or ownership affected credit at all. Paine claimed that it would. Because assets would be placed on the market to meet the levy, prices would fall, and there would be 'a dislocation and disturbance of trade and credit as might shake the latter to its very foundations and bring about the most serious financial panic the country has ever known.'[42] But the weight of such an argument was more apparent than real. Not only did Stamp insist that a great deal of paper property had no active economic function – railway shares lying in a strong box were non-functioning security – but further, that transference of ownership did not affect economic contribution to the community. As Stamp argued, 'Surely a man can keep as many people in employment on £100,000 of capital of which £70,000 belongs to him and £30,000 is borrowed, as on the original £100,000, all of which belongs to him.'[43]

And so when economists looked at private property in its economic contribution to the community, they did not much mind who owned it, so long as it was accessible to business. This is indeed how Stamp saw the levy working from the point of view of the holder of funds from newly-redeemed war loan – he would be exchanging a claim on future tax revenue for a claim on industrial production.[44] The key question, as we shall see, was the differing effects on incentives of income and capital taxes.

The capital levy, then, was seen as a perfectly practicable

proposition, and the opposition tended to drift away from utilitarian arguments, as Sidney Webb noted after dinner-table discussion with Robert Brand, a banker, and Reginald McKenna: 'It was quite clear that, whilst finding intellectual reasons for their objection, they really objected to increased taxation of the rich.'[45] Those who were content to parade nineteenth-century views about the virtues of thrift, or what Brand called the 'Gladstonian notion of allowing the money of the country to fructify in the pockets of the people' usually received short shrift; Stamp, for one, 'could never understand how gold could fructify in anyone's pocket'.[46] The widely-held view that the levy hit the patriotic saver against the profligate spender also did not get very far. Most large accumulations did not reflect assiduous thrift or morally superior savings but were achieved without effort or sacrifice, through inheritance, tricks or luck.[47] More importantly, businessmen's savings were seen to be much less strategic than they had once been, because of the diminishing significance of the private company against the joint stock enterprise. Traditional views about protecting large accumulations of private savings because of their direct application to business no longer carried so much weight: 'The real rival to nineteenth-century saving is the saving which goes on silently through company reserves, and never becomes anyone's spendable resources at all.'[48] The proposal for a capital levy by the Labour Party therefore gained considerable legitimacy because it tackled private or personal wealth and not corporate assets.

* * *

The drift of economic argument then, was not at all unsympathetic to a capital levy. A large national debt put strain upon the budget and limits upon social spending. The capital levy, itself a provocative device, was none the less brought into public debate precisely because of the operation of an allegedly more virtuous strategy, the return of the currency to its prewar parity. Yet in the end opinion outside the Labour Party thought that a levy was not worth the trouble, and the scheme was lost. The levy was thought to be 'not worth it' for three reasons: the actual yield a levy would bring; the assumptions about psychology; the perceived resilience of the British economy to high taxation.

The debate over the actual yield of a levy was one of those instances of the way in which taxation proposals, while superficially attractive for political action upon wealth, might be fraught with difficulty if their implications were not fully thought out. The particular point which deflated the yield of a levy was the loss of subsequent tax revenue. A tax levied on accumulated wealth would remove such wealth from subsequent taxes – income tax, super-tax and death duties. Stamp calculated that of the £140 million saved on annual interest payment to debt-holders, only about £50 million would remain as a net yield, the rest going to make up loss of revenue from other forms of taxation.[49] Such a net saving was equivalent to roughly 1 shilling [5p] on income tax, and it was often argued that the upheaval of a levy was not worth it if the result was going to be so small. This point certainly had a powerful influence upon Keynes: 'In the earlier discussion of the capital levy I do not think anyone was quite alive to that [the modest net return] – I certainly was not – and the force of those figures is very great.'[50]

Here the Labour side came off unnecessarily badly. Dalton dealt with the loss of future tax revenue from a levy but the argument circled around alternative figures – a net saving of one shilling [5 p] according to Stamp, or 1s 6d [7½ p] according to Dalton. Dalton's perfectly reasonable point, that a levy which reduced subsequent annual taxation would have a beneficial dynamic effect on the economy and so on tax revenues was a plausible corrective to Stamp's deflection of the scheme, but of course, not susceptible to statistical proof.[51] Stamp's status as a tax expert had an easy but not wholly deserved victory over Labour's claims.

The apparently narrow benefit of a levy once the net gain was established could have been widened by a more severe tax on capital, perhaps one which touched corporate assets. But this opened up the whole question of the levy and socialism, which Labour's economists were unwilling to pursue. Throughout the election campaigns of 1922 and 1923 Labour speakers tried to drain the proposal of any socialist content. Both MacDonald and J.H. Thomas described it as a 'purely business proposition', and Snowden referred to it as 'rendering unto Caesar the things that are Caesar's'.[52] Arthur Henderson promised that there would be no appeal to class feeling.[53] The *Daily Herald* argued throughout the 1922 campaign that the levy was a means of cutting direct taxation and encouraging thrift. The only attempt to place a more aggressive gloss upon the scheme came from G.D.H. Cole, who wanted to tear up the securities surrendered under the levy as a means of reducing the claims of shareholders upon the profits of companies.[54] Despite the desire to assuage the fears of businessmen and property-holders, the Labour Party found the levy hard to handle at the hustings. Although it had suited Dalton very well to campaign on the levy at the 1922 election, by the beginning of 1923 he discovered that 'the subject is astonishingly fertile of misunderstandings as to what is proposed and how it would work.'[55] For the 1923 campaign it was agreed 'to soft-pedal, by saying that we will submit it to experts to work out a scheme in detail, in consultation with bankers, businessmen, etc.'.[56]

A severe levy, of course, cold not have stood by itself, for it would have threatened the overall volume of savings in a way which the more modest version did not. A substantial transfer of wealth therefore through a much heavier levy would have required some prior control over allocating resources for investment; as Keynes suggested, 'it ought to be the last, rather than the first step in any transition from individualistic capitalism to a new order of society.'[57] But however anodyne and guarded the presentation, however much it was *not* a preface to socialism, it still suffered because of the disturbance it would cause, which would hardly be worthwhile with a modest net gain. The degree of 'disturbance' related to the 'psychology' of capitalism, and of the City in particular. The opposition to the levy, defeated by economic science, reappeared triumphant because of the weight attached to irrational factors in predicting economic behaviour.

Keynes argued that the levy involved far more disturbance than any other tax in proportion to its yield, because 'you are insulting, by it, a set of very strong irrational feelings in men' and so the ill consequences of a levy would 'be due to psychological rather than to economic or technical causes.'[58] Stamp made much the same point in 1921:

> It is a nice balance. It all depends on the prevailing psychology in financial circles at the time when it is introduced. It is what people imagine that will rule the issue, not what they ought to think.[59]

The precise impact of the psychological fears about a levy in the City was spelled out in a Board of Inland Revenue memorandum:

> So long as the City believes (either rightly or wrongly) that the scheme represents the end of the world . . . the City atmosphere might easily induce, upon the announcement of a heavy capital levy, such a landslide in capital values and such a hold up of credit as would constitute a national disaster. . . . It is the consideration of these psychological results which causes the economic argument to incline heavily, perhaps even decisively, against the proposal.[60]

As we have seen, economists did not take seriously the fears of a slide in values at the time of a levy, except as an irrational result.

And so even when any socialist purpose or character was removed from the levy and it was seen simply as a way of shifting burdens from future to current savings, from more to less strategic forms of wealth, a question of political balance still remained. How much could tolerably be handed over to the *rentier* capitalist from the active producer? There was no precise answer to this. Even when the capital levy scheme appeared to be dead and buried, the fundamental problem was as alive as ever. Churchill when Chancellor of the Exchequer saw the debt and associated taxation as a 'vast wet blanket across the whole process of creating new wealth by new enterprise', and he was worried that a 'really well-argued political campaign' to get rid of that burden would be difficult to answer.[61] Stamp felt that only the fact that the revenue from direct taxation slightly outweighed the expenditure on debt interest prevented it from becoming 'a very serious question indeed'.[62]

The striking of the balance was not a purely statistical one but a matter of qualitative judgement. Put quite simply, economic opinion was willing to accommodate the unreasoning fears of the City about credit and accumulated wealth, and yet was adamant in overriding business opinion about the impact of taxation upon industry. Within 'economic opinion' there was a convergence between those operating from a Marshallian perspective (albeit misinterpreted) and those from a proto-Keynesian one which argued that business was resilient to existing taxation, even though businessmen insisted that they were not.

When businessmen claimed in the 1920s that industry was being stifled by heavy taxation (on their salaries and upon undistributed company profits) they meant that the incentive to extend production was diminished.[63] Economists and civil servants – those advising the Chancellors of the Exchequer in replies to deputations of businessmen, and quizzing their representatives before inquiries – argued that, since income tax fell on profits it could not affect the prices of goods. Prices were fixed by competition, and production went on until the last unit contributed no element of profit, and it was this unit which determined prices. Therefore a tax on profits alone could not affect prices or economic behaviour. It would not distort patterns of supply and demand; it could not weaken the incentive to a salaried businessman to seek the highest profit.[64] Industrialists could make little headway against this point of view, and like the property-holders we have examined above, had to fall back on the view that, even if a tax was not in theory injurious it would become so because of the 'psychological' effect.[65] Whereas economists had been reasonably sure that the City's views about a collapse in share values following a levy were not rationally based, because sellers would match buyers, there was some difference of opinion about the impact of taxation on industry. The Cambridge economist D.H. Robertson, for example, argued that the confident repudiation of the businessmen's fears was based on misapplication of the Marshallian theories which were being wheeled into the debate. The costs which entered into the determination of price might well include an element of profit; businessmen might legitimately hold back from extending production in the face of high taxation, and to the extent that some part of the tax was passed on in prices, it would diminish net profits through a fall in demand.[66] But, interestingly, Robertson did not believe that this misapplication of theory should affect the level of taxation: first, because businessmen's expectation might well adapt to new levels of taxation (as in the past they had accommodated the restraints of trade unions and social legislation) and second, because the benefits of a high income tax might outweigh the psychological impact:

> A high income tax, the proceeds of which are devoted partly to debt reduction and partly to measures of public health and education may well have a beneficial effect on the sources of both saving and business enterprise far outweighing any discouraging effect it may exercise on the incentives to display those activities.[67]

Furthermore, the re-evaluation of the role of savings in a depressed economy, which marked off the ideas of Robertson from those of Stamp and of Dalton (where defence of savings was a cornerstone) still pointed in the same direction:

> The time has come to substitute reasoned judgements about what proportion of our national income it is proper for us to save for the blind fear of doing anything which may make that proportion less than it might have been.

Because of this robust view about the resilience of the economy to taxation, the situation anticipated by Keynes – that the pursuit of orthodoxy through deflation would make the payments to war loan holders too burdensome – never arose, even though the burden of the debt and the possibility of a property tax were persistent features of debate in the 1920s. It never arose because the level of income tax was seen as supportable even when, in depressed economic conditions, businessmen said that it was not. It was because of these judgements that the levy was not considered worthwhile, and the 'psychology' of the City deemed worthier of protection than the 'psychology' of business. Because the Labour Party was unwilling to run ahead of opinion, it did not depart from this judgement, even though, in 1931, it paid the heaviest price of all for its neglect of a dilemma of the 1920s. The levy remained therefore, in Cannan's word, 'A jolly good subject for the fat boy who wants to make the flesh creep.'[68]

## *Notes*

1. S. Pollard, *The Development of the British Economy 1914–67* (Edward Arnold, London, 2nd edn, 1973), p. 201. This essay is concerned with the internal debt.

2. A.T.K. Grant, *A Study of the Capital Market in Britain 1919–36* (Cass, London, 1967), pp. 179–180; H. Campion, *Public and Private Property* (Oxford University Press, 1939), p. 105.
3. J.M. Keynes, Lecture to the Institute of Bankers, 5 December 1922, in *The Collected Writings of John Maynard Keynes*, ed. D. Moggridge, (Royal Economic Soceity, 1981), XIX, pp. 47–8 (hereinafter *JMK*). Institutions as well as individuals held war loan, and payments of interest to companies would not necessarily have made their way through to the dividends paid to individual shareholders. But the national debt question was always seen in terms of transfers between individuals. The image of the unadventurous *rentier* would seem to have some substance, to the extent that war loan interest was re-invested in gilt-edged stock. *The Economist*, Stock Exchange Report, 8 December 1923, p. 1018.
4. Letter of 11 April 1916, in Cannan Papers, British Library of Political and Economic Science, 1023, f. 40.
5. For views within the Bank of England, see R.S. Sayers, *The Bank of England 1891 – 1944* (Cambridge University Press, 1976), vol. 1, pp. 113–14.
6. H. Dalton, *Call Back Yesterday* (Muller, London, 1953), p. 128.
7. T. Jones, *Whitehall Diary 1916–25*, ed. K. Middlemas (Oxford University Press, 1969), pp. 114–15. Select Committee on Increase of Wealth (War) (1920), vii. The distinction between the capital levy and war wealth tax is clearly brought out in Dr Mary Short's excellent thesis, 'The Politics of Personal Taxation: budget-making in Britain 1917–31' (Cambridge University PhD., 1985), pp. 68 ff.
8. *JMK*, XIX, p. 62.
9. J.C. Stamp, in evidence before the Macmillan Committee on Finance and Industry, 3 April 1930, q. 3810. On undesirable transfers see, for example, R.G. Hawtrey, *The Economic Problem* (Longmans, London, 1926), pp. 373 ff.
10. Keynes wrote in June 1927 of a 'general tendency to exaggerate the importance of national capital as compared with national income. It is the flow of current income and current savings which really matters.' 'The Colwyn Report on the National Debt and Taxation', in *JMK*, XIX, p. 688.
11. 'The Conscription of Wealth', 1918, in Treasury Papers, Public Record Office (hereinafter PRO), T 171/167.
12. Dalton, *Call Back Yesterday*, p. 128; F.W. Pethick-Lawrence, *Capital Levy* (Labour Party pamphlet, 1920), p. 1.
13. Cannan, to City Editor of *The Times*, 20 February 1924, Cannan Papers, 1028, f. 75.
14. *The Economist*, 15 December 1923, p. 1040.
15. *JMK*, XIX, pp. 63–4.
16. Bernard Mallett to R.H. Brand, 15 February 1924, Brand Papers, Bodleian Library, Box 67. MacDonald's appreciation that, in order to fulfil this purpose, the Committee had to cast its net widely – 'we must bring these people with us, and not enable them to say they were never consulted at all' – makes its material a valuable source for

views about taxation and the economy. MacDonald to Snowden, 14 February 1924, MacDonald Papers, PRO 30/69, 1169, f. 249. W.L. Coates, 'The Labour Surtax', *The Banker*, March 1928, p. 405. For the role of J.H. Thomas in killing the levy, see Short, thesis, pp. 248–49.

17. Royden Harrison, 'The War Emergency National Workers' Committee', in A. Briggs and J. Saville (eds.), *Essays in Labour History 1886–1923* (Macmillan, London, 1971), pp. 251 ff. See also Short, thesis, pp. 38 ff.
18. *Hansard*, 105, col. 894 ff. Arnold was a stockbroker who moved over to the Labour Party in 1922. Opinions about Arnold were affected by views about the levy. Dalton was favourable: 'He [Arnold] has a good deal of useful knowledge on this [the capital levy] and other financial questions and is helping the Party in the House.' But H.W. Massingham, urging MacDonald to drop the levy, warned him against Arnold: 'On the capital levy he is simply a fanatic, he thinks of nothing else, and such men in such moods are not good counsellors.' Dalton, *Diary*, March 1923; Massingham letter 10 November 1923, MacDonald papers, PRO 30/69, 1167, ff.65–7. Illustrations of anxieties elsewhere can be found in Baldwin's presentation of £150,000 of war loan to the government, and later, in the report by Riddell of Lloyd George speaking 'not unsympathetically of the capital levy'. K. Middlemas and J. Barnes, *Baldwin* (Weidenfeld, London, 1969), pp. 72–4; *Lord Riddell's Intimate Diary of the Peace Conference and After 1918–23* (Gollancz, London, 1933), p. 396.
19. G.D.H. Cole to A. Henderson, 28 May and 17 June 1919, J.S. Middleton Papers, Labour Party Archive, Fin/23 and 27.
20. In its 1922 form, the levy would have taken 5 per cent of that part of an individual's estate amounting to £5000 – 6000, rising to 25 per cent of estates of £20,000 – 30,000, and 60 per cent of estates of £1 million or more. The greatest number of estates falling under the levy would have been in the range £10,000 – 25,000, and their owners would have had to surrender 10 – 14 per cent of their wealth. Appendices to Colwyn Committee evidence, XXII, and XXIII, presented by Board of Inland Revenue.
21. See F.Y. Edgeworth, *A Levy on Capital for the Discharge of the National Debt* (Clarendon Press, Oxford, 1919), p. 18; T. Carlyle Gifford, 'Inflation of Credit and a Tax on Capital', in *The Accountants' Magazine*, June 1918, p. 239. Edgeworth was Drummond Professor of Political Economy in Oxford, 1891 – 1922; Gifford was a director in the 1920s, with Keynes, of the Independent Investment Company.
22. For the use of this by the opposition see H. Cox, *The Capital Levy: Its Real Purpose* (The National Unionist Association, London 1923), pp. 68–9. Dalton, *The Capital Levy Explained* (Riverside Press, Edinburgh, 1923), p. 39 n.
23. Dalton, *Colwyn* evidence, qs.6956–58.
24. Stamp, *Colwyn* evidence, q.5201.

25. *Will Capital Leave the Country?* (ILP pamphlet, 1924), p. 12.
26. Dalton, *Colwyn* evidence, q.5494; J.C. Stamp, *Fundamental Principles of Taxation* (Macmillan, London, 1921), pp. 155–65, for the effects of a levy on different patterns of saving.
27. H. Groves, ed. D.J. Curran, *Tax Philosophers: Two Hundred Years of Thought in Great Britain and the United States* (University of Wisconsin Press, Madison, 1974), pp. 64–5.
28. *Fate Has Been Kind* (Hutchinson, London, 1943), p. 34.
29. *Call Back Yesterday*, p. 58.
30. S. Webb, *National Finance and a Levy on Capital* (Labour Party pamphlet, 1919), p. 15.
31. Royal Commission on Income Tax, evidence, (Cmd.288), q.19082 (Miners' Federation) q.6879 (S. Webb); G.W. Carter and H.W. Houghton, 'Income Tax on Wages by Quarterly Assessment', *Economic Journal*, March 1918, pp. 31–2; J. Stamp, 'The Special Taxation of Business Profits in Relation to the Present Position of National Finance', *Economic Journal*, December 1919, p. 409.
32. R.C.O. Matthews, C.H. Feinstein and J.C. Odling-Smee, *British Economic Growth, 1856–1973*, (Oxford University Press, 1982), p. 314. The quotation comes from the Inland Revenue memorandum 'Industry and Taxation', January 1922, in PRO T 172/1230.
33. TUC, *Colwyn* evidence, para. 22, p. 588, qs. 3356, 4948.
34. *The Times*, 20 November 1923. The Cambridge professor was A.C. Pigou in *A Capital Levy and a Levy on War Wealth* (Oxford University Press, 1920); the businessman was W.L. Hichens of Cammell, Laird and Co. in *The Observer*, 8 February 1920.
35. In a review of Stamp's *Studies in Current Problems in Finance and Government* (King, London, 1924) in *Economic Journal*, June 1925, pp. 260–1. See also the assessment by J.M. Mogey in *International Encyclopaedia of the Social Sciences* (Collier-Macmillan, USA, 1968), 15, pp. 142–3; and the biography by J.H. Jones, *Josiah Stamp: Public Servant* (Pitman, London, 1964).
36. 'The Christian Ethic and Economics' in *Criticism and Other Addresses* (Benn, London, 1931), p. 79.
37. 'Special Taxation', p. 411; Hobson, *Colwyn* evidence, qs. 1647–9.
38. 18 November 1919, in JSM/Fin/50.
39. Cannan to Hartley Withers, editor of *The Economist*, 17 September 1917, Cannan Papers, 1023, f. 89; J. Bradbury, 'The Conscription of Wealth', 1918, in PRO T 171/167.
40. *The Economist*, 12 June 1920, p. 1281.
41. *Colwyn*, evidence, qs. 5199–201.
42. *The Case Against a Capital Levy* (Wilson, London, 1918) p. 9.
43. *Colwyn*, evidence, q. 5247.
44. 'A Levy on Capital: Theoretical and Academic Aspects', PRO IR 75/109.
45. In a letter to Beatrice Webb, 10 February 1923, in *Letters of Sydney and Beatrice Webb*. III, eds, N. and J. MacKenzie (Cambridge University Press and LSE, 1978), pp. 169–70.
46. *Colwyn*, evidence, para. 5, p. 105, and q. 7729.

47. Inland Revenue, 'A Levy on Capital'.
48. J.C. Stamp, 'Inheritance as an Economic Factor', *Economic Journal*, September, 1926, p. 356.
49. J.C. Stamp, *Current Problems*, pp. 250–70.
50. *Colwyn*, evidence, q. 7558. Keynes's view rested on the reduction which had already taken place in income tax from 6 shillings [30 p] to 4 shillings [20 p] 1920–25.
51. Dalton, *The Capital Levy Explained*, pp. 80–5.
52. For MacDonald see *The Times*, 24 November 1923; for Snowden and Thomas, the *Yorkshire Post*, 9 November and 4 November 1922.
53. *The Times*, 2 November 1922.
54. *Daily Herald*, 30 October, 6 November 1922; 'Unemployment and the Capital Levy', in the *New Leader*, 3 November 1922.
55. Diary, 15 November 1922, 19 January 1923.
56. Diary, 6 November 1923.
57. *Colwyn*, evidence, para. 2, p. 534.
58. *Colwyn*, evidence, q. 7612; para 4, p. 535.
59. *The Economist*, 17 September 1921, p. 431.
60. 'Proposed Capital Tax in France', Board of Inland Revenue (1919), in PRO IR 63/86. I am grateful to Dr A. Offer for this reference.
61. In a letter to O. Niemeyer, Controller of Finance at the Treasury, 26 January 1927, in M. Gilbert, *Winston S. Churchill, 1922–29, A Companion: the Exchequer Years* (Heinemann, London, 1979), pp. 924–6.
62. J. Stamp, *Financial Aftermath of the War*, (Benn, London, 1932), pp. 126–7.
63. R. Glenday, for the Federation of British Industries, *Colwyn*, evidence, paras. 50 and 56, pp. 350–1, qs. 4772–3, 4850–5.
64. W. Layton, *Colwyn*, evidence, q. 2544; Board of Inland Revenue.
65. Deputation of FBI to Chancellor, after the Report of the Colwyn Committee, 9 March 1927, in PRO T 172/1411. Churchill in reply confessed to 'pricks of scepticism' about the line of argument in the report which suggested that industry was not being unduly harmed by existing levels of taxation.
66. 'The Colwyn Committee, the Income Tax and the Price Level', *Economic Journal*, December 1927, pp. 566–81.
67. p. 580. It should be pointed out that Keynes also did not believe that the level of income tax was a cause of industrial depression. *Colwyn*, Evidence, q. 7578.
68. Cannan to Withers, 17 September 1917, 1023, f. 89. The capital levy issue was not confined to Britain, and taxes on capital were actually levied in Czechoslovakia (1919), Austria (1919), Italy and Germany (1920) and proposed in Switzerland in 1922. While some interest was taken in what was happening abroad, few lessons were drawn, because tax systems there were less developed and more tolerant of the kind of approximate valuations likely under capital taxes than was the case in Britain, where income tax, the 'final stage' in the evolution of taxation, was longer established. The case for a levy in

Britain had to be made without support from continental practice, which gives the whole debate a rather insular appearance.

# 7 The 'Social Psychology' of Unemployment in Interwar Britain

*R. I. McKibbin*

In 1938 P.F. Lazarsfeld and P. Eisenberg published a 'final' statement of the social-psychological theory of unemployment and so completed the only systematic analysis of the effects of unemployment on the individual and the family.[1] The theory suggested that men and women went through 'stages' in their reaction to unemployment from optimism to resignation and despair, and these stages were accompanied by a progressive deterioration in the individual's social and intellectual capacities. Social engagement was succeeded by social withdrawal; political activity by apathy; and mental interests by inertia. Differences of personality and temperament influenced only the timing, not the progression of the stages. Here I shall examine how far the literature available to Lazarsfeld supports such a theory. I have used only that material cited by Lazarsfeld and Eisenberg in their 1938 article or which was otherwise accessible to them, together with some more recent work when that does not seem anachronistic; and I have ignored the problem of physical deterioration with which the psychological literature was only obliquely concerned.[2]

## *I*

The theory was elaborated in three remarkable publications of which the most celebrated was the first, *Die Arbeitslosen von Marienthal* (1933), written by Marie Jahoda, Paul Lazarsfeld and Hans Zeisel.[3] Marienthal was a small industrial village about 30 km from Vienna whose workforce, entirely dependent on a textile mill which closed in 1929, was almost completely unemployed by 1930. The team, all social psychologists from the University of Vienna, attempted a 'total' study of the lives of the unemployed and this they did by an imaginative and eclectic technique of personal observation, sample budgets and diets, autobiographies, essay competitions for schoolchildren and questionnaires. It was the single most influential study of the unemployed of the interwar years.

The second, by Lazarsfeld and Zawardski, is the most striking, if also the most eccentric.[4] In 1930–31 the Institute of Social Economy in Warsaw published 57 autobiographies of unemployed men. The autobiographies, of which there were many hundreds, had been elicited by competition. The contributors were asked to record the course of their daily lives; the management of the household budget; the diet of the family; the effect of unemployment on health. The most vivid autobiographies alone were accepted; 'colourless' ones were excluded.[5]

The third was the Lazarsfeld–Eisenberg article of 1938, a bibliographical piece which attempted to collect and make sense of the international literature on unemployment. These two concluded that

> all writers . . . seem to agree on the following points. First there is shock, which is followed by an active hunt for a job, during which the individual is still optimistic and unresigned . . . Second, when all efforts fail, the individual becomes pessimistic, anxious and suffers active distress; this is the most crucial state of all. And third, the individual becomes fatalistic and adapts himself to his new state but with a narrower scope. He now has a broken attitude.[6]

Lazarsfeld was part-author of all three publications and it was thus not accidental that 'all writers' conformed almost exactly to the findings of *Marienthal* and Zawardski–Lazarsfeld.[7] Thus Jahoda *et al* divided their families into four categories: 'unbroken', 'resigned', 'in despair' and 'apathetic'.[8] The great majority (70 per cent) were 'resigned'. Families did not react in different ways, rather, they progressed from hope to despair and these were 'stages' through which all, or nearly all, must go. Zawardski–Lazarsfeld detected six stages:

> (1) As a reaction to dismissal, there comes generally a feeling of injury; sometimes strong fear and distress; sometimes an inpulse towards revenge; hatred, indignation; fury. (2) Thereafter comes a stage of numbness and apathy which is gradually (3) Replaced by calming down and an increase in steadiness, bringing one again to a relative mental balance. This mental stage is characterized by a resumption of activity; the unemployed become calm as they see that things go along somehow and adapt themselves to circumstances; they trust in God, fate, or in their own ability, and try to believe that the situation will improve very soon. (4) But this hope becomes constantly weaker, when they see the futility of effort. (5) When the situation becomes harder, the old savings and new sources exhausted, then comes the hopelessness which expresses itself at first in attacks of fear . . . (6) After these outbreaks comes either sober acquiescence or dumb apathy and then alternation between hope and hopelessness, activity and passivity, according to the momentary changes in the material situation.[9]

These conclusions anticipated those of Lazarsfeld–Eisenberg in 1938. 'From our biographies', Zawardski and Lazarsfeld argued in 1935, 'it appears that the basic attitudes stated in . . . *Die Arbeitslosen von Marienthal* namely: the *unbroken*, the *resigned*, the *distressed*, and the *apathetic*, can be seen clearly in our material, a fact indicating that these basic conceptions are sound.'[10] That a 'stage' theory of unemployment should have emerged fully formed in 1938 was, therefore, not surprising. Although Lazarsfeld later had some doubts about its conceptual sohpistication,[11] Professor Jahoda has not,[12] and, as Kelvin and Jarrett comment, 'a notion which was little more than an afterthought in *Marienthal* has since become a basic concept in accounts of the psychological effects of unemployment.'[13]

This theory argues one other proposition: that is, the fundamental importance to people's lives of formal work. Not only does worklessness lead to intellectual and social disintegration, but, by abolishing a sense of time, particularly for men, it makes life aimless, and 'demoralises' the unemployed individual. Furthermore, demoralisation undermines the capacity or the desire to seek work and renders the unemployed helpless to devise alternative structures. Apathetic men and women cannot generate new routines because these demand personal autonomy and self-dependence. The theory thus describes an emotional progression through which the unemployed seemed fated to go: a social fact – unemployment – becomes transformed into a universally observable series of mental states.

The stage-theory, partly because it is the only psychological theory of unemployment, has been very influential,[14] perhaps more in the United States – the Lynds' *Middletown in Transition* was clearly affected by it[15] – than in Britain.[16] But even in Britain it directly stimulated one of the most important studies of interwar unemployment, Beales and Lambert's *Memoirs of the Unemployed*. 'The idea of collecting the present volume of *Memoirs*', they wrote in its Introduction, 'arose as a result of the experiments which certain continental countries have begun to make in the investigation of the psychological effects of unemployment.' Specifically, they note the Polish autobiographies and the work of 'a group of Viennese psychologists'. The evidence thus collected 'at these two different sources bears sufficient marks of similarity to show that the subject is worth pursuing in our own country'.[17] In the event, the memoirs were decidedly ambiguous in their implications, and the authors made no real attempt to impose a pattern on them; it would, none the less, not have been difficult to have extracted a stage-theory from the material. If true, the theory could explain much of the apparent behaviour of the unemployed in interwar Britain: political quiescence, geographical immobility and a widely observed languor in personal and collective life; very indirectly, if true, it might even support the more extreme neoclassical interpretations of unemployment. How far does the evidence support such a theory?

## *II*

To begin with, there was nothing particularly startling in this description of unemployment: it was the plain man's view and seemed to cohere with experience. In 1911 Rowntree and Lasker recorded that

> even men of strong character tell us how exceedingly difficult it is to resist this demoralisation . . . [The unemployed] suffer psychically because of the depression amounting to acute despair, which comes after days and weeks spent in tramping the streets and meeting with nothing but disappointments and refusals.[18]

It was what many unemployed felt. 'A young casual labourer in London' told Beales and Lambert that he and his unemployed 'chums'

> usually play draughts or dominoes. We are just about able to play games like those, which don't require much thought. You stop and talk in the middle, and in any case the games never last very long. Card games want too much patience and attention.

He was interested in football when in work but 'I have not been to a match for years and don't feel much interested in reading up the sports news. . . . Besides the results seem to matter so little to me.'[19] Max Cohen felt the same inertia. His brother-in-law kept urging him to join organisations: but in his 'unhealthy state of mind' he felt unable to.[20] Even when some sort of routine was established people were conscious of a slippery slope. 'I was one of a gang', a young unemployed man from Lancashire wrote:

> We used to stay in bed late in the mornings so as not to need breakfast. I used to have a cup of tea, and then we would all go down to the library and read the papers. Then we went home for a bit of lunch, and then we met again at the billiard hall where you could watch the play for nothing. Then back for tea and to watch the billiards again. In the evening we all used to go to the pictures. That was how we spent the dole money. In the end I thought I'd go mad if I went on like that.[21]

'Deterioration' or 'demoralisation' was nearly always noticed by outsiders, however amateur or professional was their acquaintance with the unemployed. Ruth Durant, in her study of the new LCC estate at Watling, thought that the 'depression of 1929' more or less finished off what little communal life there was, just when it was most needed: 'People were too worried to develop social interests, and often too tired to seek entertainment.'[22] The well-known Save the Children Fund Study argued that parental neglect of children – late waking, sending children to school without breakfast – 'may be symptomatic of a gradual change of character. Inertia and lack of vitality among some of the unemployed are a common story among the answers to the questionnaire'.[23] The London social worker, S.F. Hatton, described the phenomenon in terms an Edwardian would have recognised:

> Three or four months on the streets, and what difference there is in the appearance and the general attitude of the lad. From the bright, keen youngster eager to work and make his way in the world, he rapidly declines into a lazy, livery street lounger.[24]

Even so pragmatic a sociologist as A.D.K. Owen saw 'stages'. After a man's repeated failure to find a job 'a fatalistic stage appears to be reached during which many men are ready to turn to some new interest sometimes with great enthusiasm. But often as not apathy and listlessness have by this time obtained a stronghold.'[25]

If the professionals thought this it was almost inevitable that the interested observer should have done so as well. Everyman's view was well represented by Beveridge's evidence to the 1930 Royal Commission on Unemployment Insurance.

> I think [he was asked] you have frequently in your Memorandum used the word 'demoralisation'? – Yes. Do you think that it is an inevitable sort of cause and effect – so many months unemployment, so much demoralisation? – No, I do not think there is any mathematical relation; obviously there is not. But I should think that it was absolutely inevitable that you cannot go on being idle indefinitely without becoming less fit for work – beyond a certain point that is clear. . . . I am not blaming the men, but we all know you cannot be idle for two or three years without losing some of your taste for work, or without losing interest in life – none of us can be.[26]

It must be said that Everywoman was not far behind. 'Personally, I would prefer to write a book than to be absolutely unemployed and I should be very disconcerted if I had not a book to write,' Mrs Sidney Webb said:

> But directly you get to the young person in whom you have actually encouraged the habit of not working, of course he prefers not to work. Most people at some time, and some people at all times, prefer to lounge rather than to work . . . I know nothing more melancholy, than the sight of idle young men in the mining villages of South Wales and Durham, with their listless unoccupied look. You can see that many of them will obviously take to bad practices . . . It is a terrible, an awful tragedy.[27]

As evidence this tells us as much about the progressive classes as about the unemployed but it also demonstrates how well entrenched a stereotype of unemployment was.

Like all stereotypes, it was as much ideologically determined as based upon observation, though at one level it was a not unreasonable description. It was the nature of worklessness to drive unemployed men (but not unemployed women) out of doors and this was as true of an area of high casual but low long-term unemployment like Greenwich as one of very high long-term unemployment like Brynmawr. E. Wight Bakke thought that the streets, even more than the cinemas, were where the unemployed spent their spare time. And the streets meant 'loafing', or such was the impression which outsiders formed of what the unemployed actually did. Furthermore, the men did not seem to talk together. An 'outstanding feature' of loafing in Greenwich was the silence:

> Men stood alone more often than in groups. The young men were more sociable; so were the older men who, I suppose, were pensioners. The middle-aged men were perfectly willing to talk, when I approached them, but more often than not I found them alone.[28]

It seemed the same in Brynmawr. When not visiting the Labour Exchange, Hilda Jennings wrote,

> some men stand aimlessly on the Market Square or the street corners content apparently with a passive animal existence, or with the hour-long observation of passers-by, varied by an occasional whiff at a cigarette.[29]

This was the public face of unemployment, either in Greenwich and Brynmawr or in Marienthal, where observers concealed themselves behind curtained windows so as to measure the pace at which the unemployed idled up the street.[30] As much as bookies or dockers the unemployed had their stands. They gathered in public libraries, labour exchanges, outside football matches, lolled on street corners and leant against lamp-posts. Lamp-posts, indeed, became one of the folk-myths of unemployment; even absorbed into the gallows humour of the unemployed themselves. Thus one workless rural carpenter thought the lot of the town unemployed almost enviable: they 'have at least got lamp-posts . . . to loll up against.'[31] To some the unemployed simply resembled old cars: J.A. Newrick of the Iron and Steel Trades Confederation commended trades-based exchanges on the grounds that their use stopped the unemployed 'standing at the streets and deteriorating'.[32] The view that the unemployed lounged about looking aimless, that they seemed 'listless' and 'apathetic' and that this was a 'demoralised' condition, was, therefore, to some extent factually grounded. That is what unemployment must have looked like to those who were not unemployed. The *Marienthal* conclusions were in part a systematic account of what was apparent. In fact, it was a misleading view and once known to be so. In 1909 Chapman and Hallsworth, describing Edwardian loafers, had concluded that 'they flock to the towns where relief funds are being dispersed, hang on to street processions, and being always in evidence . . . *confound public opinion about the nature of the problem of unemployment*'.[33] Since the stereotype was also an ideological one that was one of the lessons of history people rarely learnt.

## *III*

But the unemployed were not lounging 24 hours a day, and when they were lounging, they did not all lounge at once. Much of the life of the workless was concealed from the public and the evidence which supports 'demoralisation' is actually very intractable. Lazarsfeld and his colleagues, however, did try to go beyond appearances. 'Demoralisation', they argued, showed itself in four ways: in the disintegration of daily routines, in an inability to devise alternative 'work', in the progressive collapse of intellectual interests and in the abandonment of direct political activity. Let us examine these.

First routines. It seems obvious that unemployment will disrupt routines established in work; in practice, it is not so obvious. For casual labourers whose work was intermittent anyway, it was likely that routines were always flexible. For skilled workers, experiencing both first-time and long-term unemployment, the *initial* effects could have been disorienting. Sinfield found that men never before workless 'will often be very eager to talk about the injustice and outrage'; in contrast 'the unskilled man in his forties, now in his second or third spell out of work this year, may be laconic to the extent of disconcerting the most experienced interviewers'.[34]

In fact, after the first shock when men might show signs of going to pieces, routines of a sort were re-established. 'Signing on' at the labour exchange twice a week was obligatory and changeless: then, even in areas where it was usually pointless, there was the business of finding a job. As Bakke noted, 'hunting a job is the "job" of the unemployed worker'.[35] He calculated that the average Greenwich man spent 4–5 hours a day looking for one. This was a fairly inflexible procedure; skilled men went as far afield as the cheap tram would take them; unskilled men as far as they could walk. Much of the apparent aimlessness of unemployed life was due to the fact that unskilled men often looked for jobs in an aimless way. Skilled men had better contacts, and pen and paper.[36] In the 1970s Sinfield found that amongst the unemployed he interviewed it was

> very evident that there is no single 'right way' to look for work and what is seen as luck has often tended to dominate the job-search. . . . This helps to account for the fatalistic attitude expressed by many men without skills.[37]

But that they were fatalistic did not stop them seeking work; they merely looked purposeless while doing it. Furthermore, this kind of unrewarding 'job' made men very tired, and tiredness was easily mistaken for apathy.[38]

If anything, such new routines were too inflexible. Max Cohen remembered the week being divided into 'more or less rigid periods';[39] a 'longing for something diverting, exciting and stimulating, constantly torments the one unemployed'.[40] In some cases the frantic anxiety to find a job could disrupt routines established after the loss of work. Marsden cites the example of 'Mr Vickers' whose 'work' in his garden-shed, which was very important to him, fell apart as his 'obsession' about joblessness became more severe.[41] Max Cohen, though he found life on the dole 'unendurable',

> had at any rate settled into a sort of routine. I had become established in a definite lodging. I had become acquainted with different people, had even begun to strike up friendships here and there. And then I had shattered all the slowly built up edifice and cast the pieces away, in order to migrate to Newslum to get a job.[42]

Many women simply continued old routines or had new

routines imposed on them. If they were married domestic duties expanded to fill the day; if unmarried and living at home much the same happened. Single women living away from home, about whom we know little, may have been more disorientated than anybody.[43] 'Hunting a job' became a routine because there was no diminution of the desire for work. The stage-theory is ambiguous here; Lazarsfeld appears to have believed that demoralisation on the one hand and the dole on the other inhibited job-search. Many classical and neoclassical economists, of course, have argued that the dole almost infinitely prolonged job-search.[44] None, however, of the contemporary 'sociological' evidence to which either Lazarsfeld or the economists might have had recourse supported this. Every Ministry of Labour study of the period denied it.[45] Neither the Blanesburgh Committee (1925–27) nor the Holman Gregory Commission (1930–32) received any convincing evidence that it was so and much positive evidence that it was not. R. C. Davison, who knew the unemployed well, thought the danger was not that men would not seek work but that they would too readily degrade skill – the real point at issue: 'unemployed men are themselves really eager to work, at wages even below their own usual standards.'[46] J. J. Astor's committee went out of its way to dismiss the notion that job-search was either prolonged or non-existent:

> The anxiety of the individual to get back to work, attested by employers, Employment Exchange officials, trade union secretaries, and the individual workmen whom our investigators interviewed, that flocking after the bare report of a job of which they discovered many instances, the application of the men on relief work to which they were unaccustomed . . . are all evidence to the contrary.[47]

What was probably true was that men became reluctant to do small jobs for fear that they would be reported to the exchanges; but that is because the dole was too mean, not too generous. Bakke thought the dole, by keeping body and soul together, actually facilitated job-search, and he concluded that without it men and women would have starved in exactly the same places where they just scraped by with it.[48] Thus, even in areas where looking for a job was often futile new routines were apparent. This is not to suggest they were satisfactory substitutes for work; simply that there *were* new routines and that people retained a surprising hold over life.

Second: were the unemployed willing to find substitutes for ordinary work? The stage-theory suggests not; it does so not on grounds of poverty – that the unemployed were simply too poor to afford alternative work, which might be a fair proposition – but on grounds of 'demoralisation'. After a certain point people did not *want* alternative work. *Marienthal* noted as an example of this the unemployed's loss of interest in allotments and in rabbit-breeding, both once enthusiastically followed.[49] But the evidence from Britain cannot support this.

To start, for most unemployed women finding alternatives was not a problem. They either had to or were expected to continue household work; how they reacted depended partly on temperament and on the demands of the home. For some, unemployment could be liberating while for others a disaster. A conventional division of labour often doubled the miseries; men would not do housework and had to find other ways to kill time, while women could not, therefore, get relief from domestic duties which unemployment might otherwise have procured them.[50] The position of single women living away from home is unclear. Caradog Jones concluded that 'hobbies seem . . . to be unknown among women and artistic pursuits are rarely followed by female manual workers'.[51] They were, however, according to the Pilgrim Trust, more gregarious than unemployed men and this may have mitigated the isolating effects of unemployment. The remarkable success of (say) the 'keep fit' movement among women had no male equivalent. But for many single women manual workers unemployment could have been desolating, not because of 'demoralisation' but because of the material and cultural impoverishment of their ordinary life.

As to men, where alternative work was available they did it. This had probably always been so. The Rowntree and Lasker diaries suggest that for unemployed skilled workers hobbies and home repair could be therapeutic. One of their sample wrote that when he returned home at night 'foot-sore with tramping about all day' he often found that

> some little item wanted attention, one in particular being the chimney, which was causing us annoyance with smoking very badly. So, on making a careful inspection, I found a soot-door in the attic which no doubt was for cleaning purposes, and naturally I grasped the idea at once; and after carefully covering the fireplace I took some water and poured it through the soot-door, which I am proud to say had the desired effect.[52]

A 'skilled millwright' told Beales and Lambert that 'though there is nothing I can do to keep myself efficient', he liked to do 'odd jobs, like mending boots, chopping up boxes for firewood and repairing things'.[53] Even in down-at-heel Brynmawr men worked where they could; they 'work on allotment or garden, tend fowls or pigs, or do carpentry in their backyard or kitchen, making sideboards out of orange boxes'.[54]

For many men gardens and allotments were obviously a godsend; how far they created an 'alternative life' out of them partly depended on how far they had previously been absorbed in their work. Of the saving value of gardens to those who had them there seems little doubt. Walter Brierley's unemployed miner 'Jack' hated winter and even spring since he could do

> nothing but walk around the garden; everything was in but nothing yet ready for coming out. . . . He would be glad when the early potatoes were ready so that he could stay in the garden for whole mornings or whole afternoons . . . When he worked at the pit he could finish the garden in a month and only work in it in the evenings and on the occasional holidays . . . gardening had then never been a delight in itself . . . But for the last two springs he had almost been too slow, too careful.[55]

Terence Young noted the popularity of allotments amongst the unemployed on the LCC estate at Becontree.[56] The Pilgrim Trust believed that the unemployed Durham miner 'had not a perpetual sense of grievance, but . . . rather a determination to make the best of things; to make his allotment or his poultry holding a life for himself.'[57] In the Special Areas 'they are to a large extent providing a fairly full "alternative life" for younger men.'[58]

It is unlikely that for many men make-work adequately stood in for ordinary work, though it might for some.[59] For older men, particularly those who had a long history of continuous skilled or semi-skilled work, an intensification of hobbies was probably never adequate. One unemployed man, who had a wide range of hobby interests, wrote that 'sports and pastimes banish depression whilst they are taking place but when I get to bed at night, I lay and imagine every silly possible thing that may happen.'[60] The problem was that make-work activities usually lacked association; very few, as Kelvin notes, 'demand the interdependence, on a continuing basis, which is of the essence of most work relationships'.[61] None the less, where circumstances made access to alternative work possible, the unemployed took the chance and were anxious to do so.

If this is right, it seems likely that *Marienthal*'s conclusions about the intellectual interests of the unemployed are, as a rule, equally suspect. Jahoda *et al* used as their principal index the increasing reluctance of the unemployed to read newspapers and books, even when public library charges were either abolished or reduced, and a growing readiness to occupy themselves with passive pastimes, like going to the cinema: 'one can mention in this connection the well-known fact that people unsuccessful in their search for a job usually end by going to a movie'.[62] It would be surprising if some of this were not true and evidence can be mobilised to support it. The Marienthal data on newspaper and book reading have to be accepted, and the objection that poverty alone might explain them can probably be discounted.[63] Indeed, the cinema, like the lamp-post, was part of folk-wisdom. The cinema, Bakke thought, was the 'most prominent feature of the spare-time activity of the employed and unemployed alike'.[64] Of Brynmawr Hilda Jennings wrote: 'at nights, there are the pictures, and the long queues outside the "Picture House" probably account for more of the "pocket-money" of the unemployed than do the public houses.'[65]

In fact, again, much British evidence did not support *Marienthal*. It did not suggest that the unemployed 'read' less than they did previously; if anything they read more. A Welsh miner thought the one thing that kept him 'from doing something desperate' was that he now read a lot.[66] Another of the Beales and Lambert autobiographers, a millwright, wrote: 'I read a lot more and enjoy it; I buy the *Daily Herald* and borrow as many other papers and magazines as I can, and I am able to borrow books from the county library.'[67] Bakke argued that unemployed workers read at least as much as they previously had and that newspaper reading had probably risen.[68] On Merseyside at the height of unemployment, 'it has been usual to find the reading-rooms full all day of unemployed men'.[69] The rooms were warm, free, they possessed the newspapers and the newspapers contained positions vacant columns and (where censorious librarians had not excised them) the racing results. The scene in a principal Liverpool library was typical of much of urban Britain:

> Some [unemployed men] come to look for vacancies in the newspapers; others read trade and technical papers, detective stories or magazines. Three of those reading rooms have a special arrangement by which urgent vacancies for workers are reported to them by telephone from the Employment Exchange and are posted up.[70]

Like the labour exchanges they were markets of gossip but since they were also where books reposed, books were often read. They were ideal for someone like this embittered engineer who thought only of 'warm sheltered places like the public library, where I like to read revolutionary novels'.[71] For both cultural and economic reasons the library in Marienthal did not perform these functions with, presumably, the consequences Jahoda *et al* record.

As to the cinema, it is unlikely that the unemployed went to it any more than they did when in work. The Pilgrim Trust's survey, indeed, seemed to show that unemployed men in the large towns went to the pictures less than they used to;[72] and Bakke, though he admitted that skilled workmen were very reluctant to abandon the cinema, thought they would do so if they had to. Like Jennings, he believed the unemployed were more likely to desert the pub than the picture palace.[73] The important point, however, is simply that cinema-attending was a very popular working-class pastime; that the unemployed continued going showed nothing except that they wanted to do what they had always done.[74]

Equally, what constitutes intellectual interests depends

partly upon cultural definitions. The pervasiveness of racing-talk and betting amongst the unemployed was noticed by everybody but whether it was regretted or not depended on *a priori* assumptions. One assumption, argued specifically by Zawardski and Lazarsfeld, was that the passion for betting was a 'pathological' consequence of unemployment.[75] To the unemployed the future was dominated by fortune; the best a man could hope for was good luck. Bakke also thought this: 'The worker sees all about him experienced and skilled men with no work to do. If he is in work, he feels lucky. If he is out of work he is the victim of hard luck.'[76] It is not surprising if the unemployed thought good luck as likely to find a man a job as anything else, since in many places clearly it was. It is doubtful, however, if betting can be explained in the same way. I have argued elsewhere that betting, both for the employed and the unemployed, *was* an intellectual activity where the minimising of luck was part of the satisfaction.[77] Furthermore, if, as to many unemployed they were, the operations of the labour exchange appeared random and vindictive, it was not 'irrational' to trust in fortune's smiles. One employed man 'actually drew a contrast between the fairness of the pools and the alleged favouritism of the Exchange'.[78]

Betting had another obvious function. It allowed physical and emotional excitement when comparative poverty deprived people of other 'stimulation'. Max Cohen thought that people's 'stamina' was 'undermined' when they were denied stimulants, tea and cigarettes in his case: 'Anyone who is deprived of a stimulant to which he has become accustomed suffers, in the early stages, at any rate, from a weakening of the faculties.'[79] Betting might also have helped to compensate for the loss of what was politely called 'romantic' interests, something the unemployed felt keenly but about which it was still thought not nice to enquire.[80] In fact, the appeal of betting to the unemployed was straightforward: it was culturally sanctioned, it permitted a genuine intellectual activity and it induced physical excitement.

The last and most important of the stage-theory's conclusions concern the political activities and associationalism of the unemployed. The authors of *Marienthal* measured the unemployed's growing disinclination to retain, let alone seek membership of clubs and organisations, and a diminution of both political activity and partisanship.[81] They concluded that this was accompanied by a disintegration of ideological solidarity. Zawardski and Lazarsfeld wrote:

> This fact of the disassociation of feelings of solidarity among the proletarians, the shift in class consciousness, the split in the masses, *explains the weakness of the unemployed as a mass: the masses cease to exist as such when the social bond – the consciousness of belonging together – does not hold any longer*. There remain only scattered loose, perplexed, and hopeless individuals. *The unemployed are a mass only numerically, not socially*.[82]

The unemployed's explanation for their plight is thus individualistic and not structural. Their anger was directed not against capitalism or 'the system' but against the lucky, those in work.[83]

As a description, much of this was true. Not only did trade union membership decline (which could, however, be explained on a number of grounds) but there appears to have been considerable hostility to the unions among the unemployed: largely because they seem helpful only to those in work. The Beales and Lambert autobiographies are eloquent here. A South Wales miner, asking himself what effect unemployment had on him, replied:

> It has definitely lessened my interest in politics, because it has led me to believe that politics is a game of bluff and that these people do not care a brass farthing for the bottom dog. . . . The same applies to the trade unions; when it comes to a real test they are hopeless.[84]

A 'skilled millwright' said he 'had no wish to attend political meetings',[85] an unskilled labourer was simply 'not interested in politics'.[86] Furthermore, some unemployed or their families might well have directed their bitterness against the employed, as did the wife of Walter Brierley's hero.[87]

The stage-theory argues, in effect, that the unemployed have no politics. The elimination of political interests is no doubt gradual but it is inexorable: the last stage of unemployment extinguishes the last flickerings of political enthusiasm. This is the conventional wisdom and a good deal of the literature has attempted to explain why the unemployed were so apolitical. But *everyone* has a politics. The question is not why the unemployed were apolitical but whether their politics was appropriate to their circumstances.

In brief, beyond wanting employment, the political aims of the unemployed in Britain were twofold: to defend personal privacy and to maintain unemployment benefit. The theatre of their politics was the labour exchange and its agents were the claimants, the clerks, the supervisors, the interviewing officers, the court of referees and the 'means test man'. The exchanges themselves were politically contentious; however benignly they behaved they were regarded by the unemployed as enemy territory. The first reason for that was material; being under-financed the exchanges were grim and shabby. To the unemployed these impressions were powerful and unforgettable. 'The inside of the Exchange was dingy and repellant to the eye,' Max Cohen remembered. 'There appeared to be a large number of notices forbidding one to do this and warning one of the penalties of doing that.'[88] The Ministry of Labour was aware of this. 'We are not at all proud of the premises we are in,' J. F. G. Price told Margaret Bondfield, 'and we are always doing our best, without being extravagant, to get more suitable accommodation for our work. Some of our premises are certainly not a credit to us.'[89] On the whole, they remained not a credit to them for another forty years. Though men and women usually adjusted, despite their fears, to the dole queue and real or imagined stigmas, to the horrors of the exchanges themselves, they hardly ever adjusted:

> Well, it's the way they treat you, somehow. It's the way the chairs are arranged. You go in and you sit down on a chair and you find its bolted down to the floor and you can't move it. And when you come up to the counter, if you want to speak to the guy you've got to sit forward on the edge of your chair, and he's behind a little window, and he says 'Speak up' . . . I don't mind them messing me about, but the trouble is there are some genu-ine claimants up there, and they get messed about as well.[90]

The second reason was the individuals they had to deal with. The clerks at the exchanges were in an impossible position. They were under constant pressure from on high (as they are still) to detect abuse and this could become almost obsessional.[91] Before the abolition of the 'genuinely seeking work' clause in 1930 the unemployed were subject to 'a futile and sometimes brutal ritual' in which few believed.[92] After 1931 new discriminations were introduced, *inter alia* the means test, even more resented. The result was that however helpful or willing were the overworked clerks, however well intentioned the supervisors and means test officers, however fair the courts of referees, they all were servants of 'them', all trying to do down the unemployed. Unemployed men particularly were disposed to regard the exchanges as hostile from the outset, even if for the great majority most of the time the collection of benefit was automatic.

> If he has been out of work for some time, [Jennings wrote] each Friday he will have a short period of sickening anxiety lest the clerk should single him out and tell him he is to be sent to the 'Court of Referees'; then will follow a few days' consequent dread lest his benefit should be stopped and he be cast on to the Poor Law, have to do 'task work' for his maintenance, and take home less to his family in return for it.[93]

The clerks themselves did not help – 'pleasantness soon wears off when forty to fifty men step up to [his] box every fifteen minutes.'[94] Their permanently interrogatory air accounts for their unpopularity.

> And the bloody blokes [Bakke records one man saying] wouldn't have their jobs if it wasn't for us men out of a job either. That's what gets me about holding their noses up.
>
> They treat you like a lump of dirt they do. I see a navvy reach across the counter and shake one of them by the collar the other day. The rest of us felt like cheering.[95]

The dislike of the unemployed for the interviewing officers (who investigated claims of dubious eligibility) and the courts of referees was probably more justified. The interviewing officers, even more than the clerks, were on the hunt for scroungers; success on the job was measured by disallowed claims. Bakke noted of the officers

> There is an altogether disproportionate sense, on the part of the men connected with the interviewing with whom I came in touch, of their ability to 'size up' their man by a sort of intuition. It was a significant fact to me that the source of satisfaction which seemed to be most prominent was the ability to detect the 'non-genuine' cases rather than the ability to be really helpful to a man in his search for work.[96]

The result was that the unemployed person was ready for war if summoned before the officer. 'He goes in a defensive state of mind prepared to engage in a battle of wits.'[97] The unemployed responded with considerable ingenuity. What a particular officer wanted to hear was quickly transmitted down the line and successive 'candidates' met him with increasing confidence.

The unemployed were most likely to come before the court of referees when they went on to transitional benefit. For the state this marked an important boundary; for the men and women it signified only that all insurance contributions had been exhausted. The court was supposed to discover whether the claimant was in practice seeking work. Neither court nor claimant actually knew what was meant by that; whether (say) a skilled worker *should* accept unskilled labour. Furthermore, the courts were overburdened, ill-informed about the applicant, and composed of people whose acquaintance with the life of the unemployed was, to say the least, second-hand.[98] The unemployed approached the court as

> *an individual* who during the last quarter was the same man with the same qualifications and the same worth, save for the very important fact that at the moment he is not able to show thirty stamps on his cards during the last two years.[99]

He thus bore the courts the same hostility he bore the interviewing officers and adopted the same tactics. As to the means test officers, little needs saying. However many individual officers were found helpful and pleasant, as representatives of a system which intruded humiliatingly into working-class privacy they were hated.

The third reason for the dislike of the exchanges was their failure as exchanges. Throughout the 1930s only about one-fifth of adult vacancies were filled through them. There seems little doubt that the unemployed lacked faith in them as places to find work; a scepticism shared by those many employers who made no attempt to use them. The result was, as Llewellyn Smith observed, that the

> unemployed worker who relies on the Exchange becomes disheartened . . . Sometimes even the Exchange appears to him as an obstruction standing between him and a job.

'The Labour Exchange is closing down to-day
And father's going to work to-morrow morning'
is the refrain of a popular East End song.[100]

The exchanges became simply instruments for state hand-outs; normally given but (it appeared) grudgingly, and by hostile officials able to withdraw them at whim. The attitude of the unemployed to the exchanges was, therefore, almost wholly negative; *pro tanto* so was their attitude to similar government agencies and to philanthropic bodies such as the National Council for Social Service. The Pilgrim Trust study, written under the influence of the National Council, admitted that the 'queue' created an unemployed 'community' and generated a powerful 'opinion':

> Evidently the unemployed clubs are in many places the subject of unemployed gossip in the queue, and the frequency with which the laconic criticism 'dope' is made against them, suggested that it was also an idea originating in this way. It looks as if many of the unjustified views of the Unemployment Assistance Board regulations are derived from the same source. Many unemployed men, for instance conceal small occasional earnings for which no deductions would be made from their allowances. The printed leaflet stands little chance against this strong public opinion.[101]

All this was certainly an introverted and local politics but it bears little resemblance to Lazarsfeld's account of the political apathy of the unemployed. It was actively hostile not so much to the general policies of the state – though they also were disliked – as to its agents. Miss Jennings, who thoroughly disapproved of this sectarianism, none the less admitted that it was effective politics:

> For the mass of the unemployed, local politics in South Wales only concentrate their thoughts more firmly on the material problems of their existence. 'Vote Labour, and put an end to poverty, misery, and Courts of Referees' is the popular slogan, not 'Stand together and assert the value of man and his right and duty to express himself by work.'[102]

Its governing dictum was 'always believe the worst' and it was assumed, rightly or wrongly, that the unemployed were engaged in a perpetual struggle to win their due. Four years after writing the *Unemployed Man* Bakke concluded that 'workers who have been without jobs for long periods in all parts of the country begin to look upon the protection of their benefit at a maximum rate as their main object'.[103] Whether you approve of this politics or not depends on what possibilities you think were available to the unemployed. On a pessimistic reading of events it was perfectly appropriate. They were socially and geographically isolated; they were poor or very poor; they were largely excluded from conventional political life, and they were a minority. Nothing they said or did was likely to change overall government policies and if much of their anger was directed at those in work this was not an unreasonable response to a government one of whose implied strategies after 1931 was the attempted mobilisation of those in work against those out of it. The unemployed had few political weapons; one they did have was other people's guilt. Society might not have been ready to create jobs for them but it did not deny all responsibility: the dole was the ransom property was prepared to pay. Furthermore, by localising politics, by confining it to the exchanges and their personnel, the unemployed maintained some command over the political structure of their lives and ensured that psychological tension which is an essential part of successful political action. A more 'revolutionary' politics almost certainly would have failed, and by failing have discredited politics altogether. Even Hannington tacitly recognised this and 'unemployed struggles' became increasingly a struggle to maintain benefit 'at its maximum rate.'[104] The 'uprising' of the unemployed in 1934–35, when the government imposed the new standard rates, the successful way they exploited social guilt, and the speed with which the rates were then withdrawn, shows how correctly they had judged what was politically open to them.

## *V*

What then remains of the stage-theory? Not much. And what can be rescued is largely truistic. There was never any reason to doubt that the lives of most men and women were in some sense work-centred. Nor is it surprising, therefore, that the loss of work could cause dismay and even despair. But it is hard to go beyond that. We cannot convincingly argue that the unemployed disintegrated, that their mental faculties withered, that they lost interest in work, that they became apolitical or that there was some sort of progressive decline. What is surprising, rather, is how little any of these things happened. We are left with a thesis which is at best descriptive, at worst misleading and with almost no explanatory power.

What went wrong? The empirical basis upon which the thesis was built was much too slight. It was difficult to generalise from Marienthal itself. The town had 77 per cent unemployment, high even by depressed area standards, and was small, smaller than Brynmawr. It was unusual in having extremely high rates of both male and female long-term unemployment. In addition, the study was of the residual population. There was no attempt to look at those who had gone to find work in Czechoslovakia or other parts of Austria; nor did the authors make much allowance for the fact that it was a residual survey. *Marienthal* is, therefore, a rather hit-or-miss *description* of a single industry village of exceptionally high long-term unemployment from which limited conclusions can be drawn.

The Polish autobiographies, though they make compelling reading, have negligible value as historical evidence. Their commissioning was itself a dubious enterprise. The sample was not established with any rigour; indeed, almost the reverse is true. The main criterion for selection was the writer's ability to 'express himself'. Although Zawardski and Lazarsfeld admitted their contributors were of the 'higher' strata of the unemployed and perhaps not statistically representative, they contented themselves with the alarming observation that the writers were 'phenomenologically representative': their 'utterances give a vivid picture of the experiences of those who are less able to express themselves'.[105] The result is a collection of autobiographies embodying the more deeply existential experiences of those who wrote them, and little else.

Further, Lazarsfeld and his colleagues had no clear idea of what questions should be asked. Lazarsfeld originally wanted to look at working-class leisure; it was Otto Bauer who put him on to unemployment.[106] But the study was never put in a cultural context; at no point did they ask what the *employed* life of Marienthal had been like. An unemployed community was abstracted from its history and a series of secondary effects described. In part, this was due to the then nature of social psychology. In 1934, the American social psychologist, Hadley Cantril, in a famous article, suggested that the questions the social psychologist should ask of unemployment included: to what extent did it affect the unemployed man's sense of time, personal appearance, attitude to shaving – women did not become unemployed in 1934 it seems – washing, sexual behaviour, reading, etc. These questions, though interesting, all concerned secondary effects.[107] Only an inquiry into the cultural and social circumstances in which the unemployed lived prior to unemployment could make these secondary effects intelligible.

What should the first questions have been? Bakke suggested that the way a man reacted to unemployment was influenced by eleven variables[108] but we probably need to look only at five, recognising that in practice all overlap; income, length of unemployment, degree of skill, the sex of the unemployed person, and (above all) the occupational and associational culture from which the unemployed came.

The first – degree of poverty – was largely overlooked by Lazarsfeld and his colleagues. This was important since the economic conditions of the unemployed differed widely. The workless of Marienthal were paid a dole even after their insurance contribution had been exhausted; the Polish received nothing after 13 weeks. The British unemployed lived under yet a different economic regime, a bit more above the margin, and their preoccupations were thus somewhat different. The ability to cope with unemployment is in part dependent upon existing financial resources; a hungry man, for example, is less fitted to find a job. Even now, as Kelvin and Jarrett point out, it is almost impossible to make 'the crucially important distinction between the effects of unemployment and the effects of the poverty which almost invariably goes with it.'[109] Nowhere was this distinction made adequately and often not at all in the psychological literature of the 1930s.

The second thing we would need to know was a man's experience and expectations. For an unskilled worker whose life was always one job after another even a prolonged period out of work might not seem very unusual; and we should remember that, even at the bottom of the depression, most unemployed were not long-term but typically came on and off the unemployment register. A skilled worker might be buoyed up by the hope that skills give him a premium in the market. However, he could also find unemployment more difficult than that same unskilled worker for whom it was a recurrent fact of life. In Liverpool, the Pilgrim Trust wrote, 'the importance of this must be clear to anyone who knows the sordid but easygoing and sociable atmosphere of the old districts',

> where the unemployed man has his corner, his friends, his library, and his bookmaker, where he speaks freely when you call on him, where he calls his friends in to tell you all about it, where not much is spent on rent and next to nothing on upkeep. Such an atmosphere is utterly different from that in the housing estates, where the unemployed man takes an anxious look round when you mention unemployment to him and rapidly tells you to come in.[110]

For some, usually called 'work-shy' in the literature, the distinction between employment and unemployment hardly even mattered:

> The chances are that he is mixed up with some betting concern, or that he keeps greyhounds, or picks up something here and there in addition to his Unemployment Assistance by hawking or street singing. . . . He may be dressed rather flashily and the chances are that he will complain of those men who won't work, contrasting them with hard triers like himself.[111]

They were like the hard trier interviewed by the Trust, despite a warning that he 'throws culinary articles at his parents, habitually uses filthy language, frequents gambling clubs, and is a bookmaker's tout'. ' "A real clever boy", his mother . . . described him.'[112]

Experience was also affected by skill. The skilled worker was more likely to know the ropes than the unskilled, he was probably more competent at finding a job – by writing letters, for example – and was more likely to have a union to fall back on. Since skilled men were better paid he usually had greater resources at the outset and probably more domestic comfort. He was also in a better position to devise alternative routines; more likely to have a garden or an allotment and his own tools and skills which could be converted. Kelvin and Jarrett's 1981 observation that 'we have . . . occasional fleeting glimpses of unemployed skilled men pursuing skilled activities in garden sheds, of salesmen setting out to sell themselves, of managers making an office of their dining room to manage their search for work and so on'[113] should in principle be true of the interwar years, and much of the evidence suggests that it was. (But we should not exaggerate distinctions between skilled and unskilled; 'unskilled' men could be very flexible and, in certain circumstances, might have been able to cope better than that comparatively small part of the workforce we can properly call 'skilled'.)

Although the psychological literature (and not just the psychological) made little of sex differences, it is clear that women's experience of unemployment could differ widely from that of men. This had little to do with unemployment as such. How women reacted to unemployment was largely dependent upon cultural conventions, of which family status was the most important. For an unemployed woman spinner with an unemployed husband (quite common in Lancashire) and several children receiving perhaps for the first time a comparatively secure needs-related income, unemployment could be a blessing; on the other hand, for a not very sociable single woman living in lodgings, a misery.

Finally, the way people managed unemployment was very largely determined by the life they led before they became unemployed. Lazarsfeld *et al.* were impressed by the rapid decline in the associational *capacity* of the unemployed. But in Britain there is little evidence of this. If men dropped out of clubs, or organisations dissolved, this was due largely either to poverty or to the migration of those normally most active in clubs and societies.[114] If unemployed people were aimless or isolated, this was often because their non-working lives had always been aimless or isolated. The Pilgrim Trust was struck by this: a place like Rhondda ('a hotbed of associations') gave great associational support for the unemployed because it had always led an intense collective life. Liverpool was exactly the reverse. The Trust comments:

> In the case of unemployed men . . . the sample visit suggests strongly that it is not because they spend time going to the cinema or taking part in other commercialised pleasures that in large towns it is so difficult to run effective clubs for them; but rather that in the large towns they live very much emptier lives and that they probably go less often, and not more often to the cinema . . . the real obstacle in the way of building up a good club in a large city is not the competition of commercialised amusements but the lack of any social foundations on which to begin.[115]

This was by no means the only obstacle in the way of an 'effective club' – though the Trust would not admit that – but the general point is almost certainly right. What and how much unemployed people read, went to the pictures, were politically active or joined clubs largely depended on how far they did those things when they were in work. 'Pathological' characteristics of unemployment, the passion for betting, for example, were simply 'pathological' characteristics of working-class life. Furthermore, the dole was a kind of wage and it permitted a good deal of social continuity. Consequently, as Bakke pointed out, the unemployed did not think of themselves as a class *qua* unemployed:

> The comparative security provided by the social services . . . has served well to keep them from being conscious that they have interests as a group of *unemployed* apart from their interests as *workers*.[116]

Even if not working they remained tied to many aspects of working-class life, to old habits and expectations, which they tried to preserve. That people were not wrenched from their class and community and that family life remained largely intact[117] explains why the unemployed were so resilient and, in the circumstances, so unscathed.

## *Notes*

1. P. Eisenberg and P. F. Lazarsfeld, 'The Psychological Effects of Unemployment', *Psychological Bulletin*, 35, 6 (June 1938).
2. Nor have I raised the possibly analogous question of retirement. First, 'retirement', as we understand it, was very unusual in working-class life before the Second World War and Lazarsfeld *et al.* could rightly argue that it is an unhistorical comparison. Second, it is questionable whether it is analogous. Modern retirement is, in

fact, part of the structure of employment; all of us know we must plan for it. But interwar unemployment, particularly, was often unexpected and random. It could not be planned for.

3. M. Jahoda, P. F. Lazarsfeld and H. Zeisel, *Die Arbeitslosen von Marienthal* (Leipzig, 1933), and English edn. *Marienthal: The Sociography of an Unemployed Community* (London, 1972). All references here are to the English edition.
4. B. Zawardski and P. F. Lazarsfeld, 'The Psychological Consequences of Unemployment', *Journal of Social Psychology*, VI, 2 (May 1935).
5. Zawardski and Lazarsfeld, pp. 224–5.
6. Eisenberg and Lazarsfeld, p. 378.
7. P. Kelvin and J. Jarrett, *Unemployment* (Cambridge, 1985), p. 19.
8. Jahoda *et al.*, p. 56.
9. Zawardski and Lazarsfeld, p. 235.
10. Ibid.
11. In the introduction to the English edition of *Marienthal*, Lazarsfeld wrote that he had for a long time been reluctant to consent to a translation because 'certain aspects of our approach were very naive' (*Marienthal*, p.xi).
12. M. Jahoda, *Employment and Unemployment* (Cambridge, 1982).
13. Kelvin and Jarrett, p. 113.
14. For a general discussion of the literature, see Royal Institute of International Affairs, *Unemployment: An International Problem* (London, 1935), pp. 14–15; J. A. Garraty, *Unemployment in History* (NY, 1978), pp. 178–87.
15. R. S. Lynd and H. M. Lynd, *Middletown in Transition* (London, 1937), pp. 254–6 partic. The Lynds' conclusions, however, were significantly different from those of *Marienthal.*
16. Though in America it became hopelessly confused with the debate on the 'culture of poverty' and lost much of its force. For an excellent discussion of this, particularly of Oscar Lewis's work, see C. A. Valentine, *Culture and Poverty* (Chicago, 1969).
17. L. Beales and R. S. Lambert (eds.), *Memoirs of the Unemployed* (London, 1934), pp. 9–10.
18. B. S. Rowntree and B. Lasker, *Unemployment: A Social Study* (London, 1911), p. 242.
19. Beales and Lambert, p. 227.
20. M. Cohen, *I was one of the Unemployed* (London, 1945), p. 91.
21. Pilgrim Trust, *Men without Work* (Cambridge, 1938), p. 149.
22. R. Durant, *Watling: A Social Survey* (London, 1939), p. 46.
23. Save the Children Fund, *Unemployment and the Child* (London, 1933), p. 23.
24. S. F. Hatton, *London's Bad Boys* (London, 1931), p. 72.
25. A. D. K. Owen, 'A Report on Unemployment in Sheffield', *Sheffield Social Survey Pamphlet No. 4* (Sheffield, 1932), p. 64.
26. Royal Commission on Unemployment Insurance, (1930–32) *Minutes of Evidence*, qq.6033–44.
27. Ibid., qq.10,514–18.

28. E. W. Bakke, *The Unemployed Man* (London, 1933), pp. 183–9.
29. H. Jennings, *Brynmawr: A Study of a Depressed Area* (London, 1934).
30. *Marienthal*, pp. 66–7.
31. Beales and Lambert, p. 191.
32. Report of the Unemployment Insurance Committee (1927), 11, *Minutes of Evidence*, q.647.
33. S. J. Chapman and H. M. Hallsworth, *Unemployment: The Results of an Investigation made in Lancashire and an Examination of the Poor Law Commission* (Manchester, 1909), p. 69. Italics mine.
34. A. Sinfield, *What Unemployment Means* (Oxford, 1981), pp. 37–8.
35. Bakke, p. 129.
36. Ibid., pp. 128–9.
37. Sinfield, pp. 44–5; also Bakke, p. 14.
38. Bakke, p. 71.
39. Cohen, p. 12.
40. Ibid., p. 134.
41. D. Marsden, *Workless* (London, 1982), p. 147.
42. Cohen, pp. 181–2. 'Newslum' was an outer London suburb.
43. This was the Pilgrim Trust view. Pilgrim Trust, p. 251.
44. For a rather tidied up account of contemporary 'classical' views of job search, see M. Casson, *Economics of Unemployment* (Oxford, 1983), pp. 37–61, 84–100. For the debate on the extreme neo-classical position, see D. K. Benjamin and L. A. Kochin, 'Searching for an Explanation of Unemployment in Interwar Britain', *Journal of Political Economy*, 87, 3 (June 1979), and replies in the same journal, 90, 2 (April 1982). It is worth noting that only one of the contributions, P. A. Ormerod and G. D. N. Worswick, makes any reference to the sociological material – the Pilgrim Trust survey. No one refers to Bakke.
45. R. C. Davison, *The Unemployed* (London, 1929), p. 170; J. Jewkes and A. Winterbottom, *Juvenile Unemployment* (London, 1933), p. 24.
46. Davison, pp. 192–3.
47. J. J. Astor *et al. The Third Winter of Unemployment* (London, 1923), p. 73.
48. Bakke, pp. 133–4.
49. *Marienthal*, pp. 70–4.
50. Three times a problem if the woman also gave up paid work because she 'could not bear to be the breadwinner' (Pilgrim Trust, p. 147).
51. D. Caradog Jones *et al.*, *The Social Survey of Merseyside* (London, 1934), II, p. 276.
52. Rowntree and Lasker, p. 242.
53. Beales and Lambert, p. 104.
54. Jennings, pp. 138–41.
55. W. Brierley, *Means Test Man* (London, 1935), p. 11.
56. T. Young, *Becontree and Dagenham* (London, 1934), p. 162.
57. Pilgrim Trust, p. 75.
58. Ibid., p. 216. Though not always. One of Beales and Lambert's

memoirists, an engineer's turner, regarded allotment digging as only an unsatisfactory alternative to an alternative. One of the economic consequences of unemployment, he said, 'includes the abandonment of hobbies' – in his case photography, an expensive one. 'Mending boots or digging allotments is by no means a substitute for those normal satisfactions of interests and hobbies which are the necessary antidotes to the debilitating effects of modern industrial life' (Beales and Lambert, pp. 244–5.) This is a very sophisticated analysis which defies conventional categories.

59. The Pilgrim Trust recorded the case of one Blackburn weaver in his thirties who refused to learn fancy weaving since that might have meant getting work. 'His interest was in the construction of models which he did skilfully and the member of the family who alone took his situation seriously was his wife' (Pilgrim Trust, p. 86).
60. Beales and Lambert, p. 201 ('A Carpenter's Younger Son').
61. P. Kelvin, 'Work as a Source of Identity: the Implications of Unemployment', *British Journal of Guidance and Counselling*, 9, 1 (January 1981), p. 8.
62. Eisenberg and Lazarsfeld, p. 365.
63. Because library charges were effectively abolished in Marienthal.
64. Bakke, p. 178.
65. Jennings, pp. 138–41. See also A. D. Lindsay, 'Unemployment: the "Meanwhile" Problem', *Contemporary Review* (June 1933), pp. 687–95.
66. Beales and Lambert, p. 70.
67. Ibid., p. 105.
68. Bakke, p. 194. His diarists read on average 10.7 hours a week. Eisenberg and Lazarsfeld concede that Bakke's evidence ran counter to their own (Eisenberg and Lazarsfeld, p. 364).
69. Caradog Jones *et al.*, II, p. 300.
70. Ibid.
71. Beales and Lambert p. 75.
72. See above p. 186.
73. Bakke, p. 263.
74. Kelvin and Jarrett, p. 69.
75. Zawardski and Lazarsfeld, p. 248.
76. Bakke, p. 14.
77. R. I. McKibbin, 'Working-Class Gambling in Britain', *Past and Present*, 82 (February 1979).
78. Pilgrim Trust, p. 99.
79. Cohen, p. 41. Beales and Lambert's 'skilled millwright' told them that 'perhaps' I miss cigarettes most' (Beales and Lambert, p. 105).
80. Cohen, who was a little less reticent about these things, wrote that 'young people need that interchange of experience between the sexes known as "romance". Too often unemployment makes a romantic social life impossible' (Cohen, p. 159). Although this is exactly the area where the social psychologist might have enquired, Lazarsfeld *et al.* do not appear to have done so. Zawardski–Lazarsfeld say that only two of their autobiographies mention sex, though one of those

is pretty febrile (Zawardski and Lazarsfeld, p. 234n). There is an appendix to the Beales and Lambert volume by Morris Robb on the medical consequences of unemployment. He concluded that for married men and women 'sexual congress' first increases and then decreases with unemployment. 'Additional nervous strain' is imposed on the individual by *coitus interruptus*, the cheapest form of contraception (Beales and Lambert, pp. 277–8). Perhaps this is proof of A. J. P. Taylor's famous assertion that withdrawal rendered the British a repressed nation, with all its awful consequences (A. J. P. Taylor, *English History, 1914–1945* (London 1965), p. 166).
81. *Marienthal*, pp. 38–41.
82. Zawardski and Lazarsfeld, p. 245.
83. Ibid., p. 242.
84. Beales and Lambert, p. 69.
85. Ibid., p. 105.
86. Ibid., pp. 127–8.
87. Brierley, pp. 66–7.
88. Cohen, p. 3; see also pp. 6–7.
89. Report of the Unemployment Insurance Committee (Blanesburgh), II, *Minutes of Evidence*, q.270.
90. Marsden, p. 88.
91. Kelvin and Jarrett, p. 88.
92. A. Deacon, *In Search of the Scrounger* (London, 1976), p. 61.
93. Jennings, p. 138.
94. Bakke, p. 79.
95. Ibid., p. 80.
96. Ibid., p. 98.
97. Ibid., p. 97.
98. Deacon, p. 57.
99. Bakke, pp. 106–7.
100. H. Llewellyn Smith (ed.), *The New Survey of London Life and Labour* (London, 1932), III, p. 174.
101. Pilgrim Trust, p. 161; for examples of this hostility to the clubs, see E. Wilkinson, *The Town that was Murdered* (London, 1939), pp. 233–4; A. Hutt, *The Condition of the Working Class in Britain* (London, 1933), pp. 45–6.
102. Jennings, p. 141.
103. E. W. Bakke, *Insurance or Dole* (New Haven, 1935), p. 198.
104. W. Hannington, *Unemployed Struggles* (London, 1936), pp. 298–313.
105. Zawardski and Lazarsfeld, pp. 224–6.
106. D. L. Sills, 'Paul Lazarsfeld', in *International Encyclopaedia of the Social Sciences*, 18 (1968), pp. 411–13.
107. H. Cantril, 'The Social Psychology of Everyday Life', *The Psychological Bulletin* (May 1934), 31, 5, pp. 317–18.
108. Bakke, pp. 257–8; see also A. Sinfield, 'Unemployment in an Unequal Society', B. Showler and A. Sinfield, *The Workless State* (Oxford, 1981), p. 153.
109. Kelvin and Jarrett, pp. 127–8.

110. Pilgrim Trust, p. 92.
111. Ibid., p. 173.
112. Ibid., pp. 174–5.
113. Kelvin and Jarrett, p. 56.
114. A. D. K. Owen, 'The Social Consequences of Industrial Transference', *The Sociological Review*, xxxix (1937), pp. 343–4.
115. Pilgrim Trust, pp. 275–6; see particularly, Table LIX, p. 274.
116. Bakke, p. 236.
117. The curious lack of an imaginative sympathy for the unemployed which Lazarsfeld *et al.* possessed, is almost crassly displayed here. Noting the tendency of the unemployed to indulge in 'irrational spending', they write: 'For example, it is reported that in a small group of partially unemployed Flemish workers just outside of Brussels pigeons are bought and kept at great expense because of the owner's hope that some day his pigeon will win a worthless trinket in a race. These same workers spend a good part of their annual income so that their children will have the proper outfit for communion' (Eisenberg and Lazarsfeld, p. 360).

# 8 Trade Unions and Corporatist Politics: the response of the TUC to industrial rationalisation, 1927–33

*Gordon Phillips*

It is an historical commonplace that the trade union movement in Britain set a new political course following the defeat of the General Strike of 1926. This was marked particularly by the talks which the TUC General Council held with the Mond group of employers in 1928–29. More controversially, several historians have represented the union leadership at this juncture, as turning towards 'corporatist' policies. 'In 1929–35', Keith Burgess asserts, the TUC leadership was won over to 'Keynesian economic policies and corporatist industrial strategies'.[1] In Ross Martin's view, their activities in these years helped to create 'a cautious anglicized version of the corporate state'.[2] Keith Middlemass likewise discerns 'openly corporatist themes' in the discussions with Mond, and in the subsequent contacts between the General Council and national employers' organisations an attempt 'to build their own form of institutional cooperation – corporatist in a far more subtle and flexible form'.[3] Mond and his colleagues, James Hinton argues, stood for 'the corporatist organisation of industry'; moreover, 'as in the First World War many trade union leaders found themselves drawn towards this corporatist vision of industrial organisation.'[4] In a more sustained and theoretical treatment, Alan Booth has isolated two short-lived essays in corporatist politics during the interwar period, abandoned in turn as the economic slumps of 1921–22 and 1931–33 supervened.[5]

The definition of 'corporatism' by these authors is not

always clear and may not be consistent. Where it is most deliberately defined, in the work of Booth and Middlemass, the concept embodies a distinctive method of policy-making in a capitalist industrial system. Institutions or formal means of communication are established, at national level, through which representatives of government, employers and labour seek agreement on economic and social programmes designed to accommodate their different interests. A national political consensus is thus formed, and as far as possible imposed upon their constituencies by each subscribing interest. For Booth, in particular, corporatism derives from conditions of economic and social strain, in which labour might undermine the stability of the capitalist regime. It is a political process adopted to contain that threat by judicious and limited concessions to labour's demands, and it is liable to be dispensed with once that threat recedes.

Corporatism, therefore, rests upon a tripartite relationship. Its development requires the purposeful political cooperation of government, employers and trade unionists. A desire for such cooperation may be found, however, in any one of these groups, and if influencing its outlook and behaviour sufficiently strongly may be aptly described as a corporatist 'tendency'.

This essay will examine the views of the union leadership during the Mond-Turner talks and their sequel, making only incidental reference to the standpoint of industrialists and of the state.[6] From this perspective, it will cast doubt on the historical existence of corporatism, even as a tendency. Following the General Strike, the TUC leadership did, indeed, seek a closer understanding with organised employers. They accepted thereby the tactical necessity of avoiding further large-scale strikes, and the intellectual necessity for reassessing the vitality of capitalism, which led them to endorse measures of industrial rationalisation. Yet the principal union spokesmen showed no interest, in either connection, in a partnership with government, even when a Labour administration assumed office in 1929. Under MacDonald's ministry, the unions steadily withdrew their support for rationalisation as Mond had conceived it, and reasserted the collectivist principles which they had maintained prior to 1926. In so doing, they voiced open hostility to the National Confederation of Employers' Organisations. More than this, they became increasingly critical of the government's own handling of industrial policy. Whatever else divided the TUC politically, this movement of opinion was almost universal. Both in accepting and condemning rationalisation, therefore, the unions displayed no liking for corporatist procedures. They judged it instead by its apparent impact in their main field of activity: collective bargaining. Even those leaders who wished to define bargaining anew did not doubt its primary importance for their organisations. To the extent that corporatist processes ran counter to this method of regulating industrial conditions, they were regarded with suspicion. That the two functions might be reconciled was a possibility hardly yet perceived.

## *I*

The idea of a joint national conference between capital and labour was floated even before the General Strike.[7] The General Council hesitated at first, but by 1927 was keen to promote it. The TUC chairman, George Hicks, revived the proposal at the Congress of that year, while the Secretary, Citrine, publicised it in the national and labour press.[8] Although Mond and his associates represented no official body of employers, the Council accepted their invitation to hold talks on industrial organisation and industrial relations, approving participation by a vote of 27 to 3.[9]

What benefits did the Council hope to secure? In addition to asserting its own discretionary power to speak for the movement, it had three major objectives. It wished, first, to enlist the support of influential employers in defence of endangered union rights. 'I think', Bevin reported in January 1928, 'the Conference has acted as a bit of a brake. I find there is a distinct check against the reactionary elements on the other side.'[10] Secondly, the Council envisaged the creation of permanent consultative machinery by the TUC and the official national organisations of employers. The intention to recommend a National Industrial Council was discernible in the Mond-Turner agenda, even if its *raison d'être* remained ill-defined.[11] Finally, it was anticipated that the conference might affirm the value of industrial rationalisation, and involve union representatives in its implementation. 'I am convinced', Citrine wrote on the eve of the talks, 'that the co-operation of the trade unions can be secured for the realisation of the maximum of efficiency in the employment of labour, the reduction of costs of production and the elimination of waste in all branches of production and distribution.'[12]

It was this last undertaking which was politically most original and ideologically most hazardous. The proposition that unions should collaborate with management in order to make capitalist industries more efficient was inescapably controversial. While the General Council did not repudiate the ideals of public control, they abandoned the view which the movement had asserted over the past decade, that the scientific organisation of industry was incompatible with its private ownership.[13] There is no evidence that this conversion to rationalisation was influenced by the kind of socialist theorising articulated by MacDonald in England or Hilferding in Germany, or even by its inclusion in the electoral platform of the Labour Party.[14] The Council's attitude reflected rather a pragmatic recognition that, especially in the staple industries, some rationalisation schemes had been implemented already, and union resistance was futile. 'Rationalisation', Bevin told the 1929 TUC, 'is coming in spite of us, and the question is, are we going to be inside the movement taking part in what is going on and taking our place in it?'[15] Furthermore, in trades like steel, coal mining or cotton textiles, where unemployment was already severe or rapidly worsening, reorganisation offered a safeguard against renewed attacks on working conditions. The General Council had already accepted this logic, in the coal dispute of 1926, by approving the moderate reform proposals of the Royal Commission and the Samuel memorandum. Its experience confirmed the fatuity of fighting rearguard actions in bankrupt industries. 'The ultimate policy of the movement', the Council told Congress in 1928, 'can find more use for an efficient industry than for a derelict one.'[16]

The alternative was stark; but this should not disguise the optimism with which the TUC leadership regarded rationalisation. At the Mond-Turner conference their favourite text, reiterated in the joint statement, was a resolution from the World Economic Conference of 1927 which asserted that rationalisation would bring gains to the whole community, including 'higher and steadier remuneration . . . equitably distributed.'[17] In a series of papers on unemployment to prepare the Council for discussions with the Mond group, the TUC research staff argued that prosperity could be restored to the British economy on two conditions. If the basic industries were reorganised they could look forward, with the exception of coal, to a renewal of growth; indeed, the textile and metal trades could absorb most of the quarter million workers expected to lose their jobs in mining. In addition, an expansion of the home market by means of a general rise of wages would stimulate various 'new' industries like chemicals, electrical goods and artificial fibres. Rising living standards and improvements in industrial productivity would be mutually reinforcing. 'The high wage policy, which can only be made effective by the policy of rationalisation, is not only desirable in itself but is a direct cause of increased prosperity in the industries dependent on the home market, and ultimately in the export trades also.'[18] Furthermore, enlarged consumer expenditure would generate job opportunities in the service sector. Within a few years the tide of recovery would be in flood.

The confidence expressed by TUC officials was displayed, perhaps more reservedly, by union leaders in the ailing export trades.[19] It rested partly on an awareness of the contrasting fortunes of particular firms and industries in Britain, and even more on the apparently superior performance of the highly rationalised manufacturing concerns in Germany and the USA.[20] Whatever its vantage-point, however, the General Council did not view rationalisation in Britain as a corporatist enterprise, if this be taken to imply collaboration between industry and government. The process was to advance by dint of a partnership between unions and employers, not as the result of state decisions. The TUC research papers refer to the need for government assistance, in this context, only in two cases of special difficulty: mining and agriculture. When the Mond-Turner conference drew up its report on unemployment, its chief demand upon the state was not for direct intervention in the industrial sphere but an expansionary monetary policy.[21] As for rationalisation, it had already recommended that this should be the subject of discussions between individual trade associations on the one side, and the appropriate union organisation on the other, whose aim would be to launch 'experimental' schemes featuring agreed variations in customary labour practices.[22] The procedure to be followed was that of *ad hoc* bilateral negotiation. The most that could be expected from the Mond talks, the *Labour Magazine* believed, 'is that a general programme will be evolved which the trade unions and the organisations of employers in all trades and industries can reasonably be invited to consider in relation to their own concrete problems.'[23] To its principal union advocates, in fact, rationalisation appealed chiefly as affording opportunities for extending the scope and content of collective bargaining. In a rationalised industrial system, Citrine contended,

> it lies with the union . . . to assume responsibility for such representation of the workers on works committees, joint councils, and boards of management as will follow the development of what I have called 'the politics of industry', meaning the extension of the principle of joint conference on matters of commercial policy as well as of industrial administration and regulation of wages and working conditions.[24]

The project for a National Industrial Council was of similar design. The Mond-Turner conference proposed that representatives of the General Council and of national employers' organisations would hold quarterly meetings, to discuss 'the widest questions concerning industry and industrial progress.' They were also to undertake systematic inquiries into industrial problems, and to establish machinery which would help solve recalcitrant industrial disputes.[25] Not all TUC leaders were inclined to attribute much importance to such a Council.[26] Those who did saw it, not as a corporatist institution, but as the embodiment of an autarkic industrial sector. There was thus no suggestion that the state should be involved in, or even have contact with, this body. Indeed, the conciliation scheme to be run by the Council appeared to compete with the industrial courts and mediation services provided by the Ministry of Labour, whilst its investigative activities would overlap with government inquiries like the

Balfour committee on industry and trade.[27] The NIC was intended to supplement the established and voluntary system of industrial relations, not to render that system more dependent on government. It would, Citrine hoped, ultimately form the highest tier of an integrated bargaining structure. 'Part of the scheme I have in mind', he told a union colleague during the conference, 'and which may still be possible to work, would be to have a National Industrial Council which would be representative of all the separate industrial councils in each industry.'[28] A council of this kind conformed to a pattern of industrial relations like that envisaged by the Whitley reports of 1917–18.[29] It was consistent with the TUC's conception of rationalisation as a policy that industry should pursue by means of its own devising and without government aid or interference.

## *II*

The hopes which the General Council invested in the Mond-Turner conference were disappointed. The National Confederation of Employers' Organisations and the Federation of British Industries could not be prevailed upon to join a National Industrial Council. They agreed only to the irregular discussion of topics within their respective spheres of interest, preferably relating to government policy.[30] As for the promotion of rationalisation, no trade association responded to Mond's invitation to enter negotiations to this end with the affiliates of the TUC. Further advances on this front depended on the initiatives of the second Labour government – notably the public inquiries into the problems of the steel and cotton industries set up in 1929.[31] The unions affected gave evidence to these inquiries and contributed modestly to the dialogue on reorganisation which followed, but were far from satisfied with the outcome.[32] At no stage, did they or the Cabinet involve the General Council in discussions or acknowledge its possible interest.

If rationalisation under government auspices was not subject to effective union control, in other industries it presented a still more unpleasing aspect. In 1930 the TUC rapidly abandoned the earlier, optimistic assessment of its character. They now saw the process as signifying a familiar assertion of managerial prerogatives and, worse, as a source of rising unemployment. In the setting of a rapidly deteriorating labour market the judgement of the Mond-Turner conference that this was 'not a very serious factor' in destroying jobs seemed highly questionable.[33] In April 1930 a staff report to the General Council's Economic Committee noted 'uneasiness at the present position of affairs', citing recent speeches on the effects of rationalisation by Arthur Pugh of the steelworkers, John Hill of the boilermakers, and Oswald Mosley, one of the junior ministers responsible for combatting unemployment.[34] The chorus of criticism within the union movement was to grow steadily louder.

The displacement of labour by rationalisation was a problem which had been noticed previously. Even the Geneva resolution of 1927 acknowledged that some temporary unemployment would result from this policy and necessitate 'suitable measures'.[35] The TUC research staff had considered the measures required in their memoranda in 1928–29, calling for the careful scheduling of reorganisation, the transfer of labour, the reduction of working hours and financial compensation of workers made redundant.[36] In the unemployment committee of the Mond-Turner conference both Bevin and Pugh insisted that rationalisation was already contributing significantly to the level of unemployment in some industries.[37] As yet the General Council regarded the extent of such displacement as limited and manageable. The joint statement which they signed with the Mond group in June 1929 accepted an accretion of unemployment as a temporary cost of industrial renovation; they insisted only that

> the changes involved in rationalisation should be introduced gradually, and the Trade Unions should be consulted as to the best methods of dealing with displacement. Firms or industries, where possible, should set up a Labour Reserve Fund out of profits to assist displaced workers.[38]

As its economic prognosis became less sanguine, the TUC leadership cast around for arguments to justify their change of mind about rationalisation. In a tentative fashion, Arthur Pugh stated a new thesis to the Macmillan Committee on

Finance and Industry, to which he gave evidence on behalf of the General Council in May 1930. Rationalisation in Britain, he suggested, had deviated from the best models; its application had been uncoordinated, and constrained by a narrowly competitive outlook.

> Of course, if you are going to apply all these great developments . . . to advance the undeveloped countries, and increase the standard of life of the people there, then I can see enormous advantages but, as applied to ourselves alone, I do not see what we can get out of it except a lot of unemployment which we are not going to be able to absorb.[39]

Increased industrial efficiency also required complementary public policies to expand purchasing power.[40] Ernest Bevin, among Pugh's audience on this occasion, developed similar arguments with greater cogency in a memorandum to the government's Economic Advisory Council the following month. There was no adequate evidence, he claimed, that the displacement of labour by improved methods of production was of merely short-term duration. Industrial reorganisation had not prevented a catastrophic slump in Germany and the USA, formerly held up as examples for Britain to follow. Bevin questioned whether rationalisation could create employment anywhere under conditions of general commercial crisis. Least of all would it do so if it were not associated with a simultaneous expansion of consumer demand.

> Behind all this idea of reorganisation appears to be the conception that by the cheapening of production, the concentration of labour and the introduction of scientific methods wealth will be provided in such vast quantities that it will cause the creation of new industries, and therefore the total volume of people employed . . . will more than compensate for those displaced. However, it is as well to remember that unless there is a shortening of the hours of labour, a raising of the school leaving age, pensioning, an increase of purchasing power, and the creation of demand by adding to leisure, new outlets in other directions cannot be provided.[41]

The solutions which Bevin put forward to deal with the problem of displacement were recapitulated from the unemployment programme of the Mond-Turner conference. They were stated again in two resolutions on rationalisation (one drafted by his own union) adopted by the TUC in September

1930.[42] This disquiet, however, fell short of outright condemnation. Conjoined with appropriate political and economic safeguards, rationalisation might yet elicit union support. By the time that the TUC submitted the second instalment of its evidence to the Macmillan committee, in November, its attitude had visibly hardened. Profit-making entrepreneurs were now held incapable of a 'scientific' management of the industrial economy.[43]

> We all accept the fact that our basic industries need reorganisation and that the process has to be pressed forward as rapidly as possible, but what guarantee is there that the same state of affairs will not recur? . . . It appears to us that the community must now take the responsibility of saying that industry shall not, in future, be permitted to exist in a state of anarchy, and that means should be provided whereby industrial development and progress will be supervised, regulated, and stimulated by some organ of the community as a whole.

Rationalisation could be approved, therefore, only if taken out of the hands of capitalists and placed in those of a public investment bank and public corporations. This revived collectivism in the union movement was phrased in a less abrasive way than in past years; but it was none the less definite, and over the coming months the General Council and its constituents devoted much attention to the form and content of its proposals for nationalisation and economic planning.[44]

Such criticisms of rationalisation, though obviating a political consensus, implied a closer relationship between the unions and the government. They envisaged administrative as well as statutory remedies for labour displacement. Bevin's paper, for example, proposed that government departments should collect returns on all reorganisation schemes involving works closures, and on the contingent arrangements for redeploying or compensating the workers affected. In fact, the TUC leadership exerted scarcely any pressure on the Labour cabinet to adopt such measures; they were brought forward neither in public campaigns nor in private consultations with ministers. No more did the General Council try to push the government into impetuous attempts to nationalise one or other industry.[45] They had no appetite, it seemed, even for the kind of corporatism which socialists might have been expected to favour.

This inactivity is explicable, in part, by the lack of effective communication between the TUC and the Cabinet.[46] It also displays the reluctance of the union leadership openly to challenge ministerial judgements or align themselves with the government's radical critics. It was obvious that a minority administration could not, even had it wished, proceed far with the socialisation of industry. But the government discountenanced even the more pragmatic policies which Bevin and others demanded in order to make rationalisation palatable. MacDonald told the House of Commons in February 1930 that the state could not extend special assistance to the victims of industrial reorganisation:[47]

> It would not be practicable to identify among the unemployed those whose unemployment is attributable to rationalisation even if it were desirable to differentiate in the treatment to be given to them. Rationalisation is calculated ultimately to improve the economic condition of the country, and therefore to add materially to the volume of employment generally available.

This statement subsequently became the text for all official replies to labour demands for statutory compensation for displacement. In the Economic Advisory Council the Minister of Labour, Margaret Bondfield, made a similarly discouraging response to Bevin's memorandum. Though she paid lip-service to the idea of extending retirement pensions she discountenanced compulsory redundancy payments (unless dismissals resulted directly from legislation), and evinced no interest in recording the adoption of private rationalisation schemes. Like MacDonald, she insisted that the existing unemployment insurance provisions were sufficient.[48]

The General Council timidly accepted this official verdict. It still saw its own sphere of operations as lying outside politics and in seeking palliatives for industrial displacement its natural bias carried it towards collective bargaining – notwithstanding its ideological tendency towards collectivism. In this sense the impact of the Mond-Turner conference on the tactics of the TUC leadership outlasted its intellectual influence. In May 1930, under the negotiating arrangements made in the wake of the conference, the Council asked to meet the National Confederation of Employers'

Organisations to discuss 'the displacement of labour due to rationalisation'.[49] The TUC's Economic Committee attended the first such meeting in November.

In taking this step, the General Council were consciously importuning the employers instead of confronting the government. The latter, Milne-Bailey admitted, could not discriminate in affording relief 'between workers dismissed because of higher productivity and for other reasons'. On the other hand, 'it is perhaps feasible [for industry] to treat them differently'.[50] A number of collective agreements extending concessions to workers subject to dismissal had already been made during the 1920s by Joint Industrial Councils in flour milling, gas and match manufacturing, as well as by individual firms in the confectionery, brewing and dyeing trades.[51] Some arranged to redeploy workers, others to set up funds to supplement unemployment benefit or to help men start their own businesses. Though the NCEO could not authorise such measures it might at least endorse them so that other profitable companies might consider their adoption.

This attempt at industrial diplomacy proved wholly abortive. The NCEO had little enthusiasm for pan-industry consultation, and would tolerate no encroachment on the autonomy of its constituents. Its view of the question raised by the TUC was shaped by a sterile economic orthodoxy. The talks proceeded, at funereal speed, to a second meeting in May 1931, where the employers' spokesman, Sir Arthur Dorman, made it clear that for his side no serious problem of displacement existed. He felt

> considerable doubts as to what was really meant by rationalisation. If efficiency was the principal feature of the process, was not the whole aim to lower costs and thereby increase trade? If this was so, the Confederation felt that there could not be any real displacement of labour as the result of rationalisation.[52]

The TUC's representatives were unable to carry the argument further. They were handicapped by their inability to obtain detailed information on the scale of the redundancies which they condemned. A questionnaire was circulated to affiliated organisations early in 1931 asking for reports on the effects of industrial rationalisation with respect to employment, hours and other conditions of work. But the responses were 'very incomplete' and 'on the vital matter of the amount of unemployment due specifically to rationalisation the results of the inquiry were very meagre, as the unions have indicated that they find it impossible to separate unemployment due to this cause from that arising from depressed trade and other factors.'[53] There was thus no prospect of persuading the confederation to be more constructive. 'If they relied on acceptance of the principle [of compensation] by the Confederation', Pugh told a union delegation in June, 'they would not get much further'.[54] Without being formally terminated, the talks were allowed to lapse.

The decisive rift between the NCEO and the General Council had, in fact, occurred before their meeting in May. In February 1931 the Confederation issued a public statement calling upon the government to make drastic financial economies, including a cut of one third in unemployment benefits.[55] It was obviously not about to recommend its own members to make up the difference. In April, having earlier denounced the NCEO proposals, the General Council produced a circular on the current industrial situation, which was directed to the representatives of the Confederation. This, more than any other document, acknowledged the failure of 'Mondism':[56]

> Rationalisation has been proceeding for the past few months and, except in a few instances, little or no consultation has taken place with the trade unions representing the workers directly concerned as to its application. In consequence unemployment has undoubtedly been aggravated, without any adequate provision being made for the men displaced.

Rationalisation had not brought with it a closer partnership between capital and labour. Though further discussions did take place between the General Council and the FBI, these did nothing to extend the range of collective bargaining in an industrial context.[57] The strategy which Citrine and other TUC leaders had conceived in 1927–28 was, for the moment, abandoned.

The issue of rationalisation not only isolated the unions from the organised employers but also separated them from the Labour government. While the TUC might be unwilling to press the Cabinet to relinquish this object of policy, or even to introduce palliative measures, its attitude was bound to be unsympathetic. 'In the basic industries', Bevin told the Party Conference in 1929, ' . . . for the Government at that stage to be appealing to employers, directors of factories, mines, etc., men whose only outlook in life was their sole prerogative to exercise their power in a particular industry, and trying to get them to agree on reorganisation, was not right.'[58] More outspoken dissent could be restrained, only if the political leadership upheld the principle of adequate maintenance for all unemployed. Their discussions about compensation with the NCEO and its members the Council told Congress in 1931, 'confirmed . . . its . . . view that the Rates of Unemployment Benefit should not be reduced.'[59] Their stance on the question of displacement thus significantly strengthened the General Council's resolve in the crisis of August 1931. They saw themselves as defending not just the casualties of an international trade depression, but the victims of a domestic programme of industrial reorganisation enacted by those very bankers and employers, and directed by that very Cabinet, which now demanded cuts in unemployment benefit. To surrender this ground was, from the union viewpoint, to capitulate to the least generous forces of contemporary capitalism.

## *IV*

Following the fall of the second Labour government, the TUC leadership maintained its commitment to industrial rationalisation in a collectivist form. A resolution on industrial planning was adopted by Congress in 1931 proposing, in Bevin's words, 'to transfer the very resources of nature to public ownership and national control'.[60] The motion formed the conclusion to the General Council's submission, in 1932, to the Economic Council's inquiry on rationalisation.[61] Following the same line of attack, the Council presented the TUC at its annual meeting with a report on the public regulation and control of industry and trade. Between 1934 and 1936, in cooperation with the Labour Party Executive, it drafted schemes for public ownership of coal mining, steel and cotton textiles.[62] Freed from the political inhibitions which constrained it under a Labour government the union leadership could engage in policy-making on a more ambitious scale.

A keen observer might judge the unions' idea of planning to be tinged with corporatism. The process was regarded as cooperative, bringing together specialists from a variety of backgrounds; and as having a consultative as well as a managerial dimension. In its evidence to the Macmillan Committee, the General Council had called for a planning organisation in Britain similar to the *Reichkuratorium* in Germany.[63] The report on public control revived the notion of a national industrial forum to discuss issues of economic policy:[64]

> A body of this kind, whether constituted precisely on the basis suggested by the Melchett-TUC Conference or on some other basis, would not merely provide an important piece of machinery for the consideration of the general problems of industry, but would also, through its trade union representation, be able to exercise a powerful influence on the general direction of the nation's economic and industrial policy.

To apply the term 'corporatist' to these hypothetical socialist schemes, however, distorts the meaning. There was nothing here of social consensus, of accommodating the interests of capital and labour. The blueprints, however purposeful, lacked administrative precision, and conformed rather to the demands of a party manifesto. Whether or not they can be considered practical, they certainly proclaimed a lack of familiarity with the process of government.

Two other elements in the socialist vision of rationalisation deserve notice. The first is a pervasive distrust of Whitehall officials, inherited from prewar years, and reinforced by recent experience of industrial diplomacy.[65] When Arthur Pugh was examined by the members of the EAC committee investigating the problems of rationalisation, he sought to distinguish between planning and nationalisation by reference to the presence or absence of civil servants with administrative functions: under the former, industries would be run by specialist boards of management.[66] The General Council developed this theme in its report on the control of industry:[67]

> It is doubtful, according to modern Socialist ideas, whether there is ever any advantage in conducting an industry or a commercial service by the method of direct State operation, i.e., by a Government Department. . . . The importance of flexibility and expert management on the one hand, and of freedom from party political domination, on the other hand, has so far been recognised that . . . the tendency is to secure public control and the elimination of the profit motive while keeping the actual management in the hands of a body not susceptible to party political pressure and interference.

This outlook, though following precedents set by the Labour government, also owed something to the precept articulated earlier in the 1920s as 'home rule for industry'. Industrial administration, whether capitalist or socialist, was to be left to those with a direct professional and economic commitment to its efficient conduct, and with appropriate knowledge or experience. All schemes for public ownership approved by the TUC in the 1930s accepted the principle that industries should be self-regulating and self-financing. It was never explained how this could be reconciled with the principle of centralised coordination embodied in an apparatus of national planning. Moreover these blueprints remained conventional, or at best indefinite, in their treatment of questions such as subsidies, pricing policies and trade protection, into which politics would necessarily intrude.

The trade union leadership was especially anxious to reconcile economic planning and voluntary collective bargaining. The General Council's 'control of industry' report dealt succinctly with this subject. The following year its remarks were amplified, to scotch radical demands for union participation in the management of public corporations.[68]

> [W]e think it desirable to point out the distinction between the various functions of management and control. A considerable part of the activities of industrial managements at present is concerned with the settlement of wages, hours, and all the other working conditions that most nearly affect the worker day by day. These matters are at present adjusted by negotiation between employers and trade unions. In our view, this method must continue to apply in the case of socialised undertakings. The adjustment of wages and working conditions must be undertaken by direct negotiation between the trade unions and the management of these concerns, and trade union rights, including the right to strike, must be fully maintained.

It would be impossible, Citrine pointed out, for unions to uphold a right to resist decisions to which their representatives had been a party.[69]

Even if industrial rationalisation were effected under government auspices, therefore, the unions intended to preserve their own domain, beyond the range of government. That domain was collective bargaining. From their point of view bargaining was a game for two players. Nationalisation simply meant the substitution of a public management for a private one. The role which the state played in industrial relations was traditionally limited to providing mediation or arbitration services when bilateral negotiations between management and labour had broken down. There is no evidence that the union leadership felt the least inclination to disturb this practice in the future. Dealings between a public enterprise and the unions which organised its workforce might, paradoxically, reduce the need for extraordinary government intervention rather than increase it.

## *V*

During the years 1928–33 the General Council demonstrated its capacity to debate a range of current economic issues. On industrial reorganisation, monetary policy and international trade it developed a viewpoint in some respects distinctively its own. Yet beyond the publication of its opinions, it made little or no attempt to influence government policy on these matters, even when a Labour adminstration was in office. Its overriding concern, after the General Strike, was to consolidate and expand the frontiers of collective bargaining, through a better understanding with organised employers. It endorsed industrial rationalisation with this in mind. When it failed to evoke an adequate response from the management side it turned to the establishment of a platform for a future Labour government. Its political partisanship was confirmed, after 1931, by the close relationship of the TUC and the Labour Party Executive. Even in preparing its designs for a planned economy, however, the Council gave but a slight impression of the place which the unions would occupy under the state.

If these years do not witness the development of corporatist politics in Britain the explanation does not rest primarily upon the conduct of the union leadership. Had governments of any complexion shown a strong wish to consult the unions more frankly and frequently the latter would, no doubt, have accepted their invitations. The argument presented in this essay is not that corporatism was impossible, but rather that the union leadership displayed no leaning towards it, had acquired no ingrained corporatist mentality. Naturally they were not politically isolated or ideologically irreconcilable even under right-wing ministries. But their attitude to the state was imbued with wariness and scepticism. They held to a set of prejudices, assumptions and attitudes which offered resistance to any corporatist trend: the belief that industrial relations should remain free from political control; the conviction that most politicians and civil servants knew little of the workings of industry; the suspicion that, in the politics of backrooms and corridors, their adversaries were more adept and influential than they.[70] These were dispositions which, down to the Second World War, no government sought effectively to change.

## *Notes*

1. K. Burgess, *The Challenge of Labour* (Croom Helm, 1980), p. 241.
2. R.Martin, *The TUC* (Clarendon Press, 1980), p. 216.
3. R.K Middlemass, *The Politics of Industrial Society* (André Deutsch, 1980), p. 209.
4. James Hinton, *Labour and Socialism: History of the British Labour Movement, 1867–1974* (Wheatsheaf Books, 1983), p. 142.
5. A.Booth, 'Corporatism, capitalism and depression in twentieth-century Britain', *Br.Jnl of Sociol.* 33 (1982), pp. 202–3, 208–15.
6. On the outlook of employers and governments, see R. Charles, *The Development of Industrial Relations in Britain, 1911– 39* (Hutchinson, 1973); A.Fox, *History and Heritage* (Allen and Unwin, 1985), ch.7; H. J. Gospel, 'Employers: a study of the Mond-Turner talks', *Bus.Hist.* 21(1979).
7. Fox, op.cit., pp. 325–7.
8. TUC (1927), *Report* pp. 66–7; *Labour Magazine*, October 1927; *Manchester Guardian*, 30 November 1927, reprinted in W. Milne-Bailey (ed.), *Trade Union Documents* (Bell, 1929), pp. 431–8. According to Citrine, he and Herbert Tracey helped draft this section

of Hicks's speech: Lord Citrine, *Men and Work* (Hutchinson, 1964), pp. 243–4.

9. GC mins., 23 November, 20 December 1927.
10. TUC GC archives, box 211 f262.08. The priority given by the conference to joint statements on union recognition and victimisation expressed the Council's preference.
11. Ben Turner, *About Myself* (Toulmin, 1930), pp. 148–9. The Council's proposed agenda is in GC 210 f.262.012.
12. Milne-Bailey, *op.cit.*, p. 437. Mond was a champion of rationalisation: see his *Industry and Politics* (Macmillan, 1927).
13. See especially *The Waste of Capitalism*, published by the TUC and the Labour Party in 1924.
14. D. Marquand, *Ramsay MacDonald* (Cape, 1977); *Labour and the Nation* (1928); *How to Conquer Unemployment* (1929).
15. TUC (1929), *Report* p. 385.
16. TUC (1928) *Report*, p. 209.
17. Milne-Bailey, *op.cit.*, pp. 430–1.
18. Cyclostyled copies of these reports are in the British Library of Economic and Political Science: 'Unemployment' (fHD5/51), 'Memorandum on Technological Unemployment' (fHD5/52), and 'Statement on unemployment' (fHD5/53). The quotation is from the first of these.
19. See ISTC, 'Report of EC Sub-committee on the condition of the iron and steel industry. . . . ,November 1928' (PRO BT55/98); *Precis of evidence submitted by the United Textile Factory Workers' Association to the Committee of inquiry into the Cotton Industry, 1929.*
20. The views of the TUC leadership may be contrasted with those of the International Federation of Trade Unions in 1927: 'When rationalisation is a purely technical measure or a mere reform of organisation . . . it fosters unemployment and will become a cause of social evil' (cf. *AEU Journal*, October 1927).
21. TUC (1929), *Report* pp. 188–202. Milne-Bailey laid less stress on monetary policy in the memorandum on unemployment he wrote prior to the joint discussions: 'Monetary policy is all-important in "normal" depressions but this slump is due to other and more lasting causes' (GC213 f.262.3: 'Unemployment – employers' memorandum').
22. TUC (1928), *Report* p. 229.
23. *Labour Magazine*, February 1928, p. 456.
24. Milne-Bailey, *op.cit.* See also the terms of the resolution of the International Economic Conference quoted above: '[Rationalisation] requires. . . . so far as regards the organisation of labour in the strict sense of the term, the co-operation of employees, and the assistance of trade and industrial organisations and of scientific and technical experts.'
25. GC211 f262.023, 'The prevention of industrial disputes'.
26. Cf. J. H. Thomas's comment on the Mond conference itself, which foreshadowed a permanent NIC: 'We are not asked to sacrifice

anything, but we are asked to say we can contribute in an examination of economic factors' (GC 211 f262.08).

27. This may have been one reason for the Balfour committee's opposition to an Industrial Council. Its explicit objection was to an NIC disconnected from existing bargaining institutions. See E. H. Phelps Brown, *The Origins of Trade Union Power* (Oxford University Press, 1983), p. 124.
28. Citrine to Charles Dukes, 23 October 1928 (GC235 f.575. He added, however, 'We are probably a long way off this consumation' (sic).
29. See J. B. Seymour, *The Whitley Councils Scheme* (King, 1932). Seymour indicated (p. 160) that a National Industrial Council might not be welcomed by existing Whitley Councils, or by the Association of Joint Industrial Councils.
30. GC mins., 23 April, 25 July 1929. For a full account see M. Dintenfass, 'The TUC, the FBI and British Economic Policy between the Wars', M. Phil. thesis (University of Warwick, 1980), pp. 215–16.
31. E.A.C., *Report of the Committee on the Cotton Industry*, Cmd.3615, 1930; EAC, *Iron and Steel Committee Report*, 30 May 1930.
32. *Précis of evidence submitted by the United Textile Factory Workers' Association to the Committee of Inquiry into the Cotton Industry;* PRO BT 56/33 CIA1768/20; CAB 24/217 CP 59 and 421; ISTC, *Statement of the EC of the Confederation with regard to the situation in the Iron and Steel Industry, May 1931* (Arthur Pugh), *Men of Steel* (1951), p. 456.
33. TUC (1928), *Report*, p. 229.
34. GC 235 f.575.1. See also A. Walkden, Secretary of the Railway Clerks, in *Labour Magazine*, July 1930, p. 113.
35. Milne-Bailey, op.cit., p. 430. The International Labour Office published its own study of *The Social Consequences of Rationalisation* in 1931.
36. TUC Research Department, 'Memorandum on technological unemployment'.
37. GC 210 f.262, 'Notes of joint committee on unemployment'.
38. TUC (1929), *Report* p. 200.
39. (Macmillan) Committee on Finance and Industry, Mins. of Evid., Cmd.3897 (1930), q.4689.
40. Ibid., qq.4694f.
41. CAB 58/10 EAC(H) 92.
42. TUC (1930), *Report* pp. 334–44.
43. Macmillan Committee, Mins. of Evid.; TUC Evidence Part II, paras. 10–11.
44. See below; also A. Oldfield, 'The Labour Party and planning: 1934 or 1918?', *BSSLH* 25 (1972).
45. In the steel industry, it is true, the Iron and Steel Confederation were sufficiently dissatisfied with the fruits of the official inquiry to announce, in the summer of 1931, their intention to bring their own scheme for socialisation before Parliament and the electorate. But this decision reflected the union's estrangement from government, not a mutual political intimacy. Moreover the ISTC acted indepen-

dently of the TUC and, as it transpired, with far from complete congressional backing. In the cotton industry the unions called for selective legislation on reorganisation, and for nationalisation, but failed to press either measure.

46. Citrine, *Men and Work*, p. 281.
47. Parl.Proc. (Commons) 5th ser., vol.234 (5 February 1930), cs1892–3.
48. CAB58/11 EAC(H) 110. See also BT 56/37 CIA 1770.
49. GC235 f.575.1.
50. Ibid.
51. CAB 58/177 EAC(PR)70; BT56/25, 'Rationalisation' (4 February 1930).
52. GC235 f.575.1 (19 May 1931).
53. TUC 1931, *Report* pp. 219–20.
54. GC235 f.575.1: Economic Committee meeting with representatives of certain unions, 16 June 1931.
55. GC235 f.575: 'Rationalisation and unemployment insurance'.
56. GC235 f.575.1, 'Displacement of labour due to Rationalisation', 16 April 1931. The NCEO was asked specifically whether it would cooperate in formulating safeguards, and recommend them for discussion by industrial negotiating bodies. See GC mins, 20 May 1931.
57. Dintenfass, *op.cit.*, pp. 219 ff. It is notable that the conference on labour displacement was the only one initiated at the request of the General Council rather than the employers' side.
58. Labour Party Conference (1929), *Report* p. 198.
59. TUC (1931), *Report* p. 220.
60. TUC (1931), *Report* p. 410.
61. PRO CAB58/177EAC (PR)70. In other respects the memorandum largely followed the lines of the General Council's broadside to the NCEO in April 1931.
62. TUC (1934), *Report* p. 205; (1936), *Report* p. 212.
63. Macmillan Committee, Evid. of TUC, Part II para. 12.
64. TUC (1932), *Report* p. 210.
65. See R.Roberts, 'The administrative origins of industrial diplomacy: an aspect of government-industry relations, 1929–35', in J. Turner (ed.), *Businessmen in Politics* (Heinemann, 1984).
66. CAB 58/178 EAC(PR) 81 Q.2308.
67. TUC (1932), *Report* p. 210.
68. TUC (1933), *Report* p. 210. The nationalisation schemes of 1934–36 gave the unions negotiating rights on all aspects of working conditions, including 'questions of policy relating to displacement of workers due to technical or mechanical development'.
69. Ibid.
70. Citrine, *op.cit.*, pp. 251–2, suggests that closer contacts between the General Council and leading employers after the Mond-Turner talks had indicated to the former the limited political influence of the latter.

# 9 Sweethearts and Scabs: irregular trade unions in Britain in the twentieth century

*Robert J. Waller*

There has been a tendency in labour historiography to portray the mainstream of the trade union movement as its natural course, indeed as the only legitimate form. In more militant circles progress is seen as consisting of a series of battles to increase the power of the unions – often taking the shape of confrontational strikes and other types of direct action. Organisational advances may be regarded as less spectacularly praiseworthy. The unions' connection with the Labour Party is often held to be an essential source of additional strength. The belligerent virtues of courage and struggle are praised to the detriment of accommodation and compromise.

One consequence of this treatment has been to decry the values and efforts of irregular or 'non-political' trade unionism which rejected the bellicose approach. Indeed, a plethora of pejorative phrases has been deployed: yellow unionism, company unionism, sweetheart unionism, along with the commonplace gibes of blackleg and scab. Those who stood outside the ranks of orthodoxy, like Havelock Wilson's National Union of Seamen, the Spencer unions in the coalfields after 1926, and most recently the Nottinghamshire miners' breakaway after the 1984–85 strike, have been castigated as collaborationists, bosses' unions, or even as tainted with fascism. Yet were such bodies really 'traitors to the working classes'? Or did they merely reflect a different tradition, another way of protecting and advancing the interests of their members? Perhaps it is time to redress the balance of historical reporting, locked so often into the celebration and justification of combative methods.

It should be emphasised that this essay deals only with unions in the manual working-class sectors of industry, rather than with organisations and associations where a non-socialist approach may be less surprising. Excluded, therefore, are staff associations, professional organisations such as the British Medical Association and the National Farmers' Union (which are of interest to students of pressure groups);[1] and also medium and higher grade white-collar unions (though many of these have not only grown but adopted distinctly left-wing stances in the second half of the twentieth century).

The variety of union types and structures before 1900, the diversity too in their relations with employers, are well established in historical literature. But there is often an implication that new models were emerging in the Edwardian period as closer ties developed between many unions, the TUC and the Labour Party; as Collison's Free Labour Association among dockers and seamen and profit-sharing and co-partnership schemes and company unions among gas-workers and railway-workers passed their peak; as adverse legal decisions inhibiting the unions' industrial and political activities were reserved; and as regional and local union autonomy was progressively ceded to centralised bureaucracies which would be in a stronger position to negotiate national settlements with employers (and, sometimes, with the government). Yet not every industry sees a labour organisation of this character developing. The best known examples of a dissentient or unorthodox approach among manual working-class trade unions from 1914 have been the seamen's union, the breakaway 'non-political' miners' unions of the interwars years, and in the 1980s the Union of Democratic Mineworkers. What brought such rival unions about? What principles did they adopt? Did they represent a legitimate method of safeguarding workers' interests? Do they deserve the calumny that has been heaped upon them?

The modern history of 'non-Labour' labour organisations should begin with the British Workers' League, which was founded in 1916 by Victor Fisher, A. M. Thompson and others as a successor to the Socialist National Defence Committee (1915) as an organiser of patriotic labour.[2] Financial support was forthcoming from Lord Milner, the best known advocate of the ideal of Empire. The aim of the League was to foster imperial preference and to unite working people behind the war effort. Its journal, *British Citizen and Empire Worker* (later *Empire Citizen*), first appeared in 1916, in some ways resembling the old *Clarion*. Despite Milner's patronage, the BWL did boast figures like the Bolton Labour MP Robert Tootill, of the Machine and Labourers' Union, who was a Vice-President of the BWL 1916–18; but it firmly rejected the wide aspirations of socialist theory, and in 1918 the political gap became more clear. The BWL formed an offshoot, the National Democratic and Labour Party, which put forward 27 candidates, 20 of whom were granted the Lloyd George coalition government's 'stamp of approval', the 'coupon'. Many of these candidates opposed pacifist Labour MPs who had not supported the war, such as Jowett and MacDonald, or Labour MPs who had had disagreements with the Coalition like Henderson. All three were defeated, as the NDP won ten seats. However, the impetus was not sustained. The NDP did not survive as a separate entity. Their policies were confused once the war's reckoning was over. They were divided over whether to advocate compulsory ballots among trade unionists before strikes could be called. They believed that nationalisation of industry was an acceptable aim, though the time was 'not yet ripe'. By the 1922 election all nine surviving MPs stood as Lloyd George Liberals; all nine were defeated. Their *raison d'être* had been supplied by the united war effort, and they could not maintain a separate existence as a 'patriotic Labour' Party thereafter. The NDP perished with the Lloyd George coalition, although *Empire Citizen* struggled on until 1927.

J. Havelock Wilson had been a Vice-President of the British Workers' League, and had received a CBE for his contribution to recruitment and National Savings. Possibly his hatred for the Germans owed much to the sinking of the *Lusitania* in 1915 and, thereafter, the unrestricted submarine warfare with the loss of many merchant sailors' lives. Certainly he had no time for communists or pacifists, and members of his union broke up several anti-war meetings.[3]

Wilson had enjoyed Liberal support as a Labour MP before 1914, and when he was elected as MP for South Shields in 1918, his designation was 'Coalition Trade Unionists' and Seamen's' candidate. Like the BWL or NDP candidates he stood as National Liberal in 1922 and was defeated. His name still ranks high among the gallery of villains in the demonology of the British labour movement. Yet Wilson was a pioneer trade unionist. In 1911 he organised the seamen's action in the transport strikes and was seen as 'planning an attack on the shipowners'.[4] His union for Sailors and Firemen effectively achieved a seamen's closed shop, and also won good wage rises, in 1917.[5] Wilson was a member of the trade union parliamentary committee in 1918, although he himself could best be described as an Independent in support of the Lloyd George Coalition during his period in the Commons.

The first real hints of Wilson's later reputation as a 'traitor' did not come until the early 1920s (after all, many unionists and leaders had favoured the war). Then his union met a rival in the shape of the Marine Workers, which he regarded (with some justification) as communist-led.[6] Wilson joined with the employers to exclude the Marine Workers from the Maritime Board, which regulated wages and conditions, in 1922.[7] This internecine strife helped to decide Havelock Wilson's position. Wage cuts were accepted in 1921, 1922, 1923 and 1925. The seamen's union (renamed the NUS in 1924) did not join the General Strike and, still under Wilson's leadership, gave a £10,000 interest-free loan to the non-political coal mining unions in 1927, for which they were expelled from the TUC. Wilson's hostility to the political labour movement was most clearly caught in this gesture. He had also resorted to the courts (in a suit which stimulated Mr Justice Astbury's declaration that General Strike was illegal) to restrain local officers of the NUS from calling out their men without sanction of the union executive; and he followed this up by a purge of branch officials who defied him. On the other hand, Wilson's and the seamen's singularity can be exaggerated by ignoring other groups of workers who never joined the General Strike, being either non-unionised or allowed exemption by the TUC General Council: these included sections of the road transport, textile, building and engineering trades, and local authority employees in several places (tramwaymen, electricity engineers, and workers in health services and food distribution). It was the NUS, however, claiming 74,000 members in 1928, which was seen as the major thorn in the side of orthodox unionism. Ernest Bevin set up a seamen's section of his Transport and General Workers' Union in 1929;[8] but Wilson died on 16 April of that year.

It seems doubtful whether he deserves to be regarded as an enemy of labour. He did not consistently eschew industrial action as a method of improving working conditions. He certainly chose a consolidationist course in the circumstances of the labour unrest of the 1920s, but it was the foundation of a rival seamen's union to his own that stung him into closer links with the employers. After Wilson's death the schism was quickly healed. His successor W. R. Spence led the NUS back into the TUC, where it has ever since remained as the recognised seamen's union; and the Maritime Board survived as the regulating unit for industrial relations in shipping. Most of the criticism of Wilson stems from his support of the 'wrong side' in the miners' dispute of 1926 and in its aftermath; yet the claims made concerning these 'non-political' unions themselves need closer analysis.

After the 1926 General Strike the drift back to work in a number of coalfields was coordinated by organisations which came to form the basis of separate trade unions. The best known was the Nottinghamshire Miners' Industrial Union, led by George Spencer,[9] but others were found in South Wales, and to a lesser extent in Durham and elsewhere. George Spencer was Labour MP for Broxtowe in West Nottinghamshire when he helped to unite 'back to work' committees in the autumn of 1926. The basis of the rift with the 'official' Nottinghamshire Miners' Association was the conviction in the county that it should not suffer for the sake of other less fortunate coalfields, where wage reductions and pit closures bit more deeply. This was the root of the concept of 'local autonomy' which has recurred in Nottinghamshire mining history. For eleven years the split in the county was maintained, and the NMIU's membership surpassed that of the NMA from 1932 to 1937, when it reached its peak of over 17,000. Even after the famed Harworth strike of 1936–37 led to the reunification of the NMA and NMIU in the Nottinghamshire Miners' Federated Union, Spencer remained President – and he was no nominal figurehead either.

No other breakaway miners' union approached the success of the NMIU, the so-called 'Spencer Union'. In South Wales,[10] the SWMIU was registered as a union in June 1927, but it appears never to have commanded more than 6000 members, even if it did on occasion claim a larger figure. It survived, like the NMIU, into the late 1930s, demonstrating particular strength at the Taff Merthyr pit. The Northumberland and Durham Miners' Non-Political Trade Union[11] peaked at around 4000 members between 1928 and 1930, according to the records of the Chief Registrar of Friendly Societies, and there the strength was heavily concentrated at St Hilda's Colliery in South Shields.

All these non-political miners' unions had principles in common. All believed strongly in the regional independence of unions in the various coalfields (although George Spencer was elected President of the SWMIU in April 1936). Most significantly, each preferred negotiation to confrontation with the employers, shunning strike action; and they rejected the notion of a political fund. Spencer told the Rufford branch of the NMIU as early as 28 November 1926 that 'the new organisation would tend to promote a better feeling between masters and men'[12] – antiquated terminology and, some would say, anachronistic sentiments. Yet this spirit of cooperation with the employers should not be mistaken for a disregard for miners' interests. In February 1927 a leading Spencer union official, Stan Middup,

> spoke on the propaganda of the old Federation, and the methods adopted in fermenting [sic] trouble in the industrial world and gave his reasons why capital and labour should work amicably together, and hoped that we should all work together to bring the lot of the miner up to a better standing than hitherto and to assure the future of the old miner who had spent all his energies in the industry.

The NMIU was particularly concerned with the provision of pensions for aged colliers, and Spencer's fund for retired miners still provides small sums to this day. (In 1984 the fund was alleged to be suffering from diversion into strike-breaking activities.) Spencer was renowned too for his handling of compensation cases. In 1930 alone he won over £10,000 for Industrial Union members.[13]

The methods adopted in the representation of Spencer Union members in everyday business included the extensive use of deputations sent to the management on all subjects ranging from overtime to nail shortages to the matter of issuing redundancy notices. If this procedure failed, the next step was often to call in George Spencer himself, who made a habit of talking personally to the management, when complaints were raised by men at a particular colliery. It is noticeable that the NMIU was a very 'top-heavy' union in its structure. Power was maintained in the hands of Spencer himself, his central organisation, and the branch committees. It was common for there to be as few as two general meetings of all branch members per year, at which the elected officials were chosen. The idea of general meeting sovereignty was not encouraged, presumably to eliminate the possibility of militant agitation from below.[14]

It was of course an abiding tenet of the 'industrial' unions that they should be 'non-political'. Like many other bodies of a conservative nature, the Spencer Union considered that only the advocacy of radical change such as socialism merited the description 'political', and that the defence of the status quo was not a political act. Clause 2(g) of the NMIU rules stated that 'the union is an industrial organisation and no funds of the union shall be used for any political purpose whatsoever'.[15] In March 1928 a leading union official 'in a very able speech on the policy of A. J. Cook said that in his opinion the solution of the current difficulties in the Trade Union movement was the elimination of politics.'[16] The SWMIU rules reiterated this position: 'the union shall be non-political. Any member raising a political issue at a lodge meeting shall be warned, and if he persists in his attitude the committee shall have the power to expel him from the union.'[17]

Along with opposition to political action went opposition to industrial action. None of the industrial unions ever called a strike. In November 1926 Spencer

> dealt with the late strike and explained the reasons which caused it, terming it in his opinion an experiment in elementary communism. The

new organisation . . . would provide old age pensions for all men past work and would eliminate strikes.

The official insignia of the South Wales industrial union was a representation of two hands clasped in friendship over colliery winding gear, with a miner's belt encircling the picture. In 1936 one of the founders and leading lights of the SWMIU, William Gregory, gave an interview to the journalist Montagu Slater:

Our main principle is that we do not believe in strikes . . . the main part of our programme is co-operation with the employers . . . the recent troubles [at Taff Merthyr in 1934–35] are not a fight to worsen conditions or to lower wages but a fight against communism which is taking a firm grip of the Miners' Federation in South Wales. It is a fight for the freedom, protection and liberty which we are entitled to as subjects of the great British Empire and under the British flag . . . [18]

It was asserted at the time, as often subsequently, that they were misguided in their professed belief that 'politics' could be separated from the proper representation of their members; to quote from the Nottinghamshire Miners' Association Year Book for 1935,

membership of a trade union, still the finest asset a worker can have: it is the only source through which he can make known his grievances, improve his wages, add weight to his social status, claim equality of freedom, and give protection to his family. It is difficult to understand any miner having a leaning towards a non-political organisation, when his very life depends on politics.

It is certainly true that the Spencer union was assisted by some of the big Midlands coal companies such as Stanton, Bolsover and Butterley, who naturally preferred it to the NMA.

It is also likely that there were individual connections with the Conservative Party, although when Spencer left the Labour Party in 1927 he did not cross the floor of the House but sat as an Independent. In 1928, however, at a smoking concert in Clipstone, the local Tory MP, the Marquess of Titchfield, said that he was a strong supporter of the new trade union the men had formed because it had recognised those principles which were the true principles of the

Conservative Party: 'personal possessions, religion, and the right of men to work out their own salvation in the right way . . . miners could translate those principles into action through the work that their great leader, George Spencer, had started.'[19] On occasion such advances were reciprocated.

Joseph Shooter, who became Branch Chairman of the NMIU at Rufford, proposed a vote of thanks when Baldwin visited the area with the words: 'On, Stanley, on with your splendid endeavours to serve our King, Country and Empire.'[20] Nevertheless, many Spencer union supporters must have remained as Labour voters in general elections. It is wrong to identify the industrial unions with fascism – it was rumoured in 1936 and 1937 that there were connections with Franco – or to make much of tales of a significant link between the non-political unions and the so-called Cliveden set.[21] They were not set up by the companies, they covered pits owned by more than one employer, and they were only 'bosses unions' in the sense that many other trade unionists believed that their policies failed to advance the interests of their working members. It is wrong, too, to call them the 'scab unions', as Francis and Smith do in their book, *The Fed*. Very similar politics – a return to work in late 1926 followed by negotiation and cooperation with the employers – were adopted by the Leicestershire Miners' Association, which remained within the MFGB throughout the 1920s and 1930s.[22] Lastly, it is wrong to build up the various connections into some kind of national non-political trade union 'movement'. Havelock Wilson was indeed a Vice-President of the British Workers' League, and the expulsion of the NUS from the TUC was largely a consequence of his financial support for the NMIU and other industrial unions; but Wilson and Spencer were both too parochial in their interests to rank as leader of a single organisation.

The spectre of 'unofficial' trade unionism was raised again during perhaps the most savage and long-lasting mining dispute, that from March 1984 to March 1985. Once more Nottinghamshire 'did different', and was accused of mass 'scabbing'. Once more this led to a breakaway union being formed which was supported by the majority of Nottinghamshire miners. Yet can the Union of Democratic Mineworkers, founded in September 1985, properly be placed in a tradition of anit-socialist trade unionism?

Much of its impetus derived from the early days of the strike in 1984. The NUM President, Arthur Scargill, and his Executive Committee called a national strike over the closure of pits, in particular that of Cortonwood in Yorkshire. Scargill was widely regarded as a Marxist, a militant, and a confrontationist, one of the battling school of miners' leaders. As the veteran labour politician Manny Shinwell put it, 'there always was an Arthur Scargill; in my day he was called A. J. Cook.' Scargill rose to the challenge of conflict with the Conservative government of Margaret Thatcher and with the National Coal Board Chairman, Ian Macgregor, but his methods resulted in a split in his union. Claiming that NUM standing policy on resistance to pit closures was agreed, the Executive did not arrange a national ballot but simply appealed to all areas to absent themselves from work. Right from the start, most Nottinghamshire miners did not heed the call. Their own area strike ballot rejected industrial action by 73 per cent to 27 per cent. Few Nottinghamshire pits were likely candidates for closure, and the county had done especially well over the previous decade because of productivity agreements with the NCB.

The traditional rivalry with Yorkshire was reinforced in the early days of the strike as large numbers of flying pickets drove south over the county border to attempt to prevent the Nottinghamshire men from working. The most vulnerable pit was Harworth, right on the border with the militant South Yorkshire field, the very mine which was the scene of the climactic 1937 dispute that brought the fusion of the NMA and the Spencer union. This time Harworth was closed by mass picketing for a week from 12 March 1984. Another chief target was a so-called 'big-hitting' 'super-pit', the highly profitable Ollerton Colliery in the Dukeries. On 14 March a Yorkshire picket, David Jones, died on the line outside the pit gates at Ollerton, fuelling the tension between the two counties. The number of mines working normally was reduced from 83 to 29 during the first week of mass picketing. This led to an energetic response from the police.[23] Some Nottinghamshire miners quickly responded to the intimidation and violence by secretly organising a Working Miners'

Committee: prominent was a tall, grey-haired miner known at first only as Silver Birch, who turned out to be Chris Butcher of Bevercotes Colliery near Ollerton. In time, it was made possible for the Nottinghamshire and other working miners to produce coal, but the resentment of the early days of the strike on both sides was not forgotten.

The working miners felt bullied, but did not believe that they were scabs because they were attempting to work in their own pit and they had not been consulted through a national strike ballot. The strikers considered themselves to be let down by their colleagues' lack of solidarity in the face of an enemy which would destroy mining and mining communities in many parts of the country. Pressures on minorities – strikers in working areas and working miners in coalfields where most were on strike – were almost intolerable, since ostracism was made more effective by the tight-knit nature of mining villages. Strikers faced financial hardship as no welfare benefits were made available; and it is scarcely surprising that the working miners and their leaders were ranked with those enemies whom the strike leaders naturally vilified: the government, the Coal Board, the police and the law courts – indeed the whole apparatus of the British state. The Nottinghamshire area leaders, Ray Chadburn and Henry Richardson, were jostled at Sheffield in April 1984 as they called for a ballot on the strike; but they were not absolutely opposed to industrial action, as their subsequent fate in Nottinghamshire was to make clear.

As the months passed, the resolve of the employers and the government did not crack, coal stocks did not expire, and the pickets did not prevent coal production in the working areas. The tide ebbed, and even in previously solid striking areas men began to drift back to work; but the rifts in the union were not healed. The left-wing General Secretary of the Nottinghamshire area, Henry Richardson, was stripped of his post by the area executive on 15 January 1985.[24] All over the county branch delegates who had supported the strike were replaced by those who had worked. Richardson's successor was Roy Lynk, who had been Financial Secretary of the Nottinghamshire area NUM since 1979. Another emergent leader of the Nottinghamshire men was the county agent, David Prendergast. Nottinghamshire refused to pay a 50 p per head levy for dismissed miners, and altered their rule book to make it less easy for the national organisation to impose their will. This led to a move by the NUM National Executive to expel Lynk and Prendergast from the union. This was passed by 10:9 on 14 May 1985, and the decision was confirmed by a 4:1 majority at a delegate conference at Sheffield on 4 July of the same year: 75:18 against Lynk, 73:20 against Prendergast. The Nottinghamshire men refused to pay attention to this, however, and set themselves up first as an independent county area of the NUM. On 9 July, Roy Lynk locked Chadburn out of the union headquarters at Berry Hill Lane in Mansfield. The completion of a breakaway union came on 18 October 1985 when a ballot created the UDM – the Union of Democratic Mineworkers. Nottinghamshire voted 'yes' to the new union, by 17,750 votes to 6792 – 72 to 28 per cent on a 90 per cent turn-out. The new union was a federation, including the small (1000–strong) Durham-based Colliery Trades Association and South Derbyshire, which only voted itself in by 1286 to 1260 on a 94 per cent turn-out. Nevertheless the South Derbyshire leader, Ken Toon, became President of the UDM, with Roy Lynk as General Secretary and George Hunter of the Durham CTA as Vice-President.[25]

Was the UDM the 'company union' Scargill claimed? Was it, in the vogue phrase of the day, a 'sweetheart' union, closeted in close harmony with the National Coal Board? Was it in fact a reincarnation of Spencerism? The Labour Party leader Neil Kinnock appealed to Nottinghamshire to avoid a split,[26] and the question now arose of the position of Labour Party members who also belonged to a body which was not recognised by the TUC and which was in opposition to the official miners' union. However, the UDM was not evidently anti-Labour Party. A number of local MPs supported the new union, including the formidable figure of Don Concannon, who had been Labour MP for Mansfield since 1966. UDM officials and members were not expelled from the Labour Party, and some remained local council candidates. Roy Lynk described himself as a Labour supporter in the tradition of Harold Wilson and James Callaghan. The UDM appeared to represent a species of trade unionism akin to the Electricians' and Engineers', which in

1985 were threatened with expulsion from the TUC for taking money from the government to defray the cost of organising strike ballots. On 22 October 1985, Bill Jordan, who was shortly to be elected President of the Engineers, Britain's second largest union, said that the UDM should be recognised by the TUC.[27] The possibility was mooted that an alternative union grouping might be founded should the TUC act in a hostile manner towards its recalcitrant moderates.

The impression that the UDM simply represented a different brand of trade unionism from that of the Scargill NUM was reinforced in 1986 when it became clear that the new union wished to apply for affiliation both to the TUC and to the Labour Party. There was no suggestion that there should be no political levy, or that 'politics' had no place in trade unionism. By late 1986 the future of the UDM was still unclear. Nottinghamshire can quite reasonably look forward to another lengthy period of separation from the official union, especially as Scargill was confirmed as President of the NUM for life (that is, to the age of 65, in 2003). The prospects for other constituent parts of the UDM federation are less sure. South Derbyshire had only voted narrowly to join the new union; Agecroft Colliery was the only pit in Lancashire to vote to leave the NUM (30 October 1985), and other 'moderate' areas like Leicestershire were by no means clearly and permanently lost to the NUM.

The UDM does represent a different workers' view of the coal industry from the main body of the NUM in the 1980s, reflecting the different response to the strike call of spring 1984. Perhaps links can be drawn with the NMIU or 'Spencer' union of 1926–37, for in a coalfield habits persist and history is remembered more vividly than in less homogeneous communities. The long-standing non-militancy of Nottinghamshire miners can be traced back to the nineteenth century. It can be ascribed not merely to relatively high wages and to the long life of the Nottinghamshire pits, but also to a political tradition contrasting strongly with that of neighbouring South Yorkshire.

Yet the breakaway of 1985 was not actively sought by Nottinghamshire miners. One can only surmise what might have happened if the NUM had not been led by Arthur

Scargill and his like-minded colleagues, but rather by men of the stamp of Will Lawther and Joe Gormley, previous NUM Presidents, or even what might have happened if there had been a strike ballot in spring 1984. Perhaps the Nottinghamshire miners would not have responded to such a call. More likely they may have heeded it but begun to drift back to work in the face of the intransigence of the NCB. As it was, the Nottinghamshire men could fairly claim to have been hounded out of the NUM by the union's dogmatic policies.

The UDM is not a company union or a bosses' union, though more inclined to cooperation with the NCB (renamed British Coal) than the rump of the NUM is. Nor is the UDM clearly anti-socialist or non-political, at least within its own definition of those terms. Nor does it have the hierarchic and bureaucratic structure of the NMIU. Rather, it was created by a rebellion from below which ousted pro-strike and pro-NUM branch officials, and the two leaders of the Nottinghamshire area of the NUM, Chadburn and Richardson. The UDM is not dissimilar in its approach and policy from the electricians' union of the 1970s and 1980s, personified by the right-wingers Frank Chapple and Eric Hammond, or from the engineers of the same period, led by Terry Duffy, Gavin Laird and Bill Jordan.

The portrayal of 'moderate' trade unionism as company or blackleg unionism is an understandable element in the rhetoric of confrontation practised by those who pursue class or industrial conflict. Reluctance to take disruptive action and willingness to negotiate with the employers would certainly represent treachery in war. For a Marxist, the coalition of a Tory government, the mines' management, the police and law courts during the strikes of the 1980s (or even the 1920s) encapsulated the enemy to be fought. Yet such tendentiousness ignores the variable historical experience of this country and other nations. Scabs were originally non-union labour brought in by the employers to a place of work where the regular workers were on strike. They were not employees attempting to carry out their own jobs against the opposition of secondary pickets from other parts of the country or even other industries. The notion of traitors to a working-class movement presupposes the existence of such a movement. In Britain no movement of such sweep or unity has ever existed, any more than all or nearly all working-class people have chosen to vote Labour in the twentieth century.

There were and are company unions, staff associations and professional organisations consciously divorced from labour representation and trade unionism. But it is, and should be, disputable whether this line of separation should be drawn about the UDM, the NMIU or Havelock Wilson's NUS. Non-political these were not, although their view of politics was very different from left-wing socialism. Neither did they let down the interests of their members, at least in the judgement of many of the workers themselves. On several occasions, from the 1920s through to the Nottinghamshire ballots of 1984 and 1985, voters in the coalfields demonstrated voluntary support for the breakaway unions. Variety may not be the spice of life, but even in the trade union movement there may indeed be room for different flavours.

## *Notes*

1. See H. Eckstein, *Pressure Group Politics, the Case of the British Medical Association* (Allen & Unwin, London, 1960).
2. See Chris Cook, *Sources in British Political History*, Vol. 1 (Macmillan, London, 1975), 31–2; Roy Douglas, 'The National Democratic Party and the British Workers' League', *Historical Journal* 15, 3 (1972), 533–52.
3. Basil Mogridge, 'Militancy and inter-union rivalries in British shipping, 1911–19', *International Review of Social History* 6 (1961), 375–412.
4. Hugh Clegg, *A History of British Trade Unions since 1889*, Vol. 2 (Clarendon Press, Oxford, 1985), p. 33.
5. Ibid., p. 164.
6. Ibid., p. 385.
7. Ibid., p. 328.
8. Ibid., p. 458.
9. See A. R. Griffin, *The Miners of Nottinghamshire 1914–44* (Allen & Unwin, London, 1962); idem, *Mining in the East Midlands 1550–1947* (Cass, London,1971); A. R. and C. P. Griffin, 'The Non-Political Trade Union Movement', in A. Briggs and J. Saville (eds.), *Essays in Labour History*, Vol. 3 (Croom Helm, London, 1977), 133–62; R. J. Waller, *The Dukeries Transformed* (Oxford University Press, Oxford, 1983), 108–30.
10. See David Smith, 'The Struggle against Company Unionism in the South Wales Coalfield', *Welsh History Review* 6, 3 (1973), 354–78;

Hywel Francis and David Smith, *The Fed.* (Lawrence and Wishart, London, 1980).
11. W. R. Garside, *The Durham Miners 1919–60* (Allen & Unwin, London, 1971), 232–4.
12. Waller, op. cit., p. 110.
13. Ibid., p. 113.
14. Ibid., p. 112–13.
15. Ibid., p. 110.
16. Ibid., p. 111.
17. Smith, op. cit., p. 357.
18. Montagu Slater, *Stay Down Miner* (1936).
19. *Newark Advertiser*, 25 January 1928.
20. *Newark Advertiser*, 18 January 1925.
21. Francis and Smith, op. cit., p. 125.
22. Griffin and Griffin, op. cit., p. 135–8.
23. *Sunday Times* Insight Team, *Strike* (Coronet, London, 1985), ch. 2.
24. *The Times*, 15 January 1985.
25. *The Times*, 19 October 1985.
26. *The Times*, 16 July 1985.
27. *The Times*, 23 October 1985.

# Index


Adderley, Sir Charles, 67, 87
Agecroft, 225
Aikin family, 97, 103, 113
Alford, Henry, 6
Allen, Clifford, 129, 132, 134
American:
  English, 7–9, 33, 35
  entry in war, 132–6, 140
  excess profits tax, 148
  press, 55
  unemployment, 164, 187, 196, 200
Andover, 10
Angell, Norman, 126, 128
Annan, Noel, 118
Aristotle, 34, 35, 48
Arnold, Matthew, 98
—, Sidney, 144, 157
Asquith, H. H., 39, 52, 129, 131, 133
Astor, J. J., 170
Austen, Jane, 104
Aylesbury, 62

Bakke, E. W., 167, 169–70, 173–4, 178, 180, 186
Baldwin, Stanley, 157, 221
Balfour, A. J., 39, 46, 95, 122
Bamford, Samuel, 22
Barker, Ernest, 21, 32–3
Barnes, William, 5–6
Barrie, James, 18
Barritt, Mary, *see* Thompson, Mary
Bateson, W. H., 98, 113
Bath, 93
Bauer, Otto, 182
BBC, 7–9, 55–6
Beaconsfield, *see* Disraeli
Beales, L., 164–5, 172–3, 176
Becontree, 172
Bedford College, *see* London, University
Belfast, xi
Benson, A. C., 100
Berkshire, 10
Berlin, Isaiah, xii
Bernstein, G. L., 118
Berwick-upon-Tweed, 11
betting, *see* gambling
Beveridge, W., 166
Bevin, Ernest, 194–5, 199–200, 202, 205, 217
Bewdley, 5
Bible, 7, 18–19
Birmingham, 17, 23, 133
Blackburn, 32, 189
Blackheath, 41
Blanesburgh Committee (1925–7), 170
Board schools, 7, 11, 13–15, 29
'Bobbin', 'Tim', 13
Bodichon, Barbara, 99, 112–14
Boer war, 46–8, 122
Bolton, 215
Bondfield, Margaret, 177, 202
Bonham-Carter family, 99, 103
Booth, Alan, 192–3
Booth family, 98
Boswell, James, 25
Bowra, C. M., xiv
Bradford, 23

Bradley, Henry, 6, 8, 29–30
Brailsford, H. N., 130, 135
Brand, Robert, 150
Bridges, Robert, 6–7, 9
Brierley, Ben, 5
—, Walter, 172, 176
Bright, John, 9, 43, 120
Brighton, 93
British Coal, *see* National Coal Board
British Medical Association, 214
British Workers League, 214–16
Browning, Oscar, 106
Brynmawr, 167, 173, 182
Bulley, Agnes Amy, 108
Burgess, Keith, 192
Burnley, 12, 16
Burns, Robert, 18
Butcher, Chris, 223

Cairns, Lord, 64, 80, 87
Calder valley, 11
Callaghan, James, 224
Cambridge 146–7, 154
  and Bertrand Russell, 118–21, 130, 134, 136, 138
  women's colleges at, ch. 4 *passim*.
Cannadine, David, 96
Cannan, Edwin, 141, 146, 155
Cantril, Hadley, 183
capital levy, ch. 6 *passim*
Cardiff, 133
Carlisle, Countess of, 95
Carlyle, Thomas, 34, 122
Carnarvon, Earl of, 72, 75
Chadburn, Ray, 223–4, 226
Chamberlain, Joseph, 39, 44, 46, 50, 52, 99–100, 123
Chapman, John, 99
—, S. J., 168
Chapple, Frank, 226
Cheltenham Ladies College, 92
Cheshire, 14, 16, 21
Chesterfield, 42
Chesterton, G. K., 18
Childers, Hugh, 71, 86
Churchill, Lord Randolph, 39, 45–6
—, W. S., xiii, 45, 153, 159
cinema-going, 165, 173–4, 186
Citrine, W., 194–5, 197–8, 204, 208, 211–12
Clark, G. Kitson, xv
Clarke, P. F., 118, 123–4
Cleveland, 11
Clipstone, 220
Cliveden, 221
Clough, Anne Jemima, 98
Clyde workers, 135–6
Cobden, Richard, 40, 44, 120, 123
cockney speech, *see* London
Cohen, Max, 165, 169, 175, 177
Cole, G. D. H., 152
Colne, 11
Compton-Burnett, Ivy, 104
Concannon, Don, 224
conscription, *see* military service
Conservative Party (*see also* Tory Democracy):
  organisation, 36, 41, 49–51, 54, 122
  press, 47
  and social reform, ch. 3 *passim*, 125–6
  and war, 127, 136
Cook. A. J., 219, 222
Cope, Rev. Sir William, 15–16
Cornwall, 12–13, 19, 21
corporatism, ch. 8 *passim*
Cotswolds, 13
Courtauld, Samuel, 99–100
Courtney, Leonard, 122
Couturat, Louis, 122
Crawshay family, 97
Cripps, Sir Stafford, 55, 58
Crosland, A., xiii
Cross, R. A., 69–73, 80, 85, 88–9
Croydon, 37
Crystal Palace speech (1872), 39, 49, 65, 68, 84–5
Curzon, Viscount, 30

*Daily Chronicle*, 47
*Daily Herald*, 173
*Daily Mail*, 47, 53, 55
*Daily News*, 47
*Daily Telegraph*, 42, 47
Dalton, Hugh, 143, 145–8, 151–2, 155, 157
Darlington, Thomas, 14–15

Davies, Emily, 91–2, 96, 99–100, 108, 112–13
—, E. W., 55, 58
—, Margaret Llewelyn, 126
Davison, R. C., 170
Deakin, William, xiii
Delane, J., 44
Derby, 14th Earl of, 60, 63, 88
—, 15th Earl of, 61, 66–7, 75, 77–8, 81, 84, 88
Derbyshire, 22–3, 30, 224
dialect, ch. 1 *passim*
Dicey, A. V., 98
—, Elinor, 99
Disraeli, Benjamin:
  rhetoric, 39, 41, 44, 49–50
  social reform, ch. 3 *passim*
Doncaster, 22
Donnelly, Lucy, 123, 132
Dorman, Sir Arthur, 203
Dorset, 5, 15
Duffy, Terry, 226
Durant, Ruth, 165
Durham, 28, 166, 172, 217–18, 224

Eastern Question, 39, 60, 85, 87–8
Economic Advisory Council, 200, 202, 206
*Economist, The*, 143, 148
Edinburgh, 42
Edmont, Edmond, 5
education, 13–24, 59, 62, 65, 73, 78–9, 85, 88–9
  Acts, (1870) 13–15, (1902) 123, (1944) xiii
  women's, chap. 4 *passim*
Eisenberg, P., 161–3
electricians' union, 224
Eliot, George, 5, 91–2, 99, 108–9
Ellis, Alexander, 4, 8, 10–12, 16–17, 22, 24, 26
Elworthy, F. T., 9, 28–9
empire, 6–7, 26, 49–50, 55, 61, 82, 122, 215, 220–1
Engel, A. J., 107
engineers' union, 32–3, 224–5
*English Dialect Dictionary*, 3, 26
Ensor, R. C. K., 24, 27
Esperanto, 21, 32
Essex, 10
Evans, Richard, 105
—, Sebastian, 17
Ewart, Mary, 97, 103

Fabian Society, 120–3
fascism, 221
Fawcett, Henry, 98
—, Millicent Garrett, 99
Federation of British Industries, 198, 204
*Financial Times*, 34–5
Fisher, Victor, 214
Folk-Lore Society, 4
Folk-Song Society, 4
Foot, Michael, 34
Forbes-Robertson, Sir J., 7
franchise, *see* Reform Acts
Free Labour Association, 214
Freeden, Michael, 118, 136

gambling, 175, 184, 186
Garrett, Elizabeth, 99
Gaskell, Mrs., 5
Gateshead, 93
George, David Lloyd, 39, 42, 44, 46, 55, 122, 126–7, 134–6, 157, 215–16
—, Henry, 120
*German Social Democracy* (1896), 121
Gillieron, Jules, 5
Girton College, *see* Cambridge
Gissing, George, 1–2, 23, 25–6, 30
Gladstone, W. E., xiii, 21, 32, 39–46, 52–3, 64–5, 69–70, 79, 81, 95, 97, 101, 121
Glasgow, 13, 37
Goldman, Lawrence, 82
Goldsmid family, 97
Gormley, Joe, 225
Gower, G. Leveson, 10
Greek language, 1, 108
Green, Charlotte, 99
—, T. H., 98
Greenwich, 167, 169
Gregory, Holman, Commission (1930–2), 170
—, William, 220
Grey family, 16
—, Sir Edward, 127–30
Gurney, Russell, 99

Hackney, 37

Halévy, Elie, 119, 123
Hallam, Thomas, 5
Hallsworth, H. M., 168
Hammond, Eric, 226
Hampshire, 10
Hannington, W., 181
Hardie, Keir, 24, 122
Hardy, Gathorne, 64, 67, 70, 83, 87
—, Thomas, 15
Hartley, John, 5
Hartington, Marquis of, 38, 44, 47, 74, 76, 86
Hatton, S. F., 165
Harvie, Christopher, 98, 109
Harworth, 217, 222
Hazlitt, William, 9
Healey, Denis, xiii
Heckmondwike, 23
Henderson, Arthur, 127, 152, 215
Hepburn, Walter, 44
Hertfordshire, 10
Hewins, W. A. S., 122
Hicks, George, 194
Hill, John, 199
Hinton, James, 192
Hitchin, 93
Hobbes, Thomas, 34, 48
hobbies, 171–3, 185, 189, 191
Hobhouse, L. T., 118, 122, 124
Hobson, J. A., 56, 118, 120, 127, 129, 137, 148
Holyoake, G. J., 38
Home Rule, *see* Ireland
Howarth, Janet, 101–3, 111
Hume, David, 18, 119
Hunter, George, 224
—, Rev. Joseph, 13

imperialism, *see* empire
Ipswich, 93
Ireland:
  Church of, 62, 64
  Home Rule, 51, 73–4, 78, 89, 119, 123, 125–7
  language, 1, 18–19, 24–5, 28
Iron and Steel Trades Confederation, 167, 211–12

Jago, F. W. P., 13
Jahoda, Marie, 161–3, 173–4
James, Sir Henry, 60, 68
—, Lloyd, 7, 9
—, William, 130
Jarrett, J., 163, 183, 185
Jenkins, Roy, xiii
Jennings, Hilda, 173–4, 178, 180
Jerrold, Blanchard, 37
Jones, Daniel, 7
—, David, 222
—, D. Caradog, 171
—, Kennedy, 55
Jordan, Bill, 225–6
Jowett, F. W., 215

Karolyi, Count Michael, xii
Kell, Colonel Vernon, 133, 139
Kelvin, P., 163, 183, 185
Kennedy, Benjamin Hall, 98
Kent, 10, 16
Keynes, John Maynard, 127, 139, 141–3, 147, 151–2, 154–7, 159, 192
—, John Neville, 98
Kinnear, Alfred, 45
Kinnock, Neil, 224
Kipling, Rudyard, 6, 27
Knatchbull-Hugesson, Sir Herbert, 16

Labour, Ministry of, 170, 177, 197, 202
labour exchanges, 167, 169–70, 174–5, 177–81
*Labour Magazine*, 197
Labour Party, 24, 81
  and capital levy, ch. 6 *passim*
  1929–31 Govt. and TUC, ch. 8 *passim*
  relations with 'irregular' trade unions, ch. 9 *passim*
  rhetorical appeal, 54
  rise of, 117–18, 125, 127, 131, 135–7
Lady Margaret Hall, *see* Oxford
Laird, Gavin, 226
Lambert, R. S., 164–5, 172–3, 176
Lambeth, 37
Lancashire, 16, 20, 24, 33, 37, 40, 97–8, 165, 185, 225
landlordism, 15–16, 61, 74, 87–8, 96, 119–20, 123, 131
Lasker, B., 164, 171
Law, Andrew Bonar, 37

Lawrence, D. H., 130
Lawther, Will, 225
Lazarsfeld, P. F., 161–3, 168, 170, 175–6, 180, 182–3, 185–7, 189, 191
Leeds, 11, 23
*Leeds Mercury*, 38
Leicestershire, 6, 11, 17, 221
Lennard, R., xvi
Lewes, George Henry, 99
Lewis, C. S., xiii
Liberal Imperialists, 52, 122
*Liberal Magazine*, 51
Liberal Party, 24
  organization and rhetoric, 36, 41–3, 46–56
  plural vote, 88
  press, 47
  response to Conservative social reform, ch. 3 *passim*
  debates about fall of, ch. 5, *passim*
Lincolnshire, 6, 22
Liverpool, 13, 21, 37, 43, 48, 84, 93, 97–8, 174, 184–6
London:
  speech, 10, 13, 16, 22–4, 28
  govt., 73, 80
  university, 92–4, 97–8, 102, 104, 121
Londonderry, xi
Lords, House of, 51, 119, 123–5
Louise, Princess (Marchionness of Lorne), 94
*Lusitania*, sinking of, 127, 215
Lynk, Roy, 223–4
Lyons, F. S. L., 18
Lyttelton, Edward, 19, 31
—, family, 95–6, 98

McCallum, R. B., xii–xiii
MacDonald, Ramsay, 24, 54, 125, 144, 151, 156–7, 193, 195, 202, 215
McFarlane, K. B., xi–xii
Macgregor, Ian, 222
McKenna, Reginald, 141, 150
McKibbin, R. I., 118
Macmillan Committee (1929–31), 199–201, 206
Malleson, Lady Constance, 132
Man, Isle of, 19, 31
Manchester, 17, 20, 37, 39, 41, 49, 65–8, 72, 84, 133
*Manchester Guardian*, xiii, 19–20, 124, 139
Mann, Tom, 125
Mansfield, 224
Marienthal, 161–3, 167–8, 171, 173, 175, 182–3, 187
Marsden, D., 169
Marshall, Alfred, 98, 120, 146, 148, 154
—, Catherine, 132
—, Mary Paley, 99
Martin, Ross, 192
marxism, 121, 222, 226
Masterman, C. F. G., 126
Maurice, F. D., 99
Merchant Shipping Bill (1875), 74–5, 77, 87
Meredith, George, 29
Middlemass, Keith, 192–3
Middup, Stan, 218
Midlands speech, 5, 11, 17, 28
Midlothian campaign, 39, 41, 43, 54
migration, 11, 13
military service, 12, 126–8, 132–3, 135–6
Mill, John Stuart, 99–100, 103, 119–20, 124, 181
Milne-Bailey, W., 203, 210
Milner, Lord, 215
miners' unions, 24, 125, 133–4, 136, 195, ch. 9 *passim*
mobility, social, 1–2, 12
Mond, A., 192–200, 202, 204, 206, 210, 212
Monkswell, Lady, 39
Moore, George, 11
—, G. E., 124
Morel, E. D., 127, 129, 134, 137
Morley, John, 44, 52
Morrell, Lady Ottoline, 122, 131–2
Mosley, Sir Oswald, 199
Murray, Gilbert, 125, 130
—, J. A. H., 3, 18

Namier, Lewis, xiii
National Coal Board, 222–6

National Confederation of Employers' Organisations, 194, 198, 203–5, 212
National Council for Social Service, 180
National Debt, ch. 6 *passim*
National Democratic and Labour Party, 215–6
National Farmers Union, 214
National Industrial Council, 194, 197–8, 206, 211
Newbolt Committee (1921), 20–1
Newnham College, *see* Cambridge
Newrick, J. A., 167
Nightingale, Florence, 98–9
No-Conscription Fellowship, 128, 132–3, 135–6
nonconformity, 19, 51, 97–8, 118, 123, 127–8
Northcote, Sir Stafford, 73, 77, 79, 89
Northumberland, 24, 218
Norwich, 93, 99
Nottingham, 93
Nottinghamshire, 22, 213–14, 217–27

Ogden, C. K., 130
Ollerton, 222
Orton, Harold, 22
Orwell, George, 22
Owen, A. D. K., 166
Oxford, xi-xx, 7, 21, 37–8, 96, 119, 130, 138
  women's colleges, ch. 4 *passim*
*Oxford English Dictionary*, 3, 6, 26
Oxford Essay Society, 109–10

pacifism, 122–3, 126–36
Paine, W. W., 148–9
Paley, Thomas, 103
Palmerston, Viscount, 40, 49, 62
Parliaments, Local, 37–8
Parnell, C. S., 39
Peel, Sir Robert, 35, 63, 69
Pennington family, 98
Penrith, 11
Perry, Ralph Barton, 126
Pethwick-Lawrence, F. W., 143–4, 146, 148
Philological Society, 3, 6, 8, 29
phonetics, 3–5, 7–8
Picton, James, 43
Pigou, A. C., 146, 148, 158
Pilgrim Trust, 172, 174, 180, 184–6, 188–9
Pitman, Isaac, 8, 27
Plimsoll, Samuel, 74–5
Poor Law, 36
Poplar, 24
Prendergast, David, 223–4
press, and political reporting, ch. 2 *passim*
Press Association, 43–6, 55, 58
Preston, xi
Price, J. F. G., 177
professionalisation, 105–7, 115
progressivism, 48, 109, 118, 120, 122, 124–5, 135–7
Public Worship Regulation Act (1874), 68
Pugh, Arthur, 199, 204, 206
Pure English, Society for, 6–7

railways, 12, 29, 148, 214
Raleigh, Sir Walter, 6
Rathbone family, 98
rationalisation, ch. 8 *passim*
reading habits, 5–8, 11–14, 19–20, 173–4, 183, 186, 189
Reeve, Napier, 11
Reform Acts:
  (1832) 63
  (1867) 35–6, 62–6, 72, 83
  (1884) 35–6
  (1918) 36, 53–4, 127
Regimental Exchanges Bill (1875), 73, 86
Reid, Elizabeth Jesser, 98
Reith, Sir John, 9, 55
retirement, 186–7
rhetoric, political, chs. 2–3 *passim*
Richardson, Henry, 223, 226
Ritchie, Alex, 38
Robertson, D. H., 147, 154
Rosebery, 5th Earl of, 42, 46, 121
Rothblatt, S., 106
Rothschild, Lionel de, 97
Rowntree, B. S., 164, 171
Rowse, A. L., xii, 21
Royal Holloway College, *see* London

Royal Titles Act (1876), 50, 68, 85
Rubinstein, W. D., 97
Rufford, 218, 221
Russell, Bertrand, 95, ch. 5 *passim*
—, Countess, 119–20
—, Lord John, 119

St. Hugh's College, *see* Oxford
Salisbury, 3rd Marquess of, 39–40, 45–6, 75, 87–8, 95
Salt, Thomas, 60
Samuel, Herbert, 133, 195
Save the Children Fund, 165
Scargill, Arthur, 222, 224–5
Scilly Isles, 14
Scotland, 1, 13, 18, 24–5, 28, 33, 47
*Scotsman, The*, 42, 47
seamen's union, 213–17, 227
Seebohm, Winnie, 109–10
Seeley, J. R., 108
sexual behaviour, 175, 183, 189–90
Shaen, William, 98
Shakespeare, 7, 9
Shaw, G. B., 1, 4, 7–8, 21, 122
Shaw-Lefevre, G. J., 97, 99
Sheffield, 10, 13, 23, 93, 223–4
Shooter, Joseph, 221
Sidgwick, Eleanor, 95, 99, 112
—, Henry, 95–6, 98, 100, 103, 108
Simplified Spelling Society, 8, 27
Sinfield, A., 168–9
Skeat, W. W., 8
Slater, Montagu, 220
Smiles, Samuel, 18
Smillie, Robert, 136
Smith, Benjamin Leigh, 99
—, Dorrien, 14
—, H. Llewellyn, 179
—, Paul, 83, 85, 88–9
—, Alys Pearsall, 121
—, Logan Pearsall, 7
—, W. H., 59, 88
Snow, C. P., xix
Snowden, Philip, 32, 135, 141, 144, 151
social reform, ch. 3 *passim*, 120, 123–5
socialism, 120–1, 125, 130–1, 137, 141, 144, 151–2, 201, 205–9
Socialist National Defence Committee, 215
Somerset, 9, 14
Somerville College, *see* Oxford
South Shields, 218
Spence, W. R., 217
Spencer, George, 213, 217–21, 224
—, Herbert, 59
Stamp, J. C., 142, 145, 147–53, 155
Standard English, ch. 1 *passim*
Stanleys of Adderley, 95, 113
Stead, W. T., 53
Stone, Lawrence, xiii–xv, xix
strikes:
  General, 192–4, 208, 216–17
  miners', 125, 213–14, 216–27
  seamen, 215–17
Sturt, George, 11, 28
Surrey, 10
Sussex, 10, 12
Sweet, Henry, 3–4, 8, 10
Swift, Jonathan, 25, 30
syndicalism, 130

Talbot, Edward, 95
Tariff Reform, 48, 50–1, 123, 125–6
Taylor, A. J. P., xi–xii, 130, 190
—, Helen, 100, 103
Tennyson, A., 6
Thatcher, M., 222
Thomas, Dylan, xii
—, J. H., 24, 151, 157, 210–11
Thompson, A. F., xi–xx, 56
—, A. M., 214
—, Mary, xiii, xviii
*Times, The*, 38, 40, 47
Titchfield, Marquess of, 220–1
Toon, Ken, 224
Tootill, Robert, 215
Tory Democracy, 32, 57–8
Tory Party, *see* Conservative Party
Toynbee, Arnold, 98
—, Charlotte, 99
trade unions, 24, 33, 63, 70, 73, 78, 85, 119, 176
  and corporatist politics, ch. 8 *passim*
  'irregular' types of, ch. 9 *passim*

TUC:
  and capital levy, 146–7
  and rationalisation, ch. 8 *passim*
  and 'irregular' trade unionism, ch. 9 *passim*
Treveylan, G. M., 125
Turner, Ben, 194–7, 199–200, 202, 212

unemployment:
  social psychology of, ch. 7 *passim*
  TUC reaction to, ch. 8 *passim*
Union of Democratic Control, 128, 133
Union of Democratic Mineworkers, 214, 221–7
Unionist Party, *see* Conservative Party
Unitarians, 97–8
urbanisation, 10–13
USA, *see* American

Vicinus, Martha, 97
Vienna, 162

Wald, Kenneth, 118
Wales:
  and Great War, 133–4, 146
  language, 1, 13, 19, 24–5, 28–9
  miners, 217–21
  unemployment, 166–7, 173, 176, 182, 185
Wallas, Graham, 50, 130
war:
  (1914–18) 12, 37, 54, 126–38, 140–4, 192, 214–16
  (1939–45) xi–xiii, 126, 209
Watling, 165
Waugh, Edwin, 5, 20, 27
Webb, Beatrice, xviii, 121–4, 129, 166
—, Sidney, 52, 122–3, 137, 144, 146, 150
Weber, Max, 53
Wells, H. G., 13
Westfield College *see* London
*Westminster Gazette*, 47
Weymouth, 93
Whately, Richard, 35
Whitehead, A. N., 118
Whitley Councils, 198, 211
Willis, Irene Cooper, 133
Wilson, Harold, 224
—, J. Havelock, 213, 215–17, 221, 224, 227
Wiltshire, 10
Winkworth family, 98, 100
women:
  education, ch. 4 *passim*
  speech, 16, 68
  suffrage, 42, 123–4, 127
  unemployment, 169–71, 177, 181, 183, 185, 188–90
Woodard schools, 97
Worcestershire, 15
Wordsworth, Elizabeth, 96, 102, 104
World Economic Conference (1927), 196, 199, 210
Wright, Joseph, 3–4, 26
Wyld, H. C., 2, 16–17, 19, 30

Yeats, W. B., 26
York, 11, 93
Yorkshire, 12, 22–3, 28, 37, 222, 225
Young, Terence, 172

Zawardski, B., 162–3, 176, 189
Zeisel, Hans, 161